Legitimizing Human Rights

Secular and Religious Perspectives

Edited by
ANGUS J.L. MENUGE
Concordia University Wisconsin, USA

Routledge
Taylor & Francis Group
LONDON AND NEW YORK

First published 2013 by Ashgate Publishing

2 Park Square, Milton Park, Abingdon, Oxfordshire OX14 4RN
52 Vanderbilt Avenue, New York, NY 10017

Routledge is an imprint of the Taylor & Francis Group, an informa business

First issued in paperback 2020

British Library Cataloguing in Publication Data
Legitimizing human rights : secular and religious
perspectives. -- (Applied legal philosophy)
1. Human rights--Philosophy. 2. Human rights--Religious
aspects. 3. Freedom of religion.
I. Series II. Menuge, Angus J. L.
340.1'12-dc23

The Library of Congress has cataloged the printed edition as follows:
Menuge, Angus J. L.
Legitimizing human rights : secular and religious perspectives / by Angus J.L. Menuge.
pages cm
Includes bibliographical references and index.
ISBN 978-1-4094-5002-3 (hardback)
1. Human rights. 2. Human rights--Religious aspects. 3. Secular-
ism. I. Title.
K3240.M48 2013
323.44'2--dc23

2013000854

ISBN 978-1-4094-5002-3 (hbk)
ISBN 978-0-367-60150-8 (pbk)

LEGITIMIZING HUMAN RIGHTS

Menuge has brought together a first-rate, international set of contributors to advance our reflection on the foundation, nature, and importance of human rights. This book should be studied by all those interested in human rights and who take seriously the need to inquire into the basis and justification of those rights.

Charles Taliaferro, St. Olaf College, USA

Amongst the plethora of books on human rights, this book is remarkable. Firstly, it confronts two opposite and socially important perspectives of human rights: secular and religious. Secondly, it presents dialogues from both sides and the contributors present differing viewpoints on many issues. This is what makes the book especially exciting and I recommend it with a deep conviction.

Lech Morawski, Nicolaus Copernicus University, Poland

Since the publication of the Universal Declaration of Human Rights in 1948, human rights have been an important element in bridging cultures. But what is the foundation of human rights? Can human rights be founded within secular culture or do we need religion for that? This is a central preoccupation in this interesting and important volume.

Afshin Ellian, Leiden University, The Netherlands

Taken together, the chapters collected in Legitimizing Human Rights *serve to remind atheists that if they insist on removing all traces of the law's debt to the Biblical religions, they will have also undercut the most philosophically compelling grounds for upholding the idea of human rights.*

Steve Fuller, University of Warwick, UK

One of the marks of an outstanding anthology is that its contributors confront the reader in such a way that he finds himself in an ebb and flow of dialogue, dissent, and agreement while paging through it. That's how I found myself while reading this important collection. In an age in which religious belief is not taken seriously in the rarefied corridors of the academy, this book is a welcome contribution to the literature on human rights, theology, and religious liberty.

Francis J. Beckwith, Baylor University, USA

Contents

PART III ENFORCING AND MOTIVATING HUMAN RIGHTS

Series Editor's Preface

The objective of the Applied Legal Philosophy series is to publish work which adopts a theoretical approach to the study of particular areas or aspects of law or deals with general theories of law in a way which focused on issues of practical moral and political concern in specific legal contexts.

In recent years there has been an encouraging tendency for legal philosophers to utilize detailed knowledge of the substance and practicalities of law and a noteworthy development in the theoretical sophistication of much legal research. The series seeks to encourage these trends and to make available studies in law which are both genuinely philosophical in approach and at the same time based on appropriate legal knowledge and directed towards issues in the criticism and reform of actual laws and legal systems.

The series will include studies of all the main areas of law, presented in a manner which relates to the concerns of specialist legal academics and practitioners. Each book makes an original contribution to an area of legal study while being comprehensible to those engaged in a wide variety of disciplines. Their legal content is principally Anglo-American, but a wide-ranging comparative approach is encouraged and authors are drawn from a variety of jurisdictions.

Tom Campbell
Series Editor
Centre for Applied Philosophy and Public Ethics
Charles Sturt University, Canberra.

List of Contributors

Dr. Dobrochna Bach-Golecka is Associate Professor at the Department of European Law, Faculty of Law and Administration, University of Warsaw. She holds a Ph.D. in public international law and a Ph.D. in divinity studies. Her recent publications and scientific interests include such topics as public health, regulation of services in European law, democracy and human rights, solidarity, and social values in Christian teaching. She was a visiting fellow at the Lauterpacht Center for International Law at Cambridge University in 2002, where she did research culminating in her book, *Democracy in International Law*.

Dr. Vito Breda (Ph.D. Edinburgh, LL.M. Brussels, LL.B. Milan) is lecturer of law at Cardiff Law School and holds a visiting professorship at the Faculty of Law of the Jesuit University of Deusto. His has written extensively on constitutional theory, jurisprudence, and citizenship. In 2010, he was appointed visiting fellow at the Center for European Studies at Canberra Australia National University and was one of the researchers of the FP5 EU Consent Network–Group 10 (Democracy Legitimacy and Identity). Most recently he was awarded a supervising professorship in comparative thought at the Law School of the Università degli Studi di Brescia. Before joining the Cardiff Law School, Dr. Breda worked as researcher for the Scottish Parliament.

John Calvert, J.D., has studied philosophy and has a degree in geology. However, his expertise has been in the law. For 32 years he engaged in business litigation and corporate finance with a large regional law firm in the US. During the last 11 years he has focused on US Constitutional Law, primarily as it relates to religious freedom. He has been actively involved in the debate in the US over the conduct and teaching of origins science, having appeared before legislatures, state boards of education and school boards in over 20 US states. He is the Managing Director of Intelligent Design Network, a non-profit that seeks institutional objectivity in origins science.

Professor Dr. P.B. Cliteur (b. 1955) is full-time professor of Jurisprudence, University of Leiden. He is the scholarly director of the Institute for the Interdisciplinary Study of the Law. Cliteur's research is in the field of ethics, the philosophical foundations of the law, in particular moral dilemmas around multicultural society, fundamental rights and the relationship between law and worldviews. Some recent publications are *The Secular Outlook: In Defense of Moral and Political Secularism* (Wiley-Blackwell 2010); "State and Religion against the Backdrop of Religious Radicalism," *International Journal of Constitutional Law*, 2012, 10(1), 127–52; "Female Critics of Islamism," *Feminist Theology*, 2011, 19(2), 154–67.

Dr. Paul Copan received his Ph.D. in philosophy from Marquette University, and is Professor and Pledger Family Chair of Philosophy and Ethics at Palm Beach Atlantic University. He has authored and edited over 20 books, including *Loving Wisdom: Christian Philosophy of Religion* (Chalice Press), *The Rationality of Theism* (Routledge), *The Routledge Companion to Philosophy of Religion* (Routledge), and *Philosophy of Religion: Classic and Contemporary Issues* (Blackwell). He and his wife Jacqueline live with their six children in West Palm Beach, Florida.

Dr. Hendrik Kaptein is an Associate Professor of Law and Legal Theory at Leiden University in the Netherlands (formerly at the University of Nijmegen and the University of Amsterdam). He specializes in the theory and practice of (legal) argumentation, theory of criminal law, and legal ethics. His general outlook emphasizes the importance of logic for sound argumentation, the need for reform of criminal justice in the interest of victims, anti-relativism and role-consciousness in professional ethics.

Dr. Angus J.L. Menuge was raised in England, and became an American citizen in 2005. He holds a B.A. in philosophy from Warwick University, a Ph.D. in philosophy from the University of Wisconsin-Madison, and a Diploma in Christian Apologetics from the International Academy of Apologetics, Evangelism and Human Rights. He is author of *Agents under Fire: Materialism and the Rationality of Science* (Rowman & Littlefield 2004) and many articles on the philosophy of mind, philosophy of science and Christian apologetics, and editor of several collections, including *Reading God's World: The Scientific Vocation*. His most recent work focuses on libertarian free will and the foundations of human rights.

The Honourable Mr. Justice Dallas Miller received a Bachelor of Laws in 1984 from the University of Saskatchewan and a Bachelor of Arts (History) in 1992 from Athabasca University (Alberta). He was admitted to the Bar of Alberta in 1985 and practised with Gordon, Smith and Company in Medicine Hat (1985–93) before opening his own firm (1993–2006). Mr. Justice Miller's practice expertise is in the areas of civil litigation, real estate law, wills and estates law and mediation. He has acted as a Member of the Alberta Provincial Court Nominating Committee (2004–2006), as Judicial District Representative for Medicine Hat for the Alberta Civil Trial Lawyers Association, and as Chair of the Board of Directors of International Justice Mission. In 2006, he was appointed a Judge of the Court of Queen's Bench of Alberta.

Dr. John Warwick Montgomery (Ph.D., Chicago, D.Théol., Strasbourg, LL.D., Cardiff, Dr. [h.c.], Institute for Religion and Law, Moscow) is Emeritus Professor of Law and Humanities, University of Bedfordshire, England, Distinguished Research Professor of Philosophy and Christian Thought, Patrick Henry College, Virginia, U.S.A., and Director, International Academy of Apologetics, Evangelism and Human Rights, Strasbourg, France. He is an English barrister, an *avocat à la Cour, Barreau de Paris,* and a member of the bar of the Supreme Court of the United States. His legal speciality is the international and comparative law of human rights and he regularly pleads religious freedom cases before the European Court of Human Rights. He is a U.S. and U.K. citizen, the author of some 50 books in five languages, and is included in *Who's Who in America*, *Who's Who in France*, the *European Biographical Directory*, *Who's Who in the World*, and *Contemporary Authors*.

Dr. Friedrich Toepel was a student at the universities of Munich and Freiburg, an assistant of Professor Rengier at the University of Constance (1987–89), and completed his doctorate in 1990 at Constance University. He then served as assistant at the universities of Rostock and Bonn (1993–99), and has served as Acting Professor at the University of Bonn, Guest Professor at the University of Dresden (2005–2006), Fulbright Scholar at Northwestern University, Chicago, presently serves as an Adjunct Professor of the University of Bonn.

Acknowledgements

Several of the chapters in this book represent development of initial papers presented at a working group on human rights I chaired at the 2011 IVR World Congress meeting in Frankfurt, Germany. Other contributions were solicited to improve the overall diversity and balance of perspectives and issues covered. I am very grateful to John Warwick Montgomery for helping me to see the vital importance of defending human rights, to Friedrich Toepel for his hospitality and generosity in Frankfurt, to all of the contributors for their steadfast patience throughout the editing process, and to Alison Kirk for her encouragement and help in shaping the final book.

Introduction

Angus J.L. Menuge

Human Rights are All the Rage

Human rights have never been so popular. On the one hand, they are used as ideological weapons to critique political and cultural adversaries. Liberals attack the existing marriage laws for limiting the rights of homosexuals. Conservatives charge that religious freedom has been eroded by the imposition of secularist ideology in the public square. Western democracies denounce other societies for their treatment of dissidents and religious minorities; these democracies are in turn criticized for exploiting the developing world. The United States is singled out for its use of torture and capital punishment and for its failure to provide universal health care.

On the other hand, appeal to human rights is used to advance the causes of social justice and equality. In advanced liberal democracies, this includes more and more of what citizens expect from life. Healthcare, education and sexual orientation are now increasingly viewed as fundamental to human flourishing. Yet consensus on a basic list of human rights has proven elusive. Not a few of the countries signatory to major human rights agreements exempt themselves from laws that contradict the dominant beliefs and customs of their people. And even if abuses like slavery and religious discrimination are declared illegal, the prohibition may not be enforced because the practices are culturally entrenched and ignored by law enforcement. In the West, the demand to recognize almost every strong preference as legally protected has led to contradictory rights claims. The right to life appears to be the most fundamental right of all, since, without it, no other right can be exercised. Yet elective abortion, euthanasia and even infanticide are also claimed as human rights. And while believers appeal to freedom of conscience to justify a religious voice in the public square, secularists charge that this violates their right to be free from such intrusion.

The Goal of this Collection

All this disagreement should make us ponder whether our zeal for proclaiming human rights is matched by a clear understanding of what they are. It is one thing to assert that the exercise of a particular interest is a human right. It is quite another thing to *justify* that assertion ontologically, epistemologically and pragmatically. An ontological justification must locate the basis in objective reality for asserting that human beings do have special, fundamental rights, rights that are universal, inherent and inalienable. An epistemological justification must locate an accessible, authoritative source or set of criteria we can use to identify human rights and to distinguish between legitimate and spurious human rights claims. A pragmatic justification must provide a feasible method for promoting the recognition and enforcement of human rights protections.

In each of these three cases, the quest for justification must address several fundamental questions. Basic questions of *ontological* justification include:

1. What *is* a human right?
2. Why should we think such a thing really exists?
3. What makes it the case that human beings have special rights?

Basic questions of *epistemological* justification include:

1. How can we know when something is a human right?
2. How can we know when something is *not* a human right?
3. Which worldview provides the best explanation of human rights?

Basic questions of *pragmatic* justification include:

1. How can a culture be encouraged to recognize the existence of human rights?
2. How can one reform a society with institutionalized human rights abuses?
3. How can human rights legislation be enforced?

Further, as with all rights, human rights have their limits. At what point shall we say that the exercise of an interest no longer qualifies as a right because it infringes on the equal or stronger claims of others? In justifying human rights, we must also consider their proper scope and limits. It is important to be able to show that some rights claims are spurious: they merely appropriate the language of rights to disguise an aggressive or self-serving agenda. For example a country's "right" to protect its own borders may be used to rationalize genocide, and a culture's "right" to express a preferred religion may curtail the freedom of religious minorities.

The purpose of this collection is to address these fundamental questions of the legitimacy of human rights claims and to consider the merits of both secular and religious perspectives. It is divided into three parts. The first part ("The Foundation of Human Rights") discusses the relative merits of theism and naturalism as foundations for human rights, with authors defending both sides of the question. The second part ("Religious Liberty and the Secular State") considers the nature, scope and limits of religious freedom in the West and around the world. The final part ("Enforcing and Motivating Human Rights") ponders the best way to persuade people to recognize, respect and protect human rights.

The Foundation of Human Rights

In Chapter 1, Paul Copan focuses on the primary question of ontological justification and argues that without the biblical teaching that humans are made in the image of God, no list of our natural capacities provides an adequate foundation for human rights. A major problem for non-theistic ethics is that even the best are incomplete: they simply assume humans have special dignity and worth without showing why this is to be expected on the basis of their underlying ontology. Indeed, many of the most incisive atheist philosophers (such as Bertrand Russell, J.L. Mackie and Kai Nielsen) have concluded that objective moral values cannot be grounded in an unintended physical universe. Copan further argues that as a matter of historical fact, the secular insistence on human rights itself derives from borrowed theistic capital, and that it is this capital which provides the actual foundation for our claims of human worth and dignity. At the end of his chapter, Copan offers an extensive rebuttal to the well-known Euthyphro dilemma, which seeks to show that theism cannot ground moral obligations.

In the next chapter, Paul Cliteur advances the contrary view, that human rights are the child of secularism. Cliteur argues that theism is inadequate as a foundation for human rights because it promotes the harm of other people (holy wars, stoning of homosexuals, male and female circumcision) and animals. He uses an example of the latter (unstunned ritual slaughter) to argue that the secular state has the right to limit religious freedom where it promotes cruelty, violence or other harm, or where it violates standards of equality or reasonableness. In the process, Cliteur implicitly argues for the more general thesis that secular reason can recognize a framework for evaluating human rights claims which is independent of any religious revelation. If a believer cannot demonstrate that a practice is consistent with this framework, Cliteur argues, he or she cannot expect the law to protect that practice.

It will be observed that a primary disagreement between Copan and Cliteur is whether secular reason actually can provide a framework for adjudicating conflicting human rights claims without drawing on theistic capital. If it can, then there must be some way of grounding human rights in nature (or specifically human nature) without appeal to God.

A popular way of dispensing with a theistic explanation is to argue that morality can be understood as an outgrowth of human evolution. In my contribution to this collection, I consider the prospects of Evolutionary Ethics (EE) as a foundation for human rights. My analysis distinguishes Weak EE, which claims only that our moral psychology is explained by our natural history, and Strong EE, which asserts that this history explains the existence of moral values. The main thrust of the chapter is that human rights discourse is incompatible with grounding morality in the contingencies of naturalistic evolution. If Strong EE is true, the proper conclusion is that no such things as human rights exist. There simply are no universal, inherent, inalienable rights humans have simply in virtue of being human because if humans had different biological histories these rights would not exist. For example, there cannot be a human right to life since, if we had been raised like hive bees, fratricide and female infanticide would be permissible (perhaps obligatory). On the other hand, if Weak EE is true, while human rights may exist, we are in no position to know them, since it would be at best a lucky coincidence if our moral sensibilities tracked moral reality. Either way, Evolutionary Ethics fails to vindicate the project of justifying human rights discourse by appeal to secular reason. This appears to leave a transcendent foundation for human rights as a live option.

To the contrary, in the last chapter of the section, Friedrich Toepel worries that religious pluralism makes it impractical to derive human rights from a transcendent source. After all, theistic religions have scriptures which disagree, not only about the nature of God and humanity, but also about specific human rights: for example, the prohibition of apostasy in Islamic Shariah law is regarded as a violation of religious liberty by Christians and Jews. The same problem arises for secularists, since they also have conflicting visions of the good. For example, Kantians, utilitarians and ethical egoists have fundamental disagreements about the nature of human flourishing. Toepel's conclusion is that, even if there is a correct ethical foundation for human rights, the lack of moral consensus makes this an impractical basis for implementing human rights protections. What is needed instead are credible institutions that can create a framework of positive law recognized across ideological divides. Toepel is not a pure legal positivist and does not claim that human rights can simply be reduced to what is recognized by positive law. Rather, as a "constructo-positivist," he suggests merely that, as a practical and linguistic matter, it is most helpful to restrict human rights discourse to what can be institutionalized. From my perspective, this means that Toepel's proposal is not attempting to establish the ontological or epistemological foundation for human rights. Instead, it aims to show the best pragmatic foundation—one that will maximize human rights protections in an ideologically pluralist milieu.

Religious Liberty and the Secular State

How can the state protect religious liberty and refrain from establishing a favored religious position? One of the founding ideals of the United States is that religious freedom is best protected by a secular state, one which remains neutral between religions. Yet it is not so easy to say what counts as a secular state. The word "secular" means "not religious," and that means that state neutrality between religions can only be achieved if the state operates with a correct definition of religion. In his chapter, John Calvert argues on the basis of authorities in both philosophy and law, that the correct definition of religion must be an inclusive, functional one. If the state adopts a narrow definition of "religion" as theistic belief, then the state will favor non-theistic religions, such as Secular Humanism and Atheism. This leads to the intrusion of religious bias in public schools because textbooks and instruction may contain religious material wrongly classified as secular. In fact,

Calvert argues that this has already happened. While Methodological Naturalism (the claim that science can only appeal to unintelligent causes) can have great value as a limited heuristic in many areas of science, when it is used to *define* the scientific method, students are not permitted to see the evidence that might support a theistic understanding of nature. The actual effect of this is to promote the religious views of materialist atheists (and theists who deny that God's actions are detectable in the natural world) and to discriminate against theists who believe in natural theology. This can be avoided if a broader, functional definition of religion is used, which the Supreme Court has recognized in other cases.

In the next chapter, Vito Breda considers how matters of religious liberty are complicated by the greater religious diversity of modern Western democracies. His discussion focuses on *Lautsi v. Italy*, a recent case concerning religious symbols in the classroom. In this case, the European Court of Human Rights took the view that, in the context of religious pluralism, secularism cannot simply be assumed to be the default, neutral position. This does not mean that religious expression cannot be limited (it can, as soon as there is a clear threat to public order, or evidence of coercive proselytization). Yet, Breda contends, in a pluralistic society, the mere presence of religious symbols in some classrooms can be understood as part of a cultural dialogue, rather than an attempt to impose religious belief on others. In this vein, the European Court allowed signatory states some discretion on deciding whether religious symbols can be displayed. Breda sees this as an important case, because it represents a move away from the binary conflict between a supposedly neutral secularism and "religion," to one that allows states to accommodate a plurality of religious perspectives.

Still, just when can religious freedom legitimately be restricted? In the next chapter, John Warwick Montgomery explores this thorny topic, noting that while the major human rights instruments do recognize limitations on religious liberty, they do not provide clear guidelines for discerning when these limitations apply. Today, for example, some Islamic countries either refuse to ratify human rights covenants or do so with reservations, indicating that they recognize no obligation to comply if those covenants conflict with Shariah law. If we find this dissent from basic human rights agreements unacceptable in some cases (for example, the imposition of the death penalty for apostasy), what criteria can we use to restrict these practices? As a precedent for limiting religious freedom, Montgomery considers the Mormon polygamy case, *Reynolds v. US*, and finds it wanting because it creates a false dichotomy between religious belief and religious action. This can easily rationalize the ghettoization of believers in their places of worship found in totalitarian states. Religious freedom will always entail some public expression, so the real question is at what point, and on what grounds, this expression can be restricted. Montgomery argues that this limit cannot be adequately defined by appeal to natural law (it is too vague), neo-Kantian ideas (neither individuals nor states are willing to forego their special advantages), or legal positivism (it allows obnoxious states to institutionalize religious discrimination). More generally, due to their self-interest, humans are incapable of defining universal, inalienable rights: they must come from a transcendent source. In response to concerns that this is impractical due to religious pluralism, Montgomery argues that even if the proper basis for religious freedom is found in scripture, this can still be defended on independent grounds as good for society, and that the superior textual and historical reliability of the Bible over rival religious texts can be upheld.

Enforcing and Motivating Human Rights

To say that something is a human right rings hollow if there is no effective means of redress for human rights abuses. Hendrik Kaptein explores the unpopular idea of retribution, and argues that it is best understood as the attempt (not always realizable) to restore victims to their original situation, as if no abuse had occurred. As developed by Kaptein, retribution in this sense means, in effect, doing the right that should have originally been done. So understood, retribution is not something over and above respecting human rights: it is part of what it means to say that human rights are respected. It is meaningless for a state to say that it has a commitment to human rights and then to do nothing to redress violations when they occur. Kaptein argues that the de facto gap between human rights law and actual enforcement requires urgent reform.

Justice Dallas Miller agrees, and shows that on an international level, even where human rights legislation is in place, massive abuses continue. Miller focuses on what motivates the recognition and protection of human rights. While some claim this motivation derives from the Enlightenment, Miller argues that the historical and contemporary data show that culturally effective human rights movements are most often the result of Judeo-Christian principles. Miller points out that the various secular rationales for human rights (such as utilitarianism, neo-Kantian approaches and Marxism) all fail to transform the selfish human orientations that fuel abuses. And secularist attempts to justify human rights have failed to answer the skeptical critique of cultural relativists, undercutting the rationale for human rights activism, and providing cover for tyrannical regimes. By contrast, Miller argues, the drafting of the Universal Declaration of Human Rights was significantly shaped by a Judeo-Christian worldview, and this had a lasting influence on subsequent human rights instruments. At the same time, the actual state of human rights protections is abysmal in many countries. For example, the "new slavery" and other forms of human trafficking are actually increasing. While legal remedies are needed, it is naïve to think they will be accepted or enforced unless there is widespread cultural recognition of human rights. Miller argues, however, that some of the most effective promoters of this recognition have been, and continue to be, committed Christians, who firmly believe that all people are valuable before God, and that we should treat others as we ourselves expect to be treated. Faith, Miller concludes, has an important role in producing actual human rights protections and enforcement.

Dobrochna Bach-Golecka agrees and argues that a vital player in propagating a high view of human value and dignity is the Christian Church. Focusing on the example of Catholic social teaching, she shows how the Church supports human rights recognition in three ways. First, the Church has a general influence on the moral norms a culture accepts. Second, the Church provides criteria for distinguishing right and wrong behavior. Among these, most important are the virtues of charity and solidarity: if a culture embraces these, it cannot passively accept the victimization of one group in its midst. Rather, it will stand with and for that group until its mistreatment ends. Third, while the Church has no means of coercive enforcement, it can call its members and the wider society to repentance, and can offer the peace of reconciliation. Bach-Golecka goes on to show how Catholic teaching motivates respect for human rights at several levels: the congregational (where members are influenced by social teaching), the regional (through a conference of bishops) and the international (through the Vatican). At every level, the Church promotes the interdependence and solidarity of all human beings before God, a powerful basis for opposing the oppression of the powerless and the despised.

A Continuing Dialogue

While there are many other issues and perspectives that might have been included, my chief hope for this collection of chapters is that it will reinvigorate the conversation about the proper foundation for human rights. If we seek to protect human freedom and dignity, we can only hope to make that a reality if we can convince people that fundamental human rights are real, knowable and vitally important. So it is essential to find the best possible grounding for human rights ontologically, epistemologically and pragmatically. While contributors to this volume do not all agree on the best answers here, they do share the conviction that human rights theory must translate into real-world protections. The alternative is that academics continue the comfortable path of using human rights as rhetorical *machines de guerre* for their preferred political agendas. This not only corrupts the discussion with self-serving motives, it also has no discernible impact on the widespread human rights abuses suffered disproportionately by members of developing nations. For this reason, I hope that the connection many contributors draw between the theoretical justification and the practical implementation of human rights will not merely be intellectually interesting, but will also inspire the work of lawmakers, political and religious leaders, and human rights activists.

PART I
The Foundation of Human Rights

Chapter 1

Grounding Human Rights: Naturalism's Failure and Biblical Theism's Success

Paul Copan

Introduction: The Language and Reality of Rights

The United Nations Universal Declaration on Human Rights lays out a number of universal human rights, including the freedom of religion. Here is one critical affirmation:

> Everyone has the right to freedom of thought, conscience, and religion; this right includes the freedom to change his religion or belief, and freedom, either alone or in community with others and in public or private, to manifest his religion or belief in teaching, practice, worship and observance (article 18).

What *is* a right? Human rights scholar John Warwick Montgomery describes rights as *titles*. Yet the very notion of title or entitlement expresses a *source* or *justification* of the title in question. It suggests being *rooted in* or *springing from* something—that there is some authority or power that grants such a status. He adds that we cannot *define* rights without the need to *justify* them (Montgomery 1986: 78–80).

In other words, a right is not self-standing; it is a relational title, requiring a ground or justification. Human rights are anchored in the prior status human beings have. Yet this status of dignity and worth is not free-floating; it requires metaphysical grounding to make sense of this entitlement.

Jacques Maritain, who helped craft the language of the Universal Declaration, wrote: "we agree on these rights, providing we are not asked why. With the 'why,' the dispute begins" (Maritain 1951: 77). Secularists and theists alike can concur with the notion of "inalienable rights," but what *grounds* such a claim? It is this dignity, worth, or "sacredness" that the naturalistic moral realist takes for granted rather than justifying or grounding it metaphysically. The strength of biblical theism is that it offers the requisite metaphysical foundation for human sanctity—"the image of God." This divinely bestowed worth is given to all participants in the human race. It is not measured by functionalist standards routinely used by utilitarians—levels of social adeptness, rationality, or self-awareness. Moreover, this divine "image" serves as the ground for universal human rights across all societies.

My argument in this chapter is fourfold. First, biblical theism's emphasis on the image of God furnishes us with the requisite ontological foundation for human dignity and worth (or "sanctity").[1] Secular (and non-theistic) ethical systems invariably suffer from metaphysical incompleteness at one crucial point: they are unable to ground human dignity given a context of valueless, deterministic, unguided material processes; rooting human dignity in features such as free will, reason, or self-awareness begs the question since the emergence of such capacities themselves is difficult to explain naturalistically, which many naturalists themselves acknowledge (see Copan 2013). Second, to reinforce the point about biblical ethics' greater ability to ground human dignity and worth, I comment on the historical fact that biblical theism—not "secular Enlightenment values"—has given rise both to human rights discourse, not to mention the start of the bioethics movement. Third, I address a cluster of objections springing from Plato's Euthyphro question. Finally, I address the Kantian objection to and misrepresentation of divine commands, particularly that of the command for Abraham to sacrifice Isaac.

In this chapter, I am taking for granted the existence of objective moral values—such as "Kindness is a virtue rather than a vice" or "rape is wrong" or "torturing babies for fun is evil" (see Copan 2008). I would concur with the atheist philosopher Kai Nielsen at this point:

> It is more reasonable to believe such elemental things [wife-beating, child abuse] to be evil than to believe any skeptical theory that tells us we cannot know or reasonably believe any of these things to be evil … I firmly believe that this is bedrock and right and that anyone who does not believe it cannot have probed deeply enough into the grounds of his moral beliefs. (Nielsen 1990: 10–11)

Again, the problem is not *knowing* these moral truths, but more fundamentally how we came to *be* morally responsible, intrinsically valuable, rights-bearing beings.

The Incompleteness of Non-Theistic Ethics and the Success of Theism

Overall, naturalism and various non-theistic worldviews do not lead us to expect the emergence of human dignity—the foundation of human rights—and universal benevolence. Even naturalistic/secular normative ethical systems following Aristotle, Kant, and Mill or advocating an ideal observer theory *assume* the dignity or worth of human beings. Thus, they are necessarily incomplete accounts

1 Some distinguish between *worth* or *sanctity* (which is anchored in a human's *nature* or *essence*—with all of its potentialities and capacities) and *dignity* (which is based on *merit* and takes place over time and inspires/commands respect as one's due). *Sanctity* is the ground of *dignity*, and one never outlives his sanctity (see Jackson 2005: 45–51). Here, I use *dignity* and *worth* interchangeably.

(on this, see Hare 2007). Yes, such accounts can offer much helpful guidance *epistemologically*, but they routinely fail *metaphysically*. That is, a non-theistic worldview lacks the wherewithal to produce intrinsically valuable, rights-bearing, duty-bound human beings.

For example, the social contractarian John Rawls famously advocated the inviolable rights of individual human beings: "Each person possesses an inviolability founded on justice that even the welfare of society as a whole cannot override. For this reason justice denies that the loss of freedom for some is made right by a greater good shared by others" (Rawls 1999: 3–4). But why think human beings have intrinsic moral value given a worldview in which accidental collocations of atoms, as Bertrand Russell put it, are the fundamental metaphysical starting point? By contrast, biblical theism provides the requisite metaphysical context to ground human dignity and worth. The more *natural*, less surprising context for the emergence of intrinsic dignity and worth is that of a good personal Creator rather than atoms in motion. The wrongness of rape or torture for fun presupposes the more basic fact of human dignity and worth, which makes excellent sense on theism.

Moreover, secularized "Platonic" or transcendentist approaches to morality falter as well. Atheist Erik Wielenberg claims that objective morality's foundation consists of certain brute ethical facts: they "have no explanation outside of themselves; no further facts make them true" (the ontological claim), and we can know these brute ethical facts immediately without inferring them from other known facts (the epistemological claim). Necessary moral truths did not evolve with humanity but are "part of the furniture of the universe," he claims. They "constitute the ethical background of every possible universe," creating the framework for assessing the actions of any moral agent (whether human or divine) (Wielenberg 2010: 79; on this view, see also Sinnott-Armstrong 2009).

One problem with this scenario is its gratuitous assumption that objective value has emerged from valuelessness—from accidental collocations of atoms. In Wielenberg's words, "From valuelessness, value sometimes comes" (Wielenberg 2009: 40n). But to *assert* is not to *justify*, and this claim hangs on a mere metaphysical *wish* that maybe value could emerge from valueless matter; the claim is not anchored in ontological realities. Theism does not have to lean on such a thin metaphysical reed: the emergence of value in this world is rooted in a supremely valuable being that endowed finite creatures with value. From value, value comes. Although we cannot do so here, we could rightly challenge other similar naturalistic question-begging maxims: "from non-conscious matter, consciousness sometimes comes"; "from deterministic processes, free will sometimes comes"; and "from non-rational matter, rationality sometimes comes" (see Copan 2012).

A second problem with Wielenberg's perspective is this: belief in the existence of transcendent moral facts is itself a recognition that a strict naturalism fails. One must move into some sort of non-naturalistic, Platonic realm. This position is an implicit acknowledgment that something more than naturalism is required to ground moral realism. Indeed, it is a move in the direction of theism, which can anchor such moral truths in the character of a good God, as I argue below.

A third problem is this: that moral facts existed prior to the emergence of moral value, say, when humans came on the scene, assumes a massive cosmic coincidence—one that readily dissolves given theism. The non-naturalistic moral realist in this case holds that (a) certain necessary *moral facts* exist and (b) *self-reflective, morally responsible and intrinsically valuable beings* eventually appear on the scene (through unguided, highly contingent evolutionary steps) who both can *recognize* these pre-existing facts and are *duty-bound* to them. This Platonic-like moral realm, it appears, was *anticipating* our emergence, just waiting for us to comply with it—a remarkable cosmic accident! A far simpler, less ad hoc explanation is available, however: a good, personal God—the very locus of objective moral values—created human beings with dignity and worth. Moral fact-hood and moral worth have always existed since both applied to God before his creation of human beings. Theism affords a far more elegant and natural explanation.

The same could be said about other non-theistic views found in eastern religious and philosophical traditions. These impersonal versions of the "Ultimate Reality" (for example, *Brahman*) lack metaphysical grounding to justify both individual human dignity as well as personal moral qualities. Their impersonal or abstract Ultimate Reality—whether monistic or pantheistic—leaves us wondering how human rights or personal virtues such as love, compassion, and kindness could make ontological sense. For example, Buddhism's no-self doctrine (*anatman*) affirms that humans are mere bundles of ever-changing properties rather than enduring selves. Or take Hinduism's Advaita Vendanta's monism. The self (*atman*) is identical to the Ultimate Reality (*Brahman*), resulting in the obliteration of any distinction between the rights of this and that human being. Looking eastward for metaphysical grounding for human dignity and worth does not look promising.

To add to our point, many atheists themselves recognize that God and human dignity and objective morality stand or fall together. To be without God is to be without human dignity as well as objective moral values and duties. Here's a small sampling:

- Jean-Paul Sartre: "It [is] very distressing that God does not exist, because all possibility of finding values in a heaven of ideas disappears along with Him" (Sartre 1957: 22).
- Friedrich Nietzsche: "There are altogether no moral facts"; indeed, morality "has truth only if God is the truth—it stands or falls with faith in God" (Nietzsche 1968: 55, 70).
- J.L. Mackie: "Moral properties constitute so odd a cluster of properties and relations that they are most unlikely to have arisen in the ordinary course of events without an all-powerful god to create them" (Mackie 1982: 115).

As Richard Dawkins rightly observes, in a universe of selfish genes and electrons—much like Russell's "accidental collocations of atoms"—"there is, at bottom, no design, no purpose, no evil and no good, nothing but blind pitiless indifference" (Dawkins 1995: 132–3; see Russell 1963: 41).

The naturalistic moral realist might appeal to theistic thinkers such as Richard Swinburne who take the position that moral facts do not depend on the existence of a good God (Swinburne 1977: 204). Such an appeal has its own set of concerns, and at least four replies are in order.

First, recall the astonishing "cosmic coincidence problem" for the atheist, as we saw earlier—that moral facts seemingly anticipate the emergence of duty-bound moral agents. By contrast, the existence of a good God tidily unifies this transcendent moral realm—anchored in the divine nature—and the emergence of intrinsically valuable human beings who are made in his image. Second, Swinburne holds to a very counterintuitive view that God is not a necessary being—one that exists in all possible worlds. According to Swinburne, God happens to exist. So it's no wonder, then, that the moral realm and God are disconnected. But the fact that God is indeed a necessary being dissolves such a dichotomy. Third, even if Swinburne were correct, these objective moral facts still cannot account for the emergence of intrinsically valuable, morally responsible agents. Human worth is a separate metaphysical issue—one for which a personal, good God offers a natural explanation, not so on naturalism. Fourth, the purported necessity of moral truths does not diminish their need for grounding in the character of a personal, necessarily existent God. God, who necessarily exists in all possible worlds, is the source of all necessary moral truths that stand in asymmetrical relation to God's necessity. Consider the necessary truth: "Addition is possible." This is rooted in a more fundamental necessary truth—namely, the existence of numbers, which have certain essential properties. The latter grounds the former, not vice versa—hence, the asymmetrical metaphysical relationship. Likewise, consider the statement, "Consciousness necessarily exists." This is true only because God—a supremely self-aware being—exists in all possible worlds. So, a good God's necessary existence also means that objective moral facts are necessary—that is, they exist in all possible worlds precisely because a supremely good God exists in all possible worlds. A necessarily good God's existence is explanatorily prior to these moral facts (Craig 2009: 168–73).

We have seen that biblical theism, in which a good, rational, supremely aware Creator fashions human beings in his image, makes better sense of human dignity. On naturalism, though, why think morally responsible, valuable beings would be the product of mindless, non-rational, physical, valueless, non-conscious processes? Unlike theism, naturalism's context cannot anticipate the emergence of moral value or the existence of moral duty (on naturalism's moral supervenience problem, see Plantinga 2010). Again, if naturalism is true and the universe is inherently meaningless, we simply should not expect the phenomenon of rights, dignity, and intrinsic value to emerge at all. While naturalistic moral realists readily acknowledge that humans are "accidental, evolved, mortal, and relatively short-lived" (Wielenberg 2009: 35), surely, intellectual honesty forces us to admit that human rights and universal benevolence *more naturally or fittingly flow* from a theistic universe than from a naturalistic one (see Smith 2009).

God, Human Rights, and History

While a personal, good God who creates humans with dignity and worth makes far better metaphysical sense of human rights than non-theistic alternatives, a study of modern history reveals an intimate connection between the biblical worldview and the human rights movement in the West. This movement and the emergence of modern science, sociologist Rodney Stark notes, have "rested entirely on religious foundations, and the people who brought it about were devout Christians" (Stark 2005: xi).

Note that this movement was not the product of the rationalism of the Enlightenment. Rather, talk of "natural right(s)" emerged in Catholic medieval theology—a language which itself was built on the biblical understanding of "the image of God" in all humans (see Reed 2007). This, of course, would lead to the language of rights in the Declaration of Independence (1776): "We hold these truths to be self-evident, that all men are created equal [and] endowed by their Creator with certain unalienable rights," which include "life, liberty, and the pursuit of happiness." Shortly thereafter the French Declaration of the Rights of Man and Citizen (1789) affirmed certain fundamental rights "in the presence and under the auspices" of "the Supreme Being." Both of these documents affirm a *theological*—not secular—basis for human dignity. And no wonder: the rights language found in each is indebted to philosopher John Locke himself, who asserted that humans ought not harm another "in his life, health, liberty, or possessions" precisely because humans are the property, workmanship, and servants of "one omnipotent, and infinitely wise maker" (2.6) (Locke 1690).

This fact about human equality and rights is not simply the affirmation of Christian theists, but of leading atheist intellectuals as well. Professor Jürgen Habermas, an atheist, is one of Europe's most prominent philosophers. He acknowledges the inescapable historical link between human rights discourse today and the biblical worldview:

> Christianity has functioned for the normative self-understanding of modernity as more than just a precursor or a catalyst. Egalitarian universalism, from which sprang the ideas of freedom and a social solidarity, of an autonomous conduct of life and emancipation, the individual morality of conscience, human rights, and democracy, is the direct heir to the Judaic ethic of justice and the Christian ethic of love. This legacy, substantially unchanged, has been the object of continual critical appropriation and reinterpretation. To this day, there is no alternative to it. And in light of current challenges of a postnational constellation, we continue

> to draw on the substance of this heritage. Everything else is just idle postmodern talk. (Habermas 2006: 150–1)

In like fashion, none other than the late postmodern thinker Jacques Derrida affirmed the same historical fact about the biblical faith's influence:

> Today the cornerstone of international law is the sacred, what is sacred in humanity. You should not kill. You should not be responsible for a crime against the sacredness, the sacredness of man as your neighbor … made by God or by God made man … in that sense, the concept of crime against humanity is a Christian concept and I think there would be no such thing in the loft today without the Christian heritage, the Abrahamic heritage, the biblical heritage. (Derrida 1999)

This is in keeping with human rights scholar Max Stackhouse's comment: "intellectual honesty demands recognition of the fact that what passes as 'secular,' 'Western' principles of basic human rights developed nowhere else than out of key strands of the biblically rooted religion" (Stackhouse 2004: 25; see Stackhouse 2005). What's more, Harvard's Mary Ann Glendon has documented that the chief movers establishing a Universal Declaration on Human Rights in 1948 (which speaks of humans being "endowed with reason and conscience") were primarily church coalitions and individual Christian leaders who worked closely with some Jewish rabbis to create a "new world order" of human rights (Glendon 2001).

This mindset is in keeping with the biblical tradition of all humans being made in the divine image and with the Christian tradition in particular of the Christian call to follow a suffering Savior, to be a friend of sinners, to love one's enemies. This means identifying with the less-fortunate, the disempowered, the suffering. In his book on the valuable contribution belief in God has made in Western society, agnostic political scientist Guenter Lewy contrasts the mindset of the naturalist and the theist in this regard:

> Adherents of [a naturalistic] ethic are not likely to produce a Dorothy Day or a Mother Teresa. Many of these people love humanity but not individual human beings with all their failings and shortcomings. They will be found participating in demonstrations for causes such as nuclear disarmament but not sitting at the bedside of a dying person. An ethic of moral autonomy and individual rights, so important to secular liberals, is incapable of sustaining and nourishing values such as altruism and self-sacrifice. (Lewy 1996: 137)

This reminds me of what British journalist Malcolm Muggeridge wrote after spending many years in India and Africa. There he witnessed "much righteous endeavor undertaken by Christians of all denominations." By contrast, however, "I never, as it happens, came across a hospital or orphanage run by the Fabian Society or a Humanist leper colony." Caring for the profoundly needy more readily springs from the worldview of biblical theism than from naturalism.

Furthermore, from the cradle of biblical theism and its emphasis on human rights, the field of bioethics would emerge in the early 1960s. Indeed, the impulse to defend human rights took on greater urgency in the wake of the Tuskegee syphilis experiments and the *Roe v. Wade* decision in the early 1970s. Daniel Callahan has been closely associated with the emergence of the modern bioethics movement and is co-founder of the Hastings Center; he writes of the theological context that first informed this field. "When I first became interested in bioethics in the mid 1960s, the only resources were theological or those drawn from within the traditions of medicine, themselves heavily shaped by religion" (Callahan 1990: 2–4).

So the fact that the human rights and bioethics movements emerged out of a Jewish-Christian worldview context is no accident. It is not the result of "secular Enlightenment values." Indeed, these values of human rights and equality have their metaphysical moorings in a biblical worldview. The Enlightenment created a division between theology and metaphysics, on the one hand, and ethics, on the other (Copleston 1960: 5). All of this has a bearing on how we, say, interpret (as the received narrative asserts) the "religious wars" of sixteenth- and seventeenth-century Europe. Prior to the rise of modernity in the West, Church and state were bound together. It was modernity that created the sacred-secular dichotomy: the Church's political power came to be replaced by the state's political power, which, the twentieth century showed, can be just as tyrannical. On closer inspection, the boundaries of these alleged "religious" wars were drawn primarily along political lines rather than those of sectarian affiliation (Cavanaugh 2009).

Just as secular critics have wrongly dichotomized the sacred and secular when it comes to political power, so they have done when it comes to human dignity and rights, all the while borrowing from the metaphysical capital of biblical theism. Here secular ethical theories routinely fail to distinguish between the *ordo cognoscendi* (the order of knowing) and the *ordo essendi* (the order of being). While secularists can *know* moral truth and what it is to act virtuously, they lack the resources to account for how we came to *be* morally responsible, intrinsically valuable, rights-bearing beings.

The Irrelevancy of the Euthyphro Critique

Plato's *Euthyphro* dialogue raises the question: "Is what is holy holy because the gods approve it, or do they approve it because it is holy?" (10a). In theistic terms, either God's commands are *arbitrary* (something is good *because* God commands it—and he could have commanded the opposite), or there must be some *autonomous moral standard* (which God consults in order to command). Some of theism's critics raise this purported dilemma in an attempt to show that goodness can exist independently of God, even if it turns out that there is a God. On this account, the existence of God is thus irrelevant to moral matters.

God's Intrinsically Good Character

That said, there is an abundance of literature rebutting the Euthyphro "dilemma" (for example, Morris 1987; Alston 1990; Linville 1990; Copan 2008). So it is no mild shock that atheist philosopher Louise Antony takes the Euthyphro as an "explicit and vivid" dilemma from which there is no escape (Antony 2009: 70).

In fact, the theist easily evades this false dilemma. These are not the only horns to consider: there are alternatives. The chief one is that goodness is non-arbitrarily rooted in God's necessarily good character, not in divine commands. Antony's mistaken assumption that "good = commanded by God" and therefore God could issue entirely opposite commands is strange *in excelsis*. Unlike humans, God does not have duties to follow, nor does he need them. Rather, God naturally does what is good because his character is good, loving, and just. Thus, it would be odd that God would have duties or be obligated to his own divine commands—particularly when God's personhood is the very source of goodness. While God may choose to bind himself to a promise or oath, say, to make Abraham into a great nation, it is *self*-imposed rather than *externally* imposed; God can swear by nothing greater than his own good, faithful character (Hebrews 6:13). No moral standard exists outside himself. Antony incorrectly assumes that William of Ockham's version of the divine command theory is the only game of its kind in town—that God *could* command, say, torturing babies for fun, and this would become obligatory. Antony incorrectly labels divine commands as tautologous—that "goodness" reduces to or is equated with "what God commands," and vice versa; this is a gross distortion. While God's commands are relevant to ethics, they do not define or constitute goodness. For instance, God may give certain commands (say, kosher or planting laws for national Israel) that are not permanently binding, nor is there any reason to think these are inherently good.

Furthermore, this view fails to distinguish between the *good* and the *right*. The good is the broader realm of value (axiology), which includes aesthetics, rationality, and virtues (beneficence, kindness, faithfulness). *Right*, by contrast, has to do with duty, obligation, permission (deontology). Thus, God technically has no duties, but still does what is good by nature. This failure to distinguish between *good* and *right* by many of theism's critics is a common one and has led to many unnecessary philosophical rabbit trails and cul-de-sacs.

And what of God's commanding because he loves us and because he is concerned about maximizing our ultimate well-being (Baggett and Walls 2011: 46)?

Further, because of the critic's common failure to distinguish between the *good* and the *right*, he incorrectly assumes God's character is not intrinsically good and that God could not command what is intrinsically evil. Yet a necessarily good God could not command rape or baby-torture. This would be like saying one could make a square circle or be a married bachelor, which is analytically impossible (cf. Jeremiah 19:5 [NASB]: "… nor did it ever enter My mind").

However, as the cosmic moral authority, God may command something difficult, which we fallible humans cannot adequately understand, but something for which God has morally sufficient reasons (on this, see Baggett and Walls 2011).

A wise, all-good God may on rare occasions or in dire conditions command something jarring (for example, for Abraham to offer up Isaac), which means having morally sufficient reasons for doing so (for example, to test Abraham's faith that God will show himself trustworthy to fulfill his promise, even if it means raising Isaac from the dead). That said, we do have certain unshakable intuitions that it is always wrong to rape or torture babies for fun; it would be self-contradictory that a necessarily good God would command such things. Omnipotence is not sheer brute force; rather, God possesses and exercises this quality in conjunction with other great-making properties, including intrinsic goodness. So for the critic to ask "What if God commanded something intrinsically evil?" is to propose the impossible (*contra* Morriston 2009).

Further Responses to the Euthyphro

More can be said in response to the Euthyphro, which I can only here summarize (but see Copan 2013).

First, if the naturalistic (or non-theistic) moral realist is correct about needing to have some standard external to God, then she herself cannot escape a similar dilemma, mutatis mutandis: if two entities are sufficient to establish a relation (here, between God's intrinsic goodness and morally constituted human beings), inserting yet a third entity—some moral standard independent of God to assess the connection between them—becomes superfluous. The skeptic's demand is unwarranted.

Consider atheist Michael Martin's claim that the ideal observer theory (IOT) renders a theistic account of objective morality obsolete. "Good" is what "an ideal observer would approve under ideal conditions" (ch. 3 in Martin 2002).

If torturing babies for fun is wrong because an ideal observer says so, then *is torturing babies for fun wrong because the ideal observer says so, or does the ideal observer say so because torturing babies for fun is wrong?* If we use Martin's (and Antony's) logic, we would still have a moral standard independent of the ideal observer—an IIOT!

Second, the naturalist's query becomes pointless: we must eventually arrive at some self-sufficient, self-explanatory stopping point beyond which the discussion cannot go. As we saw with the IOT, why is this "independent moral standard" any less arbitrary a stopping point than God's own intrinsically good personhood?

Third, the necessity of moral truths does not diminish their need for grounding in a necessary personal God, who exists in all possible worlds. "Consciousness necessarily exists" is so precisely because God—a supremely self-aware being—exists in all possible worlds. A necessarily good God's existence also means that objective moral values are necessary—that is, they exist in all possible worlds precisely because a supremely good God exists all possible worlds (Craig 2009: 169–71).

Fourth, God, who is essentially perfect and thus worship-worthy, does not have obligations to some external moral standard; God simply acts, and, naturally, it is good. If there were an evil, but very powerful, creator of human beings, then humans would *not* be obligated to obey or worship such a being. Maximal excellence, not sheer will or power, is sufficient to ground worship-worthiness.

Fifth, though the goodness of God's personhood grounds his commands, commands still play an important role. Divine commands may partially serve as guidance in particular instances where there would otherwise be no moral obligation (for example, certain food laws in the Old Testament to distinguish Israel from surrounding nations). Furthermore, divine commands may strengthen moral motivation (for example, a strong reminder from a loving friend that spurs us into action, though we know the right thing to do) (Zagzebski 2004; Swinburne 2009).

Sixth, the acceptance of objective values assumes a kind of ultimate goal or design plan for human beings. Why think humans have any objective end or *telos*, say, to be intellectually fulfilled or to use their talents to the fullest? On naturalism, we are the products of mindless, valueless, unguided processes. Why *ought* things be different, as this assumes some kind of design plan?

Seventh, even if there were some moral standard independent of God, it still would fail to account for how humans, given their valueless, unguided, deterministic, materialistic origins came to be morally valuable, rights-bearing, morally responsible beings. From valuelessness valuelessness comes. On theism, God, the supremely valuable being, creates finite, morally valuable creatures. Value produces value.

It is worth noting that the true believer is motivated by dedication to a personal being, not to Platonic moral facts. Ultimate happiness is not found in some crass, selfish material or hedonistic reward, as critics commonly charge, but in the enjoyment of the company of the God whom the believer has served and in whose personhood is the very standard of goodness. Thus the believer can and should be good for goodness' sake; after all, Virtue, which is maximally exemplified in God, is its own reward in that the reward for a life pursuing virtue is unselfishly enjoying the company of the One who is Virtue itself.

Kant and Divine Commands

Moral Certainty, Moral Principles, and Divine Commands

Commenting on Abraham's sacrifice of Isaac in Genesis 22, Immanuel Kant called this account a "myth." On what grounds? Because no God worthy of the name could have commanded it. In fact, wrote Kant, Abraham should have replied to this supposedly divine voice: "That I ought not kill my good son is quite certain.

But that you, this apparition, are God—of that I am not certain, and never can be, not even if this voice rings down to me from (visible) heaven" (Kant 1996a: 203–4). Kant scholar Lewis White Beck sums up Kant's perspective: "Any religion that requires anything of man other than earnest and conscientious morality is mere superstition and idolatry" (Beck 1997: 76; see also ch. 4 in Cliteur 2010).

Atheist philosopher Raymond Bradley asserts that the biblical God violates—or commands humans to violate—basic moral principles. What would otherwise appear to be murder, say, appears to be morally permissible because "God commanded it." Yet, he adds, this is in conflict with our basic moral understanding. For God to, say, strike down Uzzah for touching the ark (2 Samuel 6:7) or to command Abraham to sacrifice Isaac violates a basic moral principle any right-thinking person recognizes to be true. In the latter case, according to Bradley, for Abraham to obey God's command in violation of the principle "it is morally wrong to murder"

> would be to ally oneself with moral monsters like Genghis Khan, Hitler, Stalin, and Pol Pot. It would be to abandon all pretense to a belief in objective moral values … [This] would be tantamount to an embrace of moral nihilism. And no theist who believes in the Ten Commandments or the Sermon on the Mount could assent to that. (Bradley 2003: 144, 136)

Now, biblical theists will readily acknowledge that the Scriptures record certain difficult divine commands. Bradley, however, is simply wrong in what he claims. First, he insists heeding God's command leads to moral nihilism—that *no* action is morally wrong. Second, he claims that obeying God over against recognized objective moral principles entails that the atrocities of Genghis Khan, Hitler, Stalin and Pol Pot were not morally wrong. As it turns out, both implications conflict with the moral teachings of Scripture and what right-thinking biblical theists are committed to.

The biblical theist can readily argue that, yes, there are certain universal moral principles that should never be violated *and* that a good God would *never* command them—say, torturing babies for fun, molesting children, or raping women. Yes, certain actions are always evil, and it would be impossible for God, given his intrinsically good nature, to command them. But recall the distinction between the *difficult* and the *impossible*: a good God may—under certain conditions and for some morally justifiable reason (though not necessarily apparent to us)—command something that is difficult to square with our moral understanding.

Now, if we assume that God could never command something that challenges our moral understanding, this takes for granted our moral judgments do not ever need revising or refining. As we shall see below, a good God may command something that violates a general prima facie moral principle that is not technically exceptionless. In our own society, we recognize that certain authorities (for example, those working in the police force or penal system) are justified in exerting force that ordinary citizens would not be permitted to do. How much more would this apply to a good God and Creator of all! This exception does not mean that the general prohibition against, say, killing the innocent is no longer binding but that there may be certain unusual circumstances under which such principles can be overruled.

Take the September 11 terrorist attacks. When these terrorists hijacked planes and thus put at risk many more lives on the ground, President Bush gave orders to shoot down the planes—filled with innocent passengers—which had suddenly become weapons of large-scale murder. Again, while tragic, such a command was justified in an attempt to stop the killing of many more innocent persons. Was such an order morally justifiable? One can certainly make a good case for this.

So one can coherently embrace a view in which God commands something under extraordinary circumstances, but that does not commit us to moral nihilism, nor does this exonerate Hitler or Stalin. Unlike Abraham's surrendering of Isaac, which is founded on strong biblical and historical evidence (see Kitchen 2003), we have no good reason to think that God commanded Hitler and Stalin to act as they did. The biblical theist has good theological reason to think that such unusual commands were *sui generis*, uniquely given in the unfolding of salvation-history, which would not carry over beyond that era. This hardly renders morality arbitrary (*contra* Cliteur 2010: 212–14). Again, if God is necessarily perfect in character, then he simply would not command what is intrinsically evil. The claim that it is possible for God to command people to torture others for fun is true only if it is possible for a morally perfect person to command such an atrocious thing. But, as we have seen, this is analytically *impossible*! The very reason critics cite examples such as torturing people for fun is because these actions are paradigms of conduct that no morally good person could ever entertain or endorse. Indeed, God declares there are things he could never command: "They have built the high places of Topheth, which is in the valley of the son of Hinnom, to burn their sons and their daughters in the fire, which I did not command, and it did not come into My mind" (Jeremiah 7:31 NASB).

Moreover, let us revisit the distinction between the *good* (axiology) and the *right* (deontology). The common rejoinder by theism's critics is that if some action is wrong because God prohibits it, then God cannot be said to be good in any meaningful sense. The claim "God is good" turns into no more than the claim that "God commands"—a tautology. Now, this distinction between *good* and *right* is important because many critics assume that God, if he exists, has the same duties that human beings do—and that God has the same rights over creatures as they have over one another. For example, if humans have a duty not to take an innocent human's life, then neither can God.

This is incorrect. God does not have actual duties; he simply acts, and what he does is good. This also includes his opposition to torturing babies for fun or molesting children. The *good* is not identical to the *right* or *moral*. So it is a confused notion to say that goodness is "what God commands." No, goodness extends beyond morality, and God is not subject to his own commands. Rather, his commands spring from his good character. Again, God does not have actual duties since God's goodness is broader than this. That does not mean that God does not oppose rape or torture for fun.

God's commands do not result in good and evil trading places. Baggett and Walls refer to these as "convictions of the deepest ingression that they are truly non-negotiable, and unable to be relinquished—not just psychologically, but rationally, at least without perverting morality itself" (Baggett and Walls 2011: 135). As we have seen, human beings are fallible in their moral judgments, which regularly need revising. Yet a necessarily good God could not command what is intrinsically evil and thus morally non-negotiable. Imagine a command to kill everyone around you purely for entertainment, or a command involving the permissibility of harming, hurting, and inflicting suffering on people for no reason at all. Or consider a command to hate God and despise all other human beings. Similarly, one cannot accept a system of divine commands where every duty we believe in is declared false. Nor can we accept a system which suggests that the vast majority of our moral beliefs are mistaken.

The important question to ask is *not* whether our moral beliefs are revisable, but rather whether this or that particular moral belief is non-negotiable. Even certain general moral principles like "It is wrong to kill innocent people" are not non-negotiable. Many ethicists recognize that this can be overridden in rare circumstances of "supreme emergency"—for example, when the alternative to killing non-combatants in war is to tolerate significantly greater evils, and the consequences of refraining from killing are significantly bad (ch. 16 in Walzer 2000; Primoratz 1997). Whatever one thinks of this position, it cannot be dismissed as conceptually incoherent. If a proponent of an absolutist position on killing non-combatants examined the arguments and concluded that, in rare circumstances of supreme emergency, killing non-combatants was not wrong, then it is implausible to suggest that their concept of goodness was so radically at odds with prior beliefs that good and evil would trade places, or that their position consisted of mere word games. This position may be false, but it is not obviously incoherent. Such a principle is prima facie binding, but it is not a non-negotiable principle, as can be seen in highly unusual, extraordinary circumstances—and this could certainly apply to a good God's difficult command in unique circumstances, such as Abraham's sacrificing Isaac.

We come back to Kant. Even if it is coherent for God to issue difficult commands, the question remains: "Is it rational to obey them?" Kant thought that Abraham should have said "No!" to any perceived voice from heaven commanding the sacrifice of Isaac. Kant's argument presupposes that *whenever two conflicting claims differ in epistemic status, the claim with the lower status is to be rejected* (Quinn 2005: 316). His contention that "it is wrong to kill innocent people" is a statement of certainty, but that God commands or forbids a certain action is not—and can never be—apodictically certain. So, however coherent the possibility of difficult divine commands may be, one can never rationally accept such a claim is true.

Philip Quinn points out two problems with Kant. First, "Kant has an extremely optimistic view of our ability to attain epistemic certainty about principles of moral wrongness" (ibid.: 318). Kant thinks we can be *certain* of moral claims *across the board*. This, however, is dubious. Yes, we can be confident that it is wrong to inflict as much pain as we can on another merely for our own entertainment. We are quite certain that killing and lying are prima facie wrong, and they can only be justified if some overriding moral reason applies. However, many moral claims are far from certain. Capital punishment, what counts as justifiable war, and certain end-of-life issues are far less clear. While there are defensible and justified answers to these questions, we doubt that we can claim Kantian *certainty* about answers to these questions. Indeed, we should distinguish between objective ethical principles—which may not be exceptionless (for example, the ethical legitimacy of deceiving Nazis to protect innocent Jews)—and absolute, exceptionless ones (like the wrongness of rape or torturing babies for fun).

Second, Kant claims that we can *never* be certain that God has commanded a certain action:

> That to take a human being's life because of his religious faith is wrong is certain, unless (to allow the most extreme possibility) a divine will, made known to the inquisitor in some extraordinary way, has decreed otherwise. But that God has ever manifested this awful will is a matter of historical documentation and never apodictically certain … it is at least possible that on this point error has prevailed. (Kant 1996b: 283)

Even if this is true, Quinn notes, it "would thus seem to be well within God's power to communicate to us a sign that confers on the claim that God commands [an action] a fairly high epistemic status" (Quinn 2005: 319). It is far from clear that moral claims about the wrongness of specific actions must always have a higher epistemic status than theological claims involving God's commands.

Indeed, this has been challenged by Christopher Eberle, who observes that many skeptical worries raised about belief in God's commands apply with equal force to moral beliefs (Eberle 2002: 234–87). Eberle notes problems such as the lack of public intelligibility, public accessibility, replicability, fallibilism, external criticism, independent confirmability, and proof of reliability leveled against theological beliefs all apply to moral beliefs as well.

What's more, Kant himself had the benefit of the historical influence of biblical theism on Western culture, which has come through (to use Kant's terms) "the intermediary of human beings and their interpretation" (Kant 1996b: 283). Most Westerners' beliefs in liberal ideals, such as, the equality of women, opposition to slavery, human rights, and so on are mediated through human beings and traditions our parents bequeathed to us—indeed, traditions that have been given shape by the biblical tradition (see Schmidt 2004). It's simply not true—indeed is question-begging—that moral beliefs always have a higher epistemic status than beliefs about God's commands. What's more, it has been well argued by Alasdair

MacIntyre that Enlightenment thought's inability to ground objective moral values led to the favoring of emotivism by logical positivism and other such modernist positions (ch. 5 in MacIntyre 2007).

We can be quite certain that, *in normal circumstances*, taking innocent life is wrong. However, that it is *never under any* circumstances permissible is extremely controversial. That there are rare exceptions to rules against killing when there is some greater good involved is widely accepted in contemporary ethics: threshold deontology, act-utilitarianism, rule-utilitarianism, and Rossian deontology all accept this conclusion. *It is, at best, controversial that a principle rejected by almost all of the major ethical theories on offer today is more plausible than belief that God on rare occasions commanded the taking of innocent life.* Surely, some argument is needed before the biblical theist is required to accept this controversial claim.

There does not seem any compelling reason why a biblical theist cannot claim that God has on rare occasions, for the sake of a greater good, exempted people from the prohibition to kill by commanding them to do so.

One more matter on Kant: notice how he takes for granted something like the *imago Dei* in all human beings. While philosophers like John Hare consider Kant's argument to require God's existence (see Hare 2007), secularists who make use of him to separate God and morality must still grapple with this point: Kant's purported claim that morality is independent of God *still assumes* intrinsic human worth, but this worth exists precisely because humans have been made in God's likeness. Secularists appropriating Kant's own argumentation are only keeping the discussion at an epistemological level. In hiding behind Kant, they completely bypass any metaphysical justificatory context for human worth. Such a use of Kant simply presumes human dignity—as though it is ontologically free-floating. That is, such an interpretation of Kant still does not inspire any confidence that naturalism can ground intrinsic human worth and thus human rights. Kant so understood still does not show how morality at the deeper, metaphysical level can be detached from God.

The Narrative of Abraham and Isaac

As the Abraham story is Kant's particular focus, let us say a few words about the biblical account here (for more on this, see Copan 2011). From the outset, God had guaranteed Abraham that his offspring would bring blessing to the nations of the world (Genesis 12:1–3). Thus, this *promise* to become a great people and to bless the nations of the earth cannot be separated from God's later *command* in Genesis 22 regarding Isaac. In fact, God had already brought about a miracle by giving Abraham and Sarah the child of promise, Isaac, in their old age. Isaac and Isaac alone was the child through whom the blessing would come. Second, God had already given Abraham an earlier test, commanding Abraham to let his son Ishmael—the *non*-promise child—go into the wilderness, but only after reassuring Abraham that God would also make Ishmael a great nation (Genesis 17:20).

Given this historical backdrop, Abraham had confidence that *even if the child of promise died, God would somehow accomplish his purposes through that very child.* Abraham believed *God could even raise Isaac from the dead.* That's why Abraham told his servants before he headed to Mount Moriah with Isaac, "*We* will worship and then *we* will come back to you" (Genesis 22:5, NIV). Commenting on this passage, the author of Hebrews observed that since Abraham "had received the promises," he "considered that God is able to raise people even from the dead" (Hebrews 11:17–19, NASB).

Philosopher John Hare provides this thought experiment: what if God rearranged the world so that it had different features and thus different ways to apply moral principles? Say that God willed that at the age of 18, humans should kill each other, but that *God would immediately bring them back to life and in robust health.* In that case, killing people at this age would not be a big deal (Hare 2001: 68–9). Yes, in *the world that we know*, 18-year-olds—and non-18-year-olds—die because of blunt traumas, cancer, auto accidents, and a myriad of other killers. Because of this, killing innocent people in the actual world is wrong. That is just a fact about the world.

As we consider the Abraham story with Isaac's miraculous birth, the divine promise to make him a blessing to the nations, and the promise that Ishmael would not die but would become a great nation as well, Abraham truly knew that Isaac would live to adulthood and have offspring in fulfillment of God's promise; so, if necessary, Abraham reasoned, God would bring Isaac back from the dead: "*we* will return," Abraham promised his servants. So if Abraham *knew* God would fulfill his covenant promise, *then Abraham's taking innocent human life in this case—according to God's command—was morally permissible.*

As we've seen, our ethical understanding is partly shaped by certain facts about the world. If we lived in a world in which hitting people in the head helped improve their health rather than caused them harm and pain, then such actions would be encouraged. Yes, in the actual world, hitting people in the head typically causes harm. However, this shows that the command "Don't hit people in the head" depends on certain givens about the world. However, we know that if these facts about the world were different, then the prohibition would be irrelevant.

So, what if the facts about the world include a good God who specifically reveals himself to certain persons in salvation-history and may issue extraordinary commands in these specific, unique contexts but with morally sufficient reasons? It seems that the critic's task is to show why someone like Abraham, given all he had come to know through God's previous dealings with him, should not obey God's command. After all, Abraham knew the outcome based on his previous experience with God and that taking innocent Isaac's life would only mean that God would resuscitate him so that God's covenant promise would be fulfilled. Yes, without the historical context of God's call to Abraham and the promise of blessing as well as the miraculous birth of Isaac, Abraham would have been murdering his son, but that's not what we have in the book of Genesis (material here adapted from Flannagan and Copan 2013; and Copan 2011).

If our ethical understanding is shaped by certain facts about the world, how would our thinking be different if a maximally great supernatural being who reveals himself in history and is capable of raising the dead is part of that world's set of facts? This point would undermine, say, the criticisms of Kant's reading of Genesis 22 since Kant was operating with an incomplete understanding of the facts. God's command was not intrinsically evil since Isaac, like the 18-year-olds who instantly come back to life when killed, would have come back from the dead if necessary.

Conclusion

We have seen that human rights are best grounded in the metaphysic of biblical theism, in which a good personal being makes human beings in his image. A naturalistic worldview of selfish genes and electrons simply lacks ontological grounding for the emergence of intrinsic human dignity and worth. While naturalists can *know* moral truths, the more relevant question for our discussion on human rights is how intrinsically valuable *beings* could exist at all.

Those who attempt to utilize the Euthyphro argument to argue for objective morality without God still do not account for how beings of intrinsic worth could arise from valueless matter. Secondly, history has shown that both the human rights and bioethics movements were inspired by the biblical faith—not the secular Enlightenment. Thirdly, the Euthyphro argument is more epistemological than ontological and does not touch on the strangeness of human worth and rights given a context of valueless, unguided, non-conscious material processes. Further, critics of even a nuanced divine command ethic often fail to make proper distinctions (for example, between the good and the right), and they wrongly assume that God is not necessarily good in their claim that God "could just command the opposite morality" (that is, what is intrinsically evil). Such confusions must be addressed properly in order to more fully secure the connection between divine goodness and human rights. Finally, regarding the claim by some of Kant's interpreters that morality is theologically autonomous, this view utterly disregards the metaphysical context for how intrinsic human worth could emerge from valueless matter; such an approach keeps the discussion at the epistemological level but fails to show how an affirmation of human dignity is metaphysically justified. Moreover, the claim that God could not have commanded Abraham to sacrifice his son Isaac—in the name of Kantian moral certainty—is itself grounded in a number of philosophical and theological confusions and overstatements.

Biblical theism offers us the best hope for metaphysically grounding intrinsic human worth and thus human rights. Non-theistic alternatives, however morally insightful they may be in constructing ethical systems, necessarily remain ontologically incomplete.[2]

2 Thanks to Angus J.L. Menuge for his helpful comments on an earlier draft of this chapter and to Matt Flannagan for his input on divine command ethics.

Bibliography

Alston, W.P. 1990. Some suggestions for divine command theorists, in *Christian Theism and the Problems of Philosophy*, edited by M.D. Beaty. Notre Dame, IN: University of Notre Dame Press.

Antony, L. 2009. Atheism as perfect piety, in *Is Goodness without God Good Enough?*, edited by R.K. Garcia and N.L. King. Lanham, MD: Rowman & Littlefield.

Baggett, D. and Walls, J.L. 2011. *Good God: The Theistic Foundations of Morality*. New York: Oxford University Press.

Beck, L.W. 1997. *Six Secular Philosophers: Religious Thought of Spinoza, Hume, Kant, Nietzsche, William James and Santayana*. Bristol: Thoemmes Press.

Bradley, R. 2003. A moral argument for atheism, in *The Impossibility of God*, edited by M. Martin and R. Monnier. Amherst, MA: Prometheus Books.

Callahan, D. 1990. Religion and the secularization of bioethics, *Hastings Center Report*, 20, 2–4.

Cavanaugh, W. 2009. *The Myth of Religious Violence: Secular Ideology and the Roots of Modern Conflict*. Oxford: Oxford University Press.

Cliteur, P. 2010. *The Secular Outlook: In Defense of Moral and Political Secularism*. Oxford: Wiley-Blackwell.

Copan, P. 2008. Theism, naturalism, and the foundations of morality, in *The Future of Atheism*, edited by R. Stewart. Minneapolis, MN: Fortress Press.

Copan, P. 2011. *Is God a Moral Monster? Understanding the Old Testament God*, Grand Rapids, MI: Baker.

Copan, P. 2012. The naturalists are declaring the glory of God: Discovering natural theology in the unlikeliest places, in *Philosophy and the Christian Worldview: Analysis, Assessment and Development*, edited by D. Werther and M.D. Linville. New York: Continuum.

Copan, P. 2013. Ethics needs God, in *Debating Christian Theism*, edited by C.V. Meister, K. Sweis, and J.P. Moreland. Oxford: Oxford University Press.

Copleston, F.C. 1960. *A History of Philosophy*, 9 vols. New York: Image Books, vol. 6.

Craig, W.L. 2009. This most gruesome of guests, in *Is Goodness without God Good Enough?*, edited by R.K. Garcia and N.L. King, Lanham, MD: Rowman & Littlefield.

Dawkins, R. 1995. *River Out of Eden: A Darwinian View of Life*. New York: Basic Books/Harpercollins.

Derrida, J. 1999. “Religion and Postmodernism” conference, Villanova University (October). Available at: http://citation.allacademic.com/meta/p_mla_apa_research_citation/2/6/5/7/6/pages265765/p265765–21.php [accessed: October 19, 2012].

Eberle, C. 2002. *Religious Convictions in Liberal Politics*. Cambridge: Cambridge University Press.

Firth, R. 1952. Ethical absolutism and the ideal observer, *Philosophy and Phenomenological Research*, 12(3), 317–45.

Flannagan, M. and Copan, P. 2013. Does the Bible condone genocide? in *In Defense of the Bible*, edited by S. Cowan and T. Wilder. Nashville, TN: B&H Academic.

Glendon, M.A. 2001. *The World Made New: Eleanor Roosevelt and the Universal Declaration of Human Rights*. New York: Random House.

Habermas, J. 2006. *Time of Transitions*, trans. C. Cronin and M. Pensky. Cambridge: Polity.

Hare, J.E. 2001.*God's Call: Moral Realism, God's Commands and Human Autonomy*. Grand Rapids, MI: Eerdmans.

Hare, J.E. 2007. *God and Morality: A Philosophical History*. Oxford: Blackwell.

Jackson, T.P. 2005. The image of God and the soul of humanity: Reflections on dignity, sanctity, and democracy, in *Religion in the Liberal Polity*, edited by T. Cuneo. Notre Dame, IN: University of Notre Dame Press.

Jonsen, A.R. 1998. *The Birth of Bioethics*. Oxford: Oxford University Press.

Kant, I. 1996a. Religion within the boundaries of mere reason (1793), in *Religion and Rational Theology*, trans. A.W. Wood and G. Di Giovanni. Cambridge: Cambridge University Press.

Kant, I. 1996b. The conflict of the faculties (1798), in *Religion and Rational Theology*, trans. A.W. Wood and G. Di Giovanni. Cambridge: Cambridge University Press.

Kitchen, K.A. 2003. *On the Reliability of the Old Testament*. Grand Rapids, MI: Eerdmans.

Lewy, G. 1996. *Why America Needs Religion*. Grand Rapids, MI: Eerdmans.

Linville, M.D. 1990. On goodness: Human and divine, *American Philosophical Quarterly*, 27(2), 143–52

Locke, J. 1690. *Two Treatises of Government*. Many editions.

MacIntyre, A. 2007. *After Virtue: A Study in Moral Theory*, 3rd edn. Notre Dame, IN: University of Notre Dame Press.

Mackie, J.L. 1982. *The Miracle of Theism*. Oxford: The Clarendon Press.

Maritain, J. 1951. *Man and the State*. Chicago, IL: University of Chicago Press.

Martin, M. 2002. *Atheism, Morality and Meaning*. Amherst, MA: Prometheus Press.

Montgomery, J.W. 1986. *Human Rights and Human Dignity*. Grand Rapids, MI/Dallas: Academie/Probe.

Morris, T.V. 1987. Duty and divine goodness, and the necessity of God's goodness, in *Anselmian Explorations*. Notre Dame, IN: University of Notre Dame Press.

Morriston, W. 2009. What if God commanded something terrible? A worry for divine-command meta-ethics, *Religious Studies*, 45(2), 249–67.

Muggeridge, M. 1969. *Jesus Rediscovered*. New York: Pyramid Publications.

Nielsen, K. 1990. *Ethics without God*. Buffalo: Prometheus.

Nietzsche, F. 1968. *Twilight of the Idols and the Anti-Christ*. New York. Penguin Books.

Plantinga, A. 2010. Naturalism, theism, obligation, and supervenience, *Faith and Philosophy*, 27(3), 247–72.
Primoratz, I. 1997. The morality of terrorism, *Journal of Applied Philosophy*, 14(1997), 221–33.
Ramsey, P. 1971. The morality of abortion, in *Moral Problems*, edited by J. Rachels. New York: Harper & Row.
Quinn, P. 2005. Religion and politics, in *The Blackwell Guide to Philosophy of Religion*, edited by W. Mann. Oxford: Blackwell.
Rawls, J. 1999. *Theory of Justice*, 2nd edn. Cambridge: Harvard/Belknap Press.
Reed, E.D. 2007. *The Ethics of Human Rights: Contested Doctrinal and Moral Issues*. Waco, TX: Baylor University Press.
Russell, B. 1963. A free man's worship, in *Mysticism and Logic and Other Essays*. London: Allen & Unwin.
Sartre, J-P. 1957. *Existentialism and Human Emotions*. New York: Philosophical Library.
Schmidt, A. 2004. *How Christianity Changed the World*. Grand Rapids, MI: Zondervan.
Sinnott-Armstrong, W. 2009. *Morality without God*. Oxford: Oxford University Press.
Smith, C. 2009. Does naturalism warrant a moral belief in universal benevolence and human rights?, in *The Believing Primate: Scientific, Philosophical, and Theological Reflections on the Origin of Religion*, edited by J. Schloss and M.J. Murray. Oxford: Oxford University Press.
Stackhouse, M.L. 2004. A Christian perspective on human rights, *Society*, 41(2), 23–8.
Stackhouse, M.L. 2005. Why human rights needs God: A Christian perspective, in *Does Human Rights Need God?*, edited by E.M. Bucar and B. Barnett. Grand Rapids, MI: Eerdmans.
Stark, R. 2005. *The Victory of Reason*. New York: Random House,
Swinburne, R. 1977. *The Coherence of Theism*. Oxford: Oxford University Press.
Swinburne, R. 2009. What difference does God make to morality?, in *Is Goodness without God Good Enough?: A Debate on Faith, Secularism, and Ethics*, edited by R.K. Garcia and N.L. King. Lanham, MD: Rowman & Littlefield.
Walzer, M. 2000. *Just and Unjust Wars: A Moral Argument with Historical Illustrations*, 3rd edn. New York: Basic Books.
Wielenberg, E.J. 2005. *Value and Virtue in a Godless Universe*. New York: Cambridge University Press.
Wielenberg, E.J. 2009. In defense of non-natural, non-theistic moral realism, *Faith and Philosophy*, 26(1), 23–41.
Wielenberg, E.J. 2010. Objective morality and the nature of reality, *American Theological Inquiry*, 13(2), 77–84.
Zagzebski, L. 2004. *Divine Motivation Theory*. Cambridge: Cambridge University Press.

Chapter 2

Theism and Human Rights

Paul Cliteur

In an article on "Culture, Religion, and Gender" the Israeli professor of law Frances Raday (b. 1944) takes a clear stance with regard to religion and human rights. Human rights as we know it today, she writes, "is a product of the shift from a religious to secular state culture at the time of the Enlightenment in eighteenth-century Europe" (Raday 2003: 663). The eighteenth century was a time when the religious paradigm was replaced by secularism, communitarianism and individualism; and status by contract. According to Raday the modern concept of human rights is the child of secularism. She quotes with approval the historian Yehoshua Arieli (1916–2002) who wrote:

> The secular character of the normative system embodied in human rights doctrine is essential to its comprehension. All its premises, values, concepts and purposes relate to the homocentric world and to ways of thought freed from transcendentalist premises and from the jurisdiction of religious authority. And so, the development of the doctrine of human rights is inseverably connected to the process of secularization of Western society … . (Raday 2003: 663)

The vision of Raday and Arieli means there is a clash between human rights culture and classical theism as it manifests itself in the great monotheistic traditions of Judaism, Christianity and Islam. And this conflict will by some be interpreted as a specification of a wider conflict, namely that between modern scientific culture and ancient religion (Menuge 2001).

This view is not universally shared, to say the least. There are many authors who point out the continuous relevance of the premodern worldview of theism for our contemporary morals and culture. In *The Bible Now* Richard Elliott Friedman and Shawna Dolansky tell us that many people still study the Bible as a foundation of morality and virtue (Friedman and Dolansky 2011: xi). Reading the books of Karen Armstrong (b. 1944) or listening to a recent convert to Catholicism such as Tony Blair (b. 1953) one gets the impression that all our modern enlightened values are not only derived from religious sources but dependent thereon (Armstrong 2007, 2009a, 2009b; Blair 2010; Griffiths 2011).

There seems to be a prima facie contradiction between two groups of scholars: those who see a contradiction between modern human rights and theism and those who consider human rights to be a product of theism and dependent on it (Copan 2011).

But soon things turn out to be more complicated. Reading Elliott Friedman's and Dolansky's *The Bible Now* more closely we stumble upon sentences like "the Bible has often been misused" (Friedman and Dolansky 2011: xiii) and "people used the Bible for harm" (ibid.: xii).

Apparently, according to the authors of *The Bible Now* there is a "use" of the Bible. And "using" the Bible teaches us "the Bible is an extraordinary repository of remarkable stories, exquisite writing, and revolutionary laws" (ibid.: xi). But there is also a "misuse" of the Bible. This is the case when the Bible is used for "harm."

That means there is a third position about the relationship between theism and human rights. Theism can be "used" as a basis for harmful practices, but theism can also be used for good. The authors even tell us when that misuse is in play: when the Bible is used for "harm."

This puts us on the track of further questions like the following: is "harm" the only criterion we have at our disposal to speak of "misuse" of the Bible or are there any other criteria? Answers to this question might prove helpful because there are many discussions nowadays where freedom of religion as interpreted by orthodox religious people and human rights doctrine seem to clash. Theism seems at loggerheads with human rights in questions concerning the sanctification of violence (jihad, crusades; Kelsay 2009), male and female circumcision (Tamir 1996; Putzke et al. 2008), unstunned ritual slaughter of animals (Lerner and Rabello 2006/2007), homosexuality (Wolfenden Report 1963), the death penalty (Beckwith 2002) and many other subjects.

It is the aim of this chapter to explore this field. I want to develop criteria for the legitimate "use" of religion within the context of human rights. To illustrate my argument it is helpful to treat one of the vexing issues around the legal definition of religion. Here there is more than one option, but I choose the issue of unstunned ritual slaughter, more particularly the question whether the exemption of the general obligation to stun animals before slaughter can be justified on the ground of freedom of religion.

In the pages that follow I will first give an idea of the structure of human rights law with regard to the freedom of religion. Subsequently I will show why unstunned ritual slaughter became an issue in the Netherlands. Finally I will try to argue that unstunned ritual slaughter does not necessarily have to be considered a "religious" issue. At the end of this chapter I will present some guidelines for the legal acknowledgement of religion.

Human Rights in Treaty Law

To understand the aim of this exercise it is necessary to say something about the way human rights are protected in human rights treaties. Reading these human rights treaties will make clear that the question "what is religion?" is far from academic. This is not the case because "religion" and "religious practices" enjoy a special legal protection in the constitutions of most European states and also in international human rights treaties where freedom of religion is accepted as a basic or fundamental right.

The European Convention on Human Rights includes Article 9. This Article has two paragraphs and both are important with regard to the protection of freedom of religion. The first paragraph goes as follows:

> 1. Everyone has the right to freedom of thought, conscience and religion; this right includes freedom to change his religion or belief and freedom, either alone or in community with others and in public or private, and to manifest his religion or belief, in worship, teaching, practice and observance.

The crucial word is "religion." Like "thought" and "conscience," religion enjoys a special protection. Whether "religion" deserves that protection on an equal par with "thought" and "conscience" is not something I will address in this chapter. I will take as my point of departure that there is "freedom of religion" as a constitutional and human right. Those who argue that there should be no separate provision for freedom of religion but only for freedom of speech or freedom of conscience will consider my argument beside the point. But I will take for granted that for historical and intrinsic reasons there is special protection for religion. Subsequently, I will try to develop criteria of how to deal with that freedom of religion. If an idea or a practice is not recognized as "religious" in nature there is no chance of having this idea or practice protected as religious freedom under a human rights regime. But if it is, the person invoking that freedom can claim a special protection of his beliefs and manifestation of that belief.

But once this hurdle is taken, there is another in the second paragraph of Art. 9.

> 2. Freedom to manifest one's religion or beliefs shall be subject only to such limitations as are prescribed by law and are necessary in a democratic society in the interests of public safety, for the protection of public order, health or morals, or for the protection of the rights and freedoms of others.

On Limiting the Freedom of Religion

As follows from the foregoing paragraphs: human rights are not absolute. Most of them are limited, and those limitations have been laid down in human rights treaties. Let us focus on the limitations on the freedom of religion as laid down in paragraph 2 of Article 9 of the European Convention on Human Rights. How are we to read those clauses?

In my interpretation the clearest and least misleading way to read these limitations is to say that they express *additional necessary conditions to have freedom of religion effectively protected.* What the whole Article on the freedom of religion teaches us (in both the European Convention and also the International Convention) is that once an idea or practice is recognized as "religious," this is only a *necessary* (and not a *sufficient*) condition for an effective protection of this idea or practice under a human rights regime. To have that effective protection of a human right fully realized, another condition has to be fulfilled, namely that the expression or manifestation of this religious idea or religious practice does not violate (i) the law;[1] (ii) does not contravene democratic standards, and (iii) does not violate certain standards of public order, health or morals or the rights and freedoms of others.

Unstunned Ritual Slaughter

Now I will be somewhat more specific about the matter of slaughtering animals. In this chapter I want to reflect on the concept of "religion", as used in Article 9 of the European Convention. But I want to do this in relation to a much discussed religious practice lately, namely unstunned ritual slaughter of animals. The question is this. People use meat for consumption. There is much to say about this habit, but this is not the topic of my chapter (Regan 1980; Walters and Portmess 1999). People eat meat and we will take that for granted. But at the same time people want to assure that animals that are about to be slaughtered experience only a minimum of stress and pain during the process (at least, that is often presented as the rationale behind the legislation on humane slaughter). For that reason, many countries adopted legislation that prescribes "stunning" before the animal is killed. Only "stunned" ritual slaughter was considered to be "humane" (Welty 2007; Miller 1959; Mariucci 2008).

This legislation is challenged by religious groups (Jewish and Muslim) claiming that stunning violates their freedom of religion. Unstunned ritual slaughter is for example prescribed for the kosher *schechita*. There are also some Muslim groups who claim that halal meat requires unstunned ritual slaughter. So the question is: can those exemptions from general legislation about the slaughtering of animals be acknowledged as the expression of a religion?

Although most countries accept exemptions from the general prescription of stunning before slaughter, these exemptions are challenged by animal rights activists and veterinarians who point out that unstunned ritual slaughter is not a very animal-friendly practice. In May 2012 the British veterinarian Professor Bill Reilly, a former president of the British Veterinary Association, caused some controversy with an article in *Veterinary Record*, a publication of that same organization. Reilly criticized the—in his opinion—"unacceptable" rise in the number of animals killed in ritual slaughter. Reilly said: "In my view, the current situation is not acceptable and, if we cannot eliminate non-stunning, we need to keep it to a minimum" (BBC News 2012b). He proposed two things: (i) restricting the use of halal and kosher meat to those communities that require it

1 Which can be problematic, because we have countries where, for example, apostasy is illegal though it seems integral to freedom of religion.

for their religious beliefs and (ii) convincing those religious communities of the acceptability of stunned alternatives.

Reilly provoked many negative reactions from the religious communities he was accused of having attacked. Simon Cohen of Shechita UK contested the scholarly information that Reilly tried to convey. His research was "deeply flawed," according to Cohen. Dr. A. Majid Katme from the Islamic Medical Association joined Cohen in criticizing the assumption that science had proven that unstunned ritual slaughter was more painful for animals than stunned slaughter. She made an addition, however, discrediting the implicit religious criticism that she thought was inherent in Reilly's stance. She said: "It is arrogant for someone who is not a Muslim to presume that he can teach us the practice of our faith" (ibid.). But Reilly got support from organizations concerned with animal welfare. Joyce D'Silva, from the charity organization Compassion in World Farming, said: "Judaism and Islam believe that animals are creatures of God; science tells us that they are sentient beings, who can suffer" (ibid.).

These are all indications that the issue of ritual slaughter is highly controversial and this discussion is not likely to abate in the coming period. In the Netherlands there was a discussion on the same topic when in 2011 a legislative proposal was launched by The Party for the Animals (Tweede Kamer, Lower House of Parliament, 2009–10, 31 571, nr. 2). On June 28, 2011 in the lower house of the Dutch Parliament an overwhelming majority of 116 against 30 votes opted in favor of a bill making it obligatory to stun animals before slaughter. The exemption from the general obligation for religious groups would be eliminated from Dutch law.

I will come back to the Dutch discussion on this topic later in this chapter. Let me start with the general rule on stunning according to Dutch law: Animals to be slaughtered are required to be stunned before slaughter. But in the Dutch Health and Welfare Law ("Gezondheids- en Welzijnswet"), there was an Article 44, paragraph 3, making an exemption for religious ritual slaughter: "Slaughtering animals without pre-stunning according to the Israelitic or Islamic rites is allowed." The proposal for legislation by the Party of the Animals would change this. They proposed to change the Article in the legal code cited in the following manner: "Slaughtering animals according to the Israelitic or the Islamic rites is only allowed when the animal is stunned." This topic gained international attention. BBC News Europe reported: "Dutch MPs effectively ban ritual slaughter of animals" (BBC News 2011). But only a few months later, on December 14, 2011 the Dutch Senate decided to freeze its vote against the ban on unstunned ritual slaughter (Eerste Kamer, Bedwelming bij ritueel slachten, 31571, December 13, 2011).

The Importance of this Debate

Why is this debate on unstunned ritual slaughter important at all? One thing is certain: it is not because unstunned ritual slaughter is the most important issue regarding animal welfare. There are countless other issues that deserve more attention from the perspective of animal rights or animal welfare (Van den Berg 2012). If we would consider legislative measures concerning animal welfare, a legislative bill making it a criminal act to consume meat would be far more effective. But that is not the point of this chapter. This is about animal welfare as such. What my intention is, is to analyze one specific issue where freedom of religion (or religion) gets into conflict with the modern secular morality of human rights, more in particular with the utilitarian aim to increase the happiness in this world. The topic of unstunned ritual slaughter is one of the many issues I could have selected to make my point. My point is this: in a modern liberal democracy we can accept freedom of religion only up to a certain degree. Freedom of religion can be accepted insofar as it is in harmony with generally accepted human rights and moral standards. What I will try to do is to develop criteria that judges and legislatures can use in order to decide where freedom of religion is legitimate and where it is not. For this purpose the discussion on unstunned ritual slaughter proved a fruitful case.

For the moment, the discussion in the Netherlands may have come to a halt. But the debate brought us into the heart of the discussion about the notion of "religion." In most discussions on this subject unstunned ritual slaughter is presumed to be a "religious" prescript. With "presumed" I mean that many commentators do not contest the "religious nature" of this practice. So it is often taken for granted that the first hurdle (paragraph 1 of Article 9 ECHR and paragraph 3 of Article 18 ICCPR) for the acceptance of this religious freedom is lightly taken. What the discussion is focused on subsequently, is on the question whether there are good reasons to *limit* this religious practice (on the basis of paragraph 2 of Article 9 ECHR; Haupt 2007).

That common way of framing the dilemma is unfortunate to my mind. The thesis that I want to develop in this chapter is that there are good reasons to contest the recognition of unstunned ritual slaughter as being "religious" *at all*. We should at least consider, for example, whether it is not rather a "cultural" practice. Or perhaps it is an "ideological" custom instead of a "religious" one. So according to the approach indicated in this chapter the question is not whether those presumed religious practices can be subject to limitations as are "prescribed by the law." Nor is it whether those limitations are "necessary in a democratic society," or whether those limitations are required "in the interests of public safety, for the protection of public order, health or morals, or for the protection of the rights and freedoms of others." No, the more fundamental question is: is it "religious" in the first place? It is the first paragraph of Article 9 ECHR we must be concerned with, not the second.

This indicates that we seriously have to ponder the question what the word "religion" means in the context of human rights declarations. An important question in that context is: does this mean the same thing as the word "religion" in ordinary parlance? Or is the *legal* meaning of the word significantly different? And if so, *in what sense* is the legal meaning of religion different from religion in, for example, a social sense?

One of the most fundamental insights of the theory of interpretation is that context matters. If something is accepted as "religion" in the *social* sense, does that necessitate us to accept it as "religion" is the *legal* sense? (Fuller 1958). And if there is a difference, where does that difference lie? Is it possible, for example, to sketch the contours of a workable definition of "religion" in the legal sense?

As will be made clear in the course of my argument, this is an important question that has a much wider significance than the discussion of ritual slaughter. Whether we like it or not (and some people do not seem to like it) we simply must confront the most fundamental question: what is religion? Once this question is answered it will be clear that the answer is relevant not only for the matter of unstunned ritual slaughter but for many other controversial cases where the interpretation of religion is crucial.

What Does "Religious" Mean?

Now prima facie this focus on the meaning of the word "religion" may not seem a very promising and relevant angle to approach the matter of ritual slaughter. Is it not roughly clear what we mean by "religion"? And rituals, not only around slaughtering animals but other occurrences (think of male circumcision, for instance) as well, seem indubitably part of "religion," do they not? Yet, if one goes a little deeper into the matter of "religion" it appears a much more elusive concept than some of the other phenomena mentioned in the European Convention on Human Rights. One of the claims of this chapter is that although it is difficult to say where the limits of "free expression" (Article 10 ECHR) should lie, there is not a protracted debate about what counts as the expression of an idea or the airing of an opinion. And although one may differ about the boundaries of the "freedom of assembly" (Article 11 ECHR), there is no heated debate about the question whether a gathering of people is really an "assembly."

Strange though this may seem, this is different when it comes to "religion." There is a widespread dissensus about what ideas should be considered "religious" and which of those seemingly "religious" ideas should really be categorized as "political," "cultural," "ideological" or simply "mad." "Religion" is an—with apologies for using this threadbare concept—essentially contested concept in the sense that "speech" and "assembly" are not (Clack 2008; Yandell 1999; Hick 2004; Alston 1967). We should face this openly.

The "Religiosity" of Unstunned Ritual Slaughter

This is also pertinent to the matter of ritual slaughter. Are the rules around ritual slaughter really "religious" rules? Or are they merely "cultural" and ideological"?

Pablo Lerner and Alfredo Mordechai Rabello in their elaborate and highly relevant treatment of stances on ritual slaughter refer to a *fatwa* accepting stunning

(Lerner and Rabello 2006/7). The Mufti of Dehli stated in a *fatwa* in 1935 that stunning would not violate any religious prescript because stunning does not kill the animal (which would clearly contradict the Islamic prescriptions around slaughter), but only "stuns" the animal. The method indicated is referred to as "reversible electric stunning" which means that the animal can recover, and so is not dead. The Mufti stated that it is permissible to stun the animal as long as the animal does not die in the process of stunning.

A second authoritative Islamic declaration regarding ritual slaughter is that of the Rector of the Al-Azhar University of Cairo from 1982. Stunning would not make the practice unislamic. And on the Jewish sources Norman Solomon (b. 1933) writes: "Not all Jews are equally strict in their observance of kashrut (what is or is not kosher). Some Reformers reject the system entirely, stressing that the essence of Judaism is ethics, not diet … " (Solomon 2000: 90).

These stances are, as one may expect, contested by other sources. And then the question comes up: which interpretation of religion is right? But that is a difficult question to answer, of course, and so most interpreters try to circumvent that tricky matter. That also holds true for Lerner and Mordechai Rabello. They write:

> Any framework for the protection of religious beliefs and practices should not be sought in the "correct" interpretation of the religious text, especially when there is controversy. Theological arguments trying to adopt a narrow or broad interpretation afford no real solution to this problem; the concern of this Article is rather to explain why a ban on this practice (*i.e.* unstunned ritual slaughter; PC) may be seen by Muslims or Jews as being at odds with their faith. (Lerner and Rabello 2006/7: 12)

It is this approach I want to challenge in this chapter. Of course Lerner and Mordechai Rabello are right that a ban on the practice of unstunned ritual slaughter "may be seen by Muslims or Jews as being at odds with their faith," but this cannot be decisive (Lerner 2006/7: 12). Experience teaches us that a ban on the practice of unstunned ritual slaughter is seen by *other* Muslims and Jews as perfectly in harmony with their faith. The approach by Lerner and Mordechai Rabello taking what by some Muslims or Jews is at odds with their faith would result in a kind of *laissez faire* approach towards religious practices. There will always be religious believers who proclaim some practices as required or inspired by their religion. Especially in a world of religious diversity there are myriads of religious beliefs and practices and simply all legal duties would be floating into the air once we would make compliance with the law dependent on the question whether this would not contradict some interpretation of some religion by some religious interpreter.

This is especially relevant, as I will try to show in the development of my argument, when great new moral principles are at stake, for example the principle to minimize harm and suffering not only for human animals but also for non-human animals. Simply accepting *everything* as "religion" that some people or some religious leaders present as "religious," although seemingly sympathetic (and according to some based on "respect" for religion or religious believers), would undermine not only the idea of fidelity to the law (Fuller 1958), but also the whole idea of freedom of religion. If religious freedom is to mean anything *at all* there must be a dividing line between what can be accepted as "religious" and what not.

Yet I am perfectly aware that the road ahead of us, not only practically but also from a theoretical point of view, is full of hurdles. What criterion should one use to accept some idea or practice as "religious"? This is no easy question to answer.

One of the criteria one could adopt is: numbers count. In other words: we need a majority or substantial minority of believers who subscribe to a certain practice. But then the question forces itself upon us: why is this relevant? Why could for example a small minority not be right? This is something we can ascertain in other areas of life as well. Take science. If it were true that numbers count, the views of Darwin, Newton, Galileo or Einstein could never have prevailed. Would not the same be true in religion? If "might is right" would be the only criterion in religion, the Catholic Church would have been right and not Luther. But apparently even a minority can present something that can become a majority opinion. Taking the perspective that only numbers count would mean that from a legal perspective the Reformation is not acknowledged as a religious movement as long as it has not established itself.

So numbers cannot be decisive. But what can?

Islam-scholar Hans Jansen (b. 1942) writes: "Freedom of religion is no license for cannibalism or headhunting. Or (suicide)terrorism. Or any form of violating the freedom of movement of others" (Jansen 2011: 198). So if you say it is your religious duty to eat your fellow man, this will not be recognized as "religious" by the European Court of Human Rights in Strasbourg. If you proclaim that you have to wage religious war against the enemies of God, this is not protected "religion." If we follow Jansen we cannot accept as "religion" what violates the freedom of movement of others. We must acknowledge that civilization is evolving and blind spots of former times now seem to stand in broad daylight. Is that not part of what we call "Enlightenment"? Perhaps Frances Raday is right and not only are human rights a "product" of the shift "from a religious to secular state culture at the time of the Enlightenment," but also, the Enlightenment is still the background culture against which we have to understand human rights (Raday 2003: 663).

A Debate in the Dutch Senate

That brings us to a contemporary discussion around the interpretation of religion and freedom of religion: the matter of unstunned ritual slaughter. With regard to the suffering of non-human animals there clearly is an evolution of ideas that cannot escape us. The only thing we have to discover now is *what consequences* to draw from these new insights. That is what the discussion is about. And here we have on the one hand authors like Singer advocating a new morality (Singer 2011), taking also the lives of non-human animals into consideration, and on the other hand the traditionalists like Oderberg (2000a, 2000b) who think that reference to the way freedom of religion was traditionally understood is of overriding importance.

On December 13, 2011, in the Senate of the Netherlands there was a debate on unstunned animal slaughter (Eerste Kamer, Bedwelming bij ritueel slachten, 31571, December 13, 2011). There had already been a discussion in Parliament going on in Dutch society since the summer of 2011 when a legislative proposal was launched by The Party for the Animals (Tweede Kamer, Lower House of Parliament, 2009–10, 31 571, nr. 2). This topic gained international attention. BBC News Europe reported: "Dutch MPs effectively ban ritual slaughter of animals. And the religious sensitivity was spelled out with the words:

> The Dutch lower house of parliament has passed a law effectively banning the ritual slaughter of animals, in a move condemned by Muslim and Jewish groups. The legislation states that all animals must be stunned before being killed. But the Islamic *dhabiha* and Jewish *shechita* methods of ritual slaughter require them to be fully conscious. (BBC News 2011)

The Party for the Animals (a political party founded in 2002 having two seats in Dutch Parliament) suggested prohibiting the practice of unstunned ritual slaughter in this country. Under the new law, pre-slaughter stunning of animals would become obligatory for all forms of slaughter.

On June 28, 2011 in the lower house of the Dutch Parliament an overwhelming majority of 116 against 30 votes opted in favor of the bill. But only a few months later, on December 14, 2011 the Dutch Senate decided to freeze its vote against the ban on unstunned ritual slaughter. This was done after Jewish and Muslim groups had campaigned, saying that there is no evidence animals suffer more from ritual slaughter than in ordinary abattoirs. Moreover, and this is what concerns us here, they claimed that a prescription of stunning before slaughter would compromise the freedom of religion. For the moment, the discussion in the Netherlands may have come to a halt.

Yet the question is: will this be the final word? One may doubt that. It seems the die has been cast. It is very likely this discussion will be reopened, not only in the Netherlands, but also in other countries where animal welfare is a cause for increasing concern of the public. Here I will focus on the latest discussion on this matter, that is, the discussion in the Senate.

It was interesting to see all those accomplished legal scholars, struggling with moral questions that, somehow, their legal training had not quite prepared them for.

On the basis of the development around animal rights it seems not unreasonable to speak of a new moral principle to heed the interests of non-human animals (Rachels 1991 Regan 1983; Salt 2012). It cannot be the case that this moral development has no repercussions for the way we interpret "religion." We now interpret (and must interpret) "religion" in the light of fundamental moral principles (although we still have to inquire into the nature of those principles).

Article 13 of the Treaty of Lisbon (signed by the EU member states on December 13, 2007, and entered into force on December 1, 2009) states that animals are "sentient beings." This is the vindication of an insight formulated by John Stuart Mill (1806–73) in *Utilitarianism* (1863) that "the whole sentient creation" deserves our attention from a moral point of view (Mill 1992: 123). That does not make non-human animals completely equal to human animals. It does not annul "freedom of religion" completely as alarmist voices want us to believe, nor does it make freedom of religion totally subservient to animal welfare. And finally it does not place the interests of animals above the interests of humans. These are all common misinterpretations of the situation we have to deal with. It does no more than state that the concept of "religion" in the legal sense cannot stay fixed. "Present day religion" is something different from religion in medieval times. The judiciary and the legislature simply cannot ignore that (Cliteur 2009).

But having said that, we still have no clear-cut criteria to decide how to interpret religion in a present day context. Can we say more than that religion has to be "morally acceptable"? That it may not violate "the freedom of movement of others" (Jansen 2011: 198)? That people may not use "the Bible for harm" (Friedman and Dolansky: xii)? And if they do, this is "misuse"?

In my view we can. We can be more specific and we must be more specific. It is possible and necessary to articulate some principles that may serve as guidelines in the interpretation of present day religion.

In what follows I will try to present some guidelines for this interpretation of the concept of "religion" in a legal context.

First Principle: No Cruelty or Violence

To identify principles that may guide us with regard to what can be acknowledged as "religion" it may be helpful to reflect on some of the examples considered very "religious" and pious in ancient times and nowadays usually rejected as "caricatures," "perversions" or "misuse" of religion ("religion hijacked" for political purposes).

Prominent examples seen as manifestations of religious piety in ancient times but nowadays rejected in horror are Abraham being prepared to offer his son (Delaney 1998; Kretzmann 2001; Cliteur 2010), the burning of witches (Lehmann 1988) and the military expeditions (crusades) stimulated by the pope in Rome (Phillips 2009). We know that those activities were experienced by contemporaries as undoubtedly "religious" although many of us cannot see them that way in our own time. If that is the case it may be helpful to raise the question: *why* can we not see these practices as religious anymore? A provisional answer to that question is: because we consider these practices as immoral. That is undoubtedly true, but at the same time it may be enlightening to throw up the question *why* these acts are nowadays considered to be immoral (although highly pious in previous epochs)? Answering this question cannot be too difficult. In all three examples we recognize a common thread: violence. Why do we not accept the sacrifice of children, the waging of war in the name of God and the burning of witches? What is wrong with these things? Is not, at least partly, what we find revolting in these practices that there is a clear tendency to violence and cruelty? Could we not formulate the essence of modern civilized values as the attempt to gradually diminish violence and cruelty from this world?

This is not to endorse a Whig view of the history of the West or the adoption of a historical determinism annex belief in "linear progress." What it is, is to state the obvious: that man must create a world that is a better place for everyone, also for non-human animals. That ambition of the Enlightenment as implemented in the nineteenth century in works such as Lecky's *History of European Morals from Augustus to Charlemagne* (1869) and his *History of the Rise and Influence of Rationalism in Europe* (1865) is still on the agenda. As J.B. Bury demonstrates in his *The Idea of Progress: An Inquiry into its Origin and Growth* (1920) working for progress is not a shallow or naive ideal. Peter Singer's *The Expanding Circle* (1981), *One World: The Ethics of Globalization* (2002), and *Animal Liberation* (1975), are in that tradition.

According to the psychologist Steven Pinker (b. 1954) in his book *The Better Angels of Our Nature: Why Violence has Declined* (2011) there is moral progress in the sense that our times are less violent than foregoing ages (which presupposes, of course, that suffering is a great evil, Pinker 2011). There are many examples of practices that have died out in the cultural evolution of mankind and which have to do with violence. Think of public executions. Everyone who has read some literature of seventeenth-, eighteenth- and nineteenth-century authors knows about the sometimes vivid descriptions of public executions in Europe. On October 13, 1660 Samuel Pepys (1633–1703) noted in his *Diary*: "I went out to Charing Cross, to see Major General Harrison hanged, drawn and quartered – which was done there – he looking as cheerfully as any man could in that condition" (Rivlin 2002: 213).

Second Principle: No Harm to Others

But there is more. If we compare some of the manifestations professed to be "religious" by some believers and denied that status by others, there seems to be the problem that some people decide about other people's fate. The harm being perpetrated is not "harm to self," but "harm to others" (Feinberg 1987, 1989). When Deuteronomy 13:6–11 instructs us to stone to death our own "brother," "daughter" or "wife" if they engage in illicit religious ceremonies this sounds very "universal," as if every single member of the community has the same chance to fall victim to these prescripts. But the social reality is different. It is the weaker members of the community that are being sacrificed to whip the whole community into submission to a few strong alpha males: the "community leaders" (Benson and Stangroom 2009; Mernissi 1992; Manji 2011; Cliteur 2011).

It may be illuminating also to refer to the discussion about anesthetics and inoculation. Clergymen (and medical men inspired by the clergy) once regarded vaccination of humans as, Bertrand Russell (1872–1970) relates, "bidding defiance to Heaven itself, even to the will of God" (Russell 1935: 104). In 1885, when there was a severe outbreak of smallpox in Montreal, the Catholic part of the population resisted vaccination. As one priest said: "If we are afflicted with smallpox, it is because we had a carnival last winter, feasting the flesh, which has offended the Lord" (ibid.). Natural disasters as a punishment of God for the sins of mankind is one of the most common arguments to make sense out of the manifest cruelty of nature. How to reconcile this with the idea of an omnipotent and benevolent deity?

Another discussion arose after the discovery of anesthetics. When James Young Simpson (1811–1870) in 1847 recommended their use in childbirth, the clergy reminded him that God said to Eve: "In sorrow shalt thou bring forth children" (Genesis 3:16). Russell comments: "And how could she sorrow if she was under the influence of chloroform?" (ibid.).

A discussion ensued because Simpson met his adversaries with new theological arguments. He advanced that there was no harm in giving anesthetics to *men* because God had put Adam in a deep sleep when he extracted Eve from the rib of man. According to the ecclesiastics this only saved men and not women – so the ban on the use of anesthetics in childbirth should remain intact.

Why does this discussion strike us as absurd and unsympathetic? As a first step to answer that question let us now suppose someone would decide *for himself* not to have himself inoculated against a deadly disease because he puts his trust in God. Should the state allow this to happen? In that situation there is no "harm to others," but "harm to self." Here, as John Stuart Mill famously stated in his *On Liberty* (1859), there are strong reasons for the state *not* to interfere. In this case individual autonomy should be our loadstar. Whoever freely chooses not to take measures against his own suffering is free to do so. Harm to self should be allowed. At least in the case of persons fully conscious of that they decide. But the example of anesthetics during childbirth is not of that category. Here *men* decide for *women* that anesthetics is against the word (and therefore will) of God. And here we may say: let women decide for themselves. Or even better: let every individual decide for him/herself.

Third Principle: Equality

That brings me to a third principle that may be helpful in deciding what practices can be accepted as "religious." To gauge the significance of that third principle an example may be helpful. On December 5, 1955 Martin Luther King, Jr. (1929–1968) delivered his famous speech to the Montgomery Improvement Association about Rosa Parks (1913–2005), the woman who refused to give up her place in the bus on behalf of a white person (King 2006). King was an impressive speaker. In his characteristic style he castigates the authorities who arrested and carried to jail "one of the finest citizens in Montgomery" because "she refused to get up to give her seat to a white person" (King 2006: 516). This protest cannot be wrong, King says. And then he presents an interesting argument:

> If we are wrong, the Supreme Court of this nation is wrong. If we are wrong, the Constitution of the United States is wrong. If we are wrong, God Almighty is wrong. If we are wrong, Jesus of Nazareth was merely a utopian dreamer that never came down to earth. (King 2006: 518)

Martin Luther King may have been a great orator. But that does not *eo ipso* mean he was a clear thinker. Suppose some male chauvinists or misogynists would challenge Martin Luther King and say: "How can you be so sure that God is on the side of Rosa Parks? Did not God create man and women? And did he not in His Book several times proclaim that man is the master of the household or – which comes to the same thing – a man the master of his woman?"

The male chauvinists could back up their ideas by references to God's Word, in particular some expressions by St. Paul. In 1 Timothy 2 Paul admonishes women to "dress themselves modestly and decently in suitable clothing." They should not have their hair braided. "Let a woman learn in silence with full submission," St. Paul says and continues:

> I permit no woman to teach or to have authority over a man; she is to keep silent. For Adam was not deceived, but the woman was deceived and became a transgressor. Yet she will be saved through childbearing, provided they continue in faith and love and holiness, with modesty. (1 Timothy 2:12–15)

Martin Luther King seems to think that on the basis of the foregoing he can enlist the following institutions and persons for his feminist and anti-racist cause:

1. The Constitution of the United States;
2. God Almighty;
3. Jesus of Nazareth.

He supposes these all agree about the matter before us, but that is a dubious statement, to say the least. The Constitution of the United States has different ideas on equality than God Almighty or Jesus Christ. That is to say: the Constitution of the United States is firmly based on the principle of equality. The Bible (God and Jesus Christ) is not.

Fourth Principle: Religion Subjected to Reasonableness

So far we have seen that with regard to the interpretation of the concept of religion as it appears in Article 9 ECHR there are at least three principles that may serve as guiding ideas. To acknowledge "religion" in a human rights context, this "religion" may not:

1. be violent or cruel;
2. harm others;
3. infringe equal concern of interests.

The fourth principle I want to discuss is perhaps the most far-reaching. The question we must address is whether under the present circumstances we may demand from believers claiming the freedom of religion, that their claims are understandable to a nonreligious or differently religious audience. It is the four principles together that may serve as a "canon of interpretation" for the interpretation of "religion" when we come across that word in human rights declarations and constitutions.

These four principles are constitutive for the *legal* (or normative) concept of "religion" in contradistinction to the *social* (or descriptive) concept of religion. Unconsciously and without any methodological basis, authors like Karen Armstrong and Tony Blair followed that canon of interpretation in their discussions with the New Atheists. Their only mistake was that they thought they presented a *description* of an existing reality while what they did was tell us what they think is acceptable.

Secularism and Animal Welfare

Now let us go back to the discussion on unstunned ritual slaughter in the Dutch Senate. During the debate there were some relatively new political parties that presented fresh and interesting ideas about the controversy of unstunned ritual slaughter. One of those parties was the Independent Senate Fraction (Onafhankelijke Senaats Fractie). Its representative, Professor De Lange, an emeritus professor in chemistry from the Free University in Amsterdam, proffered a principle that has rarely been stated so clearly in the Dutch legislative assembly before. Professor De Lange explained that the considerations of his party with regard to the matter of unstunned ritual slaughter were animated by a principle that he identified as the "laïcité" or "secularism" (Weil 2009; Chirac 2004; Fourest and Venner 2003; Kintzler 2007; Cliteur 2012; Blackford 2012). His party, so De Lange said, operated on the basis of a "strict secular" foundation (Eerste Kamer 2011–12: 39). And by this he meant: Church and state have to be separated. His party respected the constitutionally protected freedom of religion of others, but nevertheless he stated that arguments that are derived from religion in the societal debate should not play a preponderant role. He also proclaimed that religion should have a "private" character.

Furthermore De Lange commented on vegetarianism. This, he said, could not be enforced by the state nor should it be. But that the slaughter of animals should be performed with a minimum of stress and anger for the animals involved would be a pertinent moral obligation. Unstunned ritual slaughter dated from a period when mankind had no means at its disposal to alleviate the suffering of animals. Now mankind has. And therefore mankind is morally obliged to use these methods (that is, stunning). Arguments based on "revelations of a supernatural being" that are by definition impossible to verify, are insufficient to annul that moral obligation. It is for that reason that his faction would not consider those religious arguments valid.

On the basis of these considerations De Lange voted in favor of the proposal to eliminate the religious exception to stun animals before slaughter.

His intervention did not solicit any comments from his colleagues in the political assembly. This is unfortunate, because his specific angle of approaching the problem of ritual slaughter was fresh and potentially far-reaching.

Is this Interpretation of Secularism not too Strict?

But perhaps his statements were too bold to be accepted in the form he stated them. Does, for example, the principle of the secular state (Blackford 2012) entail that religious arguments are no longer admissible in politics? Would not that go too far? Nevertheless, De Lange is right when he says that a serious disadvantage of religious arguments (that is, arguments that are purely religious and do not make an apologetic that is independently persuasive) is that they will not convince an auditorium that is composed of listeners with a diverse religious and nonreligious background. So in political assemblies in pluralist societies (as most societies are nowadays, especially in the Western world) those arguments are little more than an *oratio pro domo*.

In my view the principle of "laïcité" should not be interpreted in the sense that religious believers are not allowed to present religious arguments in the public sphere. They have "permission to speak," so to say. Yet, there is a more restrictive interpretation of the principle of secularism that may be more appropriate in this context. This more restrictive interpretation can hardly be considered as too demanding or put too many constraints on religious believers. It is this more limited interpretation of secularism that seems pertinent here. This limited interpretation means that when the judiciary has to ascertain what is the legal meaning of "religion" in the context of present day human rights declarations and constitutional provisions in modern constitutions, this concept of "religion" has to meet certain standards of reasonableness that at least have a potential to convince us all. Here referring to a private "revelation" is simply not enough. As Thomas Paine (1737–1809) famously explained: if something has been revealed to a certain person, and not revealed to any other person, it is "revelation to that person only" (Paine 1995: 668). The religious believer, claiming that his "religious revelations" should enjoy constitutional protection while it violates basic moral principles of a civilized society must make clear that his religion *deserves* that protection. It should not be revelation "to that person only" or "that group only."

The Burden of Proof

A consequence of the requirement stated above is that a religious believer who claims a privilege on the basis of a human right must be able to give some *reasons* why the values that he claims deserve a special status should indeed be worthy of that status.

Formulating such a requirement is certainly a break with a long established tradition that religious believers cannot be required to state the reasons for their religious belief. There is a widely shared understanding that demanding from believers to explain why they hold certain things "holy," interferes in an undue fashion with their religious freedom. But if we follow Professor De Lange's approach in the mitigated form as expounded above, I think we may safely require from someone who claims a privileged status for a "religious belief" (and on that basis exemption from the ordinary legal duties that all citizens have to conform to) that at least he provides some reasons why that belief should be classified as "religious" at all.

During the debate in the Dutch Senate this demand was voiced most categorically by the representative of another relatively new political party: Faber van de Klashorst of the Party for Freedom. Faber made clear that she comes from a butcher's family and accordingly knows what she is talking about. She soberly noticed that everyone with sound moral sense can understand that the ritual slaughtering of a healthy animal that is fully conscious of what is happening is not a very happy affair (Eerste Kamer 2011–12: 26). The animals have to be put on their backside which is an unnatural position for the animal. Instinctively the animal feels what is going to happen and it experiences fear, anger and pain. On average three to five cuts of the carotid artery are necessary before the animal loses consciousness and dies. It can last between half a minute and five minutes before the animal is really dead. Some of the animals with their neck only half cut try to stand up. "This is an awful sight. This should not happen in a Dutch slaughterhouse in 2011" (ibid.). And just as Professor De Lange did, she underscores that the religious prescripts about unstunned ritual slaughter dated from 3,000 to 1,400 years ago. Can we really claim that "best practices" of those times are still the best we can come up with in our times? If we do not accept polygamy, the stoning of adulterous women and the killing of homosexuals as legitimate expressions of religious feeling, why do we do this with unstunned ritual slaughter?

These were all pertinent questions, but her most intriguing remark was in reaction to a colleague in the Senate who spoke for a small Christian party, called the "Union of Christians" (in Dutch: "ChristenUnie"). The representative of the Christian party, Mr. Ester, contended that prohibiting unstunned ritual slaughter would put the freedom of religion under pressure (if not worse). On that occasion Faber interjected that she would like to hear why unstunned ritual slaughter was considered to be a religious prescript (ibid.: 30). Where was this written? Could her colleague show chapter and verse?

As I have made clear during the course of my argument I consider this to be a perfectly reasonable question. If someone demands to be exempted from the obligations of the law (applicable to all citizens alike, one may presume) the least one may expect is that this person is able and prepared to explain *why* he or she should enjoy a privileged status. Only referring to "freedom of religion" without being able or prepared to explain why this has something to do with religion is unreasonable and cannot be accepted in a liberal democratic regime. But the representative from the Christian party reacted as if great injustice would be done to believers if this were standard practice. He called this a "dangerous" demand, because it was not "for them," the members of the Dutch Senate, to judge what is a religious prescript and what is not. Decisions about what is a religious prescript and what not, should be left to the religious community.

As I already indicated in the beginning of this chapter this is a weak argument because the religious community is divided on the issue. Traditionally religious communities had internally identified the normative source of authority. But the problem in a pluralist society is that those sources are in disarray. Who to listen to? To the most conservative elements in the community? Or to the progressive factions? Faber did not accept Ester's answer, and rightly so. She indicated that it was at least a legitimate question whether there was a scriptural basis for the practice to kill the animal while fully conscious. And then she came with the punch line: "but you cannot show me this, because it is not written anywhere" (ibid.: 30). And Faber was right. There is no prohibition of stunning in the Torah. And therefore the claim that unstunned ritual slaughter is a "religious practice" is based on the fact that *some people* claim that this is a religious practice. But because there are also people who claim this practice is *not religious*, the judge has to decide whose arguments should prevail.

At that moment we are back at the beginning of our argument. Once we concede we can argue about what is religious and what is not, both parties have to provide arguments.

Here we see that pluralism has changed the world we live in. Religious communities do not operate as homogeneous entities in a pluralist world but *are themselves* pluralistic. It is difficult, if not impossible, to provide examples of religious prescripts that are universally shared within the religious community, and the necessity of unstunned ritual slaughter is certainly a case in point. Although orthodox believers pretend that there are clear-cut religious prescriptions representative for the religious creed of the group as a whole, this pretense is often mere nostalgia. So whenever someone has the pretense to speak for the group as a whole some skepticism is warranted.

A Common Objection: A "Dangerous" Idea

Now senator Ester and many other people feel uncomfortable with this situation because they have the feeling that respect for religion also comprises respect for the way people identify their religion. Let me return to the famous definition of religion by William James (1842–1910): "the feelings, acts, and experiences of individual men in their solitude, so far as they apprehend themselves to stand in relation to whatever they may consider the divine" (James 1982: 31). James proclaims the religiousness of a practice is dependent on whether people "apprehend themselves to stand in relation to whatever they may consider the divine." This leaves broad latitude to the individual believer to determine what he considers "divine."

This individualist approach is usually argued for as something that is required by "respect for religion" and also, even more mistaken, as respect for "the individual believer." The approach advocated by Faber, so it is often said, undermines the freedom of religion. It makes the religious freedom completely dependent on the interpretation of that freedom by outsiders, some critics contend, and this certainly animated senator Ester's reaction to senator Faber's demand to cite chapter and verse. Religion is put under the tutelage of morals and therewith basically destroyed. Is this not a "dangerous" idea, to quote Ester again?

That may be doubted. My claim is that in the end the approach by Faber is more respectful of religion than the approach by Ester. Let me summarize. We have, basically, two approaches to the concept of religion:

1. Approach Faber: some religious practices are so immoral they cannot be accepted as religious (and accordingly protected by the freedom of religion).
2. Approach Ester: what is religious and what is not, is subjected to the conviction of the individual believer.

The approach of Ester ultimately makes religion dependent on the highly individualist interpretations of sometimes quite idiosyncratic "believers" (like James argued for). It is common to view his approach as respectful to religion. But is it really? It is certainly true that the approach by Faber limits religion in the sense that it excludes some religious practices, but is that really disrespectful? Is it not, on the contrary, more respectful to religion because in the long run it saves religion from deteriorating into quite bizarre religious practices sanctioned by the most reactionary forces within the religious communities?

Again this can best be exemplified by means of an example: the official recognition of a new church and a new religion in Sweden. Recently in Sweden a new church was recognized by the Swedish government, namely the church whose central tenet is the right to file-share (BBC News 2012a). Arguably, this example shows that the approach to religion as advocated by Ester is a dead end.

Missionary Church of Kopimism

The "Missionary Church of Kopimism" (in Swedish *Missionerande Kopimistsamfundet*) claims that the act of sharing information through copying is akin, if not identical, to a religious service. The kopimists (called *Kopimists* from *copy me*) consider CTRL+C and CTRL+V (shortcuts for copy and paste) as sacred symbols. A kopimist has as the core of his professed religious belief that all information should be freely distributed unrestricted. The kopimists are opposed to the privatization of knowledge in all its forms. As they say: "in our belief, communication is sacred." This is not because they want to promote illegal file-sharing, but because this means the open distribution of knowledge for all. The church also has a spiritual leader who, elated by the recent success of his religious movement, speaks of a "large step." The church was founded by a 19-year-old philosophy student Isak Gerson who seriously hopes that now file-sharing will be given religious protection. In a statement he says:

> For the Church of Kopimism, information is holy and copying is a sacrament. Information holds a value, in itself and in what it contains and the value multiplies through copying. Therefore copying is central for the organization and its members. (BBC News 2012a)

Not everyone reacted enthusiastically, but that cannot impress the members of the new religious movement, because the Swedish government agency Kammerkollegiet finally registered the Church of Kopimism as a religious organization after three previous applications had failed.

Now the question is: what is the greatest disaster that may happen to religious freedom as protected in Article 9 of the European Convention on Human Rights? Is the greatest threat to freedom of religion that the legislature and the judiciary put limits to what can count as serious religion? Or is the greatest threat to religion that the religious community can completely determine by itself what is religious and what is not? The example of the Kopimists, in spite of the fact that they do not advocating harming anybody, may still serve as an intimidating example of what can happen with religious freedom.

Bibliography

Alston, W. 1967. Religion, in *The Encyclopedia of Philosophy*, vol. 7, edited by Paul Edwards. New York and London: Macmillan and The Free Press, 140–5.

Armstrong, K. 2007. *The Bible: The Biography*. London: Atlantic Books.

Armstrong, K. 2009a. Think Again: God. *Foreign Policy*, November/December, 55–60. Available online at: http://www.foreignpolicy.com/articles/2009/10/19/god_0 [accessed: October 19, 2012].

Armstrong, K. 2009b. *The Case for God: What Religion Really Means*. London: The Bodley Head.

BBC News 2011. Dutch MPs effectively ban ritual slaughter of animals. Available at: http://www.bbc.co.uk/news/world-europe-13947163 [accessed: October 19, 2012].

BBC News. 2012a. Sweden recognized new file-sharing religion Kopimism [Online, January 5] Available at: http://www.bbc.co.uk/news/technology-16424659 [accessed: October 19, 2012].
BBC News. 2012b. Leading vet criticizes ritual slaughter of animals [Online, May 6]. Available at: http://www.bbc.co.uk/news/uk-17966327 [accessed: October 19, 2012].
Beckwith, F. 2002. The Death Penalty, in *Do the Right Thing: Readings in Applied Ethics and Social Philosophy*, 2nd edn, edited by Francis J. Beckwith. Belmont, CA: Wadsworth, 361–4.
Benson, O. and Stangroom, J. 2009. *Does God Hate Women?* London: Continuum.
Blackford, R. 2012. *Freedom of Religion and the Secular State*. Chichester: Wiley-Blackwell.
Blair, T. 2010. *A Journey*. London: Hutchinson.
Bury, J. 1920. *The Idea of Progress: An Inquiry into its Origin and Growth*. London: Macmillan.
Chirac, J. 2004. Discours Relatif au Respect du Principe de Laïcité dans la République, Palais de l'Élysée, 17 décembre 2003, in *Guide Républicain. L'idée républicaine aujourdhui*. Paris: Délagrave Édition.
Clack, B. and Clack, B. 2008. *The Philosophy of Religion: A Critical Introduction*, 2nd edn. Cambridge: Polity.
Cliteur, P. 2009. Hard Cases in Scripture: A Reflection on Legal and Religious Interpretation, in *Holy Writ: Interpretation in Law and Religion*, edited by Arie-Jan Kwak. Farnham: Ashgate, 67–111.
Cliteur, P. 2010. *The Secular Outlook: In Defense of Moral and Political Secularism*. Chichester: Wiley-Blackwell.
Cliteur, P. 2011. Female Critics of Islamism. *Feminist Theology*, 19(2), 154–67.
Cliteur, P. 2012. State and religion against the backdrop of religious radicalism. *International Journal of Constitutional Law*, 10(1), 127–52.
Copan, P. 2011. *Is God a Moral Monster? Making Sense of the Old Testament God*. Grand Rapids, MI: Baker Books.
Delaney, C. 1998. *Abraham on Trial: the Social Legacy of Biblical Myth*. Princeton, NJ and Oxford: Princeton University Press.
Eerste Kamer (Dutch Senate). 2011. Bedwelming bij ritueel slachten, 31571, December 13. Available at: http://www.eerstekamer.nl/behandeling/20111213/voortzetting_behandeling_3/document3/f=/viwef0q2hj8w.pdf [accessed: October 20, 2012].
Feinberg, J. 1987. *Harm to Others*. New York: Oxford University Press.
Feinberg, J. 1989. *Harm to Self*. New York: Oxford University Press.
Fourest, C. and Venner, F. 2003. *Tirs Croisés: La laïcité à l'épreuve des intégrismes juif, chrétien et musulman*. Paris: Calmann-Lévy.
Friedman, R. and Dolansky, S. 2011. *The Bible Now: Homosexuality, Abortion, Women, Death Penalty, Earth*. Oxford: Oxford University Press.

Fuller, L. 1991[1958]. Positivism and Fidelity to Law – A Reply to Professor Hart. *Harvard Law Review*, 71, 630–72. Also in *Philosophy of Law*, 4th edn, edited by J. Feinberg and H. Gross. Belmont, CA: Wadsworth, 82–102.

Griffiths, R. (ed.) 2011. *Hitchens vs. Blair: Be it resolved Religion is a Force for Good in the World*. The Munk Debate on Religion, November 26, 2010. Toronto: Anansi.

Haupt, C. 2007. Free exercise of religion and animal protection: A comparative perspective on ritual slaughter. *The George Washington International Law Review*, 39, 839–86.

Hick, J. 2004. *An Interpretation of Religion: Human Responses to the Transcendent*, 2nd edn. Houndmills: Palgrave Macmillan.

James, W. 1982. *The Varieties of Religious Experience: A Study in Human Nature*, edited with an Introduction by M. Marty. Harmondsworth: Penguin Books.

Jansen, H. 2011. *Op, op, Ten strijde, Jeruzalem bevrijden!: Het ware verhaal van de* kruisvaarders. Amsterdam: Uitgeverij Van Praag.

Kelsay, J. 2009. *Arguing the Just War in Islam*. Cambridge, MA: Harvard University Press.

King, M, Jr. 2006. Speech to the Montgomery Improvement Association, in *American Speeches: Political Oratory from Abraham Lincoln to Bill Clinton*. New York: The Library of America, 516–19.

Kintzler, C. 2007. *Qu'est-ce que la laïcité?* Paris: J. Vrin.

Kretzmann, N. 2001. Abraham, Isaac, and Euthyphro: God and the Basis of Morality, in *Philosophy of Religion*. The Big Questions, edited by E. Stump and M. Murray. Malden/Oxford: Blackwell, 417–29.

Lecky, W. 1865. *History of the Rise and Influence of Rationalism in Europe*, 2 vols. London: Longman, Green & Co.

Lecky, W. 1869. *History of European Morals from Augustus to* Charlemagne, 2nd edn, 2 vols. London: Longman, Green, & Co.

Lehmann, H. 1988. The Persecution of Witches as Restoration of Order: The Case of Germany, 1590–1650. *Central European History*, 21(2), 107–21.

Lerner, P. and Mordechai Rabello, A. 2006/2007. The Prohibition of Ritual Slaughtering (Kosher Schechita and Halal) and Freedom of Religion or Minorities. *Journal of Law and Religion*, 22(1), 1–62.

Manji, I. 2011. *Allah, Liberty and Love: The Courage to Reconcile Faith and Freedom*. New York: The Free Press.

Mariucci, J. 2008. The Humane Methods of Slaughter Act: Deficiencies and Proposed Amendments. *Journal of Animal Law*, 4(April), 149–81.

Menuge, A. 2001. Lutheran Theology Meets Intelligent Design. *Dialog: A Journal of Theology*, 40(1), 61–3.

Mernissi, F. 1992. *La peur-modernité: conflit Islam démocratie*. Paris: Albin Michel.

Mill, J.S. 1989. *On Liberty, the Subjection of Women, and Chapters on Socialism*, edited by S. Collini. Cambridge: Cambridge University Press.

Mill, J.S. 1992. Utilitarianism, in *On Liberty and Utilitarianism*. New York: Everyman's Library, Alfred A. Knopf, 113–72.
Mill, J.S. 1998. Nature, in his *Three Essays on Religion*. Amherst, NY: Prometheus Books, 69–125.
Miller, A.R. 1959. Humane-Slaughter Legislation, in *Food, Drug, Cosmetic Law Journal*, 14(11), 685–94.
Oderberg, D. 2000. *Applied Ethics: A Non-Consequentialist Approach*. Oxford: Blackwell.
Paine, T. 1995. The Age of Reason, in his *Collected Writings*. New York: The Library of America.
Phillips, J. 2009. *Holy Warriors: A Modern History of the Crusades*. New York: Random House.
Pinker, S. 2011. *The Better Angels of our Nature: Why Violence has Declined*. London: Viking Penguin.
Putzke, H., Stehr, M. and Dietz, H. 2008. Strafbarkeit der Zirkumzision von Jungen. *Monatsschrift Kinderheilkunde*, 8, 783–8.
Rachels, J. 1991. *Created from Animals: The Moral Implications of Darwinism*. Oxford: Oxford University Press.
Raday, F. 2003. Culture, Religion and Gender. *International Journal of Constitutional Law*, 1(4), 663–715.
Regan, T. 1980. Utilitarianism, Vegetarianism, and Animal Rights. *Philosophy and Public Affairs*, 9, 306–14.
Regan, T. 1983. *The Case for Animal Rights*. London: Routledge and Kegan Paul.
Rivlin, G. 2002. *First Steps in the Law*, 2nd edn. Oxford: Oxford University Press.
Russell, B. 1935. *Religion and Science*. London, New York and Toronto: Oxford University Press.
Salt, H. 2012. *Animals' Rights Considered in Relation to Social Progress*. New York: General Books.
Singer, P. 1975. *Animal Liberation*, 2nd edn. London: Jonathan Cape.
Singer, P. 2002. *One World: The Ethics of Globalization*. New Haven and London: Yale University Press.
Singer, P. 2011. *The Expanding Circle: Ethics, Evolution, and Moral Progress*. With a new afterword by the author. Princeton, NJ and Oxford: Princeton University Press.
Solomon, N. 2000. *Judaism: A Very Short Introduction*. Oxford: Oxford University Press.
Tamir, Y. 1996. Hands Off Clitoridectomy. *Boston Review*, October/November, with reactions by Martha Nussbaum, Jessica Neuwirth and others.
Tweede Kamer (Lower House of Parliament), 2009–2010. 31 571, nr. 2.
Van den Berg, F. 2012. *Harming Others: Universal Subjectivism and the Expanding Moral Circle*, Ph.D. thesis. Leiden: Gildeprint Enschede.
Walters, K. and Portmess, L. 1999. *Ethical Vegetarianism*. Reprint edn. Albany, NY: State University of New York Press.

Weil, P. 2009. Why the French Laïcité is Liberal. *Cardozo Law Review*, 30(6), 2699–714.
Welty, J. 2007. Humane slaughter laws. *Law and Contemporary Problems*, 70, 175–206.
Wolfenden Report. 1963. Report of the departmental committee on homosexual offences and prostitution. New York: Lancer Books.
Yandell. K. 1999. *Philosophy of Religion: A Contemporary Introduction*. London and New York: Routledge.

Chapter 3
Why Human Rights Cannot be Naturalized: The Contingency Problem

Angus J.L. Menuge

Introduction

On the face of it, human rights can only arise from a transcendent source. This is because what we mean by a *human* right is *an inherent and inalienable entitlement* (Montgomery 1986). Inherence implies that the right arises from a human being's intrinsic nature (and not from extrinsic factors, such as birth, majority opinion, or the particular constitution adopted by a state). It is because of inherence that these rights are also inalienable: they cannot be abridged or suspended by changes in external circumstances. Yet all of this makes sense only if human beings have some special, intrinsic value worthy of protection. If the universe is a cosmic accident, it is hard to see why anything has value, and harder still to see why human beings would have rights not possessed by animals, plants and even inorganic substances. So the idea that we have a special intrinsic value seems credible only if human beings were created for some unique and important purpose by a transcendent power. Thus, to cite the clearest example, according to the Judeo-Christian scriptures, human beings were specially made in the image of God to be stewards of the rest of creation (Genesis 1:26–8). On this account, we soon learn that murder of any human being is wrong *because* that being is made in the image of God (Genesis 9:6).

Since the Enlightenment, a skeptical attitude toward revelation has made this an unpopular foundation for human rights. In its place, a number of alternatives have been proposed, including natural law, legal positivism and various neo-Kantian approaches. Yet, as Montgomery (1986) shows, all of these approaches face serious objections.[1] However, it might seem that Evolutionary Ethics (EE) provides another way of accounting for human rights without appeal to the transcendent. Proponents of EE (for example, Sober and Wilson 1998, Katz 2000, De Waal 2009) might claim that human rights claims are grounded in the natural

1 In fine, Montgomery argues that the deliverances of natural law are too vague and open to interpretation; legal positivism justifies genocide so long as it is properly legislated; and neo-Kantianism fails to explain why anyone with the power to make gains by violating the rights of others should ignore his special advantages.

history of human beings. I argue, however, that any attempt to justify human rights using EE faces a serious dilemma.

The Dilemma for Evolutionary Ethics

While a number of distinct theories fall under the umbrella of EE, a common theme is that the moral sense of human beings is the result of their natural history. For Darwin, even though the moral sense is most highly developed in human beings, this does not demonstrate a difference in kind between them and other animals. Rather, he argued that *any* animal with the right social instincts "would inevitably acquire a moral sense or conscience, as soon as its intellectual powers had become as well, or nearly as well developed, as in man" (Darwin 1998: 101). The striking implication is that the deliverances of moral sense are contingent on the accidents of natural history. Darwin drew this conclusion explicitly:

> In the same manner as various animals have some sense of beauty, though they admire widely different objects, so they might have a sense of right and wrong, though led by it to follow widely different lines of conduct. If … men were reared under precisely the same conditions as hive-bees, there can hardly be a doubt that our unmarried females would, like the worker-bees, think it a sacred duty to kill their brothers, and mothers would strive to kill their fertile daughters; and no one would think of interfering. Nevertheless, the bee, or any other social animal, would gain in our supposed case, as it appears to me, some feeling of right or wrong, or a conscience. For each individual would have an inward sense of possessing certain stronger or enduring instincts, and others less strong or enduring … In this case an inward monitor would tell the animal that it would have been better to have followed the one impulse rather than the other. The one course ought to have been followed, and the other ought not; the one would have been right and the other wrong … . (Darwin 1998: 102–3)

In Darwin's nightmare scenario, human beings might have *thought* that fratricide and infanticide were moral duties. (For similar examples, see Street 2006: 120–1.) But the important question for human rights is (F):

> (F) Would fratricide and infanticide then have *been* moral duties?

EE's answer to this question depends on whether it is construed as a weak thesis about moral sensibility, or as a much stronger claim about the origin of morality itself. In its minimal form, EE is simply a thesis of *moral psychology*: it gives an account of the origin of moral sentiments and beliefs. Call this *Weak EE*. Weak EE has no ontological implications for morality: it is consistent with there being no objective moral values, or with the existence of objective moral values radically at odds with our moral sentiments and beliefs. An ontological issue arises for EE only if it makes the further claims that (1) in general at least, our psychological states reliably track moral reality and that (2) they do so *because* what counts as a moral value itself depends on biological history. Call this *Strong EE.*

Yet EE is in trouble regardless of whether it affirms Weak or Strong EE. The dilemma for EE can be raised by focusing on its answer to question (F), for regardless of how it answers (F), EE cannot provide a credible defense of fundamental human rights. First, suppose Strong EE is affirmed (our moral sense and moral reality are shaped by our natural history), so (F) must be given an affirmative answer. Then there cannot be inalienable human rights, because changes in biological history (genes and/or the environment) can abridge or even withdraw those rights. For example, if all human beings have a fundamental right to life, this must include brothers and female infants. Yet, as Darwin points out, there are possible biological histories in which these humans have no such right, because fratricide and female infanticide are moral duties.

On the other hand, suppose Weak EE is affirmed, making it possible to give (F) a negative answer. Then although being raised like a hive-bee would not make fratricide a duty, our moral sense would tell us that it was. This leaves two alternatives: either our moral beliefs are based on our instinctive moral sense or they are not. If they are, then these beliefs clearly do not provide reliable access to moral reality, since (counterfactually) we might naturally believe fratricide was right even though it was not. So even if our actual moral beliefs about fratricide happen to be true, this is a lucky coincidence, and therefore does not constitute knowledge. But then it would follow that while there might be some inalienable human rights, we cannot claim to know it. On the other hand, if our moral beliefs are not based on our moral sense, but arise instead from reason or intuition, then since these provide access to universals truths (perhaps even Kantian universal principles of practical reason applicable to rational beings as such) which transcend the accidents of natural history, it follows that these truths are not derived from the evolutionary process, even if that process produced the faculties which make knowledge of those truths possible. Either way, Weak EE fails to account for moral knowledge.

So, the basic dilemma for EE is this. If EE is correct then either (1) human rights do not exist (the ontological problem for Strong EE) or (2) they are unknowable or knowable via means which make EE irrelevant (the epistemological problem for Weak EE). I will now further develop the ontological and epistemological problems for EE. If I am right, they show that EE cannot provide a credible foundation for human rights.

The Ontological Problem for Strong EE

For Strong EE, the skeptical question arises whether moral values, such as those underlying human rights, can really be contingent on the details of biological history. EE typically offers an account of the origin of sympathy to explain, for example, why we are moved to alleviate the suffering of others. So far, this is only Weak EE (moral psychology). But it may also be claimed that the same account also explains the origin of morality itself—for example, why it is that we *ought* to alleviate the suffering of others. This is because *ought implies can*, in the sense that the moral demand only applies to beings who have reached a certain level of social and psychological development. The failure of lions to reach this level plausibly explains why they are not obligated to alleviate the suffering of gazelles. It is then claimed that morality supervenes on the historical circumstances which make appropriate social and psychological development possible. This is the claim of Strong EE.

Thus, in Darwin's own account, there is a four-stage process which accounts not only for the emergence of humanity's moral sense, but also (it might be argued) for the emergence of creatures subject to the demands of personal and social ethics. First, since cooperation promotes the survival and propagation of human genes, it explains the appearance of the social instincts, which lead an animal to "take pleasure in the society of its fellows, to feel a certain amount of sympathy for them, and to perform various services for them" (Darwin 1998: 101). Second, as a further aid to survival, in some creatures (certainly humans), mental faculties became highly developed, so that they could review their past actions and feel dissatisfied when they acted on such temporary instinctual urges (like hunger) in opposition to their "always present social instinct" (Darwin 1998: 101). Third, when language appeared as an additional aid to cooperation, the community could express its opinion of the public good and make individuals feel accountable by relying on "sympathy … an essential part of the social instinct" (Darwin 1998: 101–2). Finally, instruction and practice led to the establishing of habitual behavior, which strengthens the social instinct.

At least on one reading, Darwin's account supports Strong EE, by showing how creatures subject to the moral demand might arise from the development of their social instincts and their intellectual and linguistic powers, and from their ability to learn moral rules by habituation (for recent accounts on these lines, see Wilson 1993, Arnhart 1998, 2005). But it also appears to follow on this account that the *specific content* of moral demands depends on the contingencies of biological history. This is because it is these contingencies that have shaped the kind of being we are, and our biological history might have endowed us with different instincts, and with different intellectual and linguistic powers, and we might have been habituated to accept different moral rules. So, for example, if we had developed like hive-bees, then we would be the kind of being for whom fratricide is a moral duty *because* (according to Strong EE) we would not only have a strong social instinct toward fratricide, but the practice would enjoy wide approval and be habitual among socially well-adjusted creatures.

This claim can be buttressed by an attempt to provide a biological definition of the *summum bonum*, the final good at which morality aims. Thus, Darwin writes:

> The term, general good, may be defined as the rearing of the greatest number of individuals in full vigor and health, with all their faculties perfect, under the conditions to which they are subjected. (Darwin 1998: 124)

On this view, morality is about biological flourishing under the historically operative conditions, and since these conditions are variable, moral demands are contingent on circumstances. However, it is precisely the contingency of the moral demand which seems to be at odds with fundamental human rights, leading to at least four main objections to Strong EE.

The Analogy with Utilitarianism

One way to see the problem with Strong EE is by analogy with a well-known objection to utilitarianism: it is easy to conceive of scenarios in which morally abhorrent behavior (for example punishing those known to be innocent, genocide, killing depressed people, etc.) would be happiness maximizing. The standard utilitarian reply is that these are "outlandish" possibilities, which do not materialize in the real world, where many people are made unhappy by such outrages. However, even if correct, the utilitarian reply is objectionable because the basic moral demands most of us recognize are made contingent on the fact that certain possibilities do not actually occur. This means, however, that the utilitarian still must say that if these possibilities were to occur, then certain horrible actions would be right; yet, most of us think, this counterfactual claim is false. What is missing from utilitarianism is an understanding of the *normative necessity* of morality, according to which genocide would still be wrong even if, for example, an efficient dictator were to succeed in brainwashing or eliminating all those who disagree with his genocidal program. It seems highly counterintuitive to claim that genocide in the actual world is wrong only because of administrative incompetence!

By analogy, the problem with Strong EE is that it must implausibly claim that widespread fratricide is wrong only because of various contingent facts, such as the fact that we did not develop like hive-bees. Strong EE must claim that if we had developed in this way, then fratricide and female infanticide would have been right, because these actions would have been conducive to "the rearing of the greatest number of individuals in full vigor and health, with all their faculties perfect" (Darwin 1998: 124). And it is easy to add further scenarios, each of which withdraws protection from another class of human beings (including sisters and male infants) until we show that even if there is no scenario in which all humans are dispensable, each human being is dispensable in some scenario or other.[2] So Strong EE implies that no human being has an unconditional right to life.

---

2 With the aid of advanced technology (banks of human eggs and sperm, artificial incubation), there are conceivable worlds in which *both* parents are dispensable. In this case,

Not only could this have happened naturally, it could be made to happen artificially. For example, a statist tyrant enamored of entomology might institute a social program under which human beings are raised just like hive-bees and in which fratricide serves the interests of biological flourishing. Under those conditions, brothers of single females would no longer have a right to life. A bizarre consequence of Strong EE is that deliberate social engineering can change fundamental moral obligations: by forcing people to live a certain way, the state can make virtually any act of killing the right thing to do. If moral demands have any normative necessity, however, it is false that for example fratricide would be right under these conditions, just as, in our actual world, it was false that the legalization of genocide by the Weimar Republic created conditions that made genocide right.

The underlying problem with Strong EE is that it has no resources for saying that any feature or behavior is intrinsically good, since what counts as "good" or "bad" depends on what is adaptive, and this varies with the environment. This holds for any adaptive feature, whether a genetic trait or a morally significant behavior. For example, it is well-known that the sickle-cell mutation (a genetic trait) confers an adaptive advantage on people living in countries with prevalent malaria (Behe 2007). So one can say that this mutation is "good" for people living in those environments, and yet it is no advantage for people living in areas with no risk of malaria (in fact, if both parents have the mutation, their children will likely develop sickle-cell anemia which will shorten their lives). Likewise, the Eskimo practice of abandoning the infirm to die (a morally significant behavior) promotes human flourishing in that environment, even though it is not necessary in ours. While the Eskimos may be justified in their practice, Strong EE has to say that it is morally *good*. More traditional ethics includes a deontological component and can say that the practice is a necessary evil, and is only "good" compared to worse alternatives. The problem is that, like utilitarianism, EE defines "good actions" as ones which are good relative to the circumstances; it cannot recognize that some of these actions are not good in themselves. This seems to be why Street (2006) concludes that only moral anti-realism, which denies the existence of moral norms independent of all our evaluative attitudes, is consistent with an evolutionary account of those attitudes. On her view, our basic evaluative attitudes depend on what happened to be adaptive for our ancestors, and as an anti-realist, she claims that moral truth is simply the "reflective equilibrium" we reach from those attitudes. Thus, the reason we do not judge that infanticide is laudable is that it was not adaptive (Street 2006: 133). Yet her account implies that were we raised like lions, who practice selective infanticide on the offspring of other lions (Street 2006: 120), then we would judge such infanticide to be right and, most likely, this would be the conclusion of reflective equilibrium, so it would also be right. While Street's view is able to embrace the central claim of EE that our evaluative

the survival of the human race would not depend on the survival of those who normally reproduce, since they would not be required for reproduction.

attitudes are shaped by natural history, it does so at the price of denying that there is a human right to life as we have defined it.

The Problem of Normativity

Some proponents of Strong EE would protest the previous argument on the grounds that an evolutionary account can ground the kind of normative claims found in the moral demand. On this view, norms are generated by biological function, and although natural selection "is not a goal-oriented process … it can produce structures and mechanisms for which talk of natural purpose and function seems naturalistically respectable" (Joyce 2007: 169). So for example, relative to what enabled mammals to survive, one can say a number of things about the value of the heart:

> Modern biology will say that the function of the heart is to pump blood, and that a healthy and good heart pumps blood well. It may even allow us to say that a heart ought to pump blood … But how close does this normative language get us to moral language? (Joyce 2007: 170)

However, Joyce points out that even if Darwinian language allows us to speak of the function of organs and what they ought to do (the latter is a highly dubious claim in my view),[3] this will not take us to the moral demands applicable to human beings. For one thing, the fact that human organs have a function does not imply that human beings *as a whole* have a function (that is a fallacy of composition), since human beings are not part of a living organism, and so their actions cannot be good for that organism. But suppose we add Darwin's claim that the flourishing of the human species is the general good which is served by all human biological functions. Perhaps we can then speak of what is good for human flourishing, just as we can say that a healthy heart is good for pumping blood.

However, as Joyce argues, this does not get us the right *kind* of normativity for morality. The fact that X is good for Y does not imply that X's doing Y is morally praiseworthy. For example, mosquitoes are good for spreading malaria, assassins are good for removing political leaders, unjust wars are good for business, gas-chambers are good for exterminating large numbers of people, and, some environmentalists argue, spreading a virus lethal to humans would be good for the global ecosystem; but this does not imply that any of these things is morally good. Likewise, given Darwin's statement that the general good is "the rearing of the greatest number of individuals in full vigor and health, with all their faculties perfect," it would seem obvious that a full plan of eugenics, including

3 All natural selection really implies is that a structure is present in an organism because it conferred an advantage on the organism's ancestors, which does not imply that conferring that benefit was a good thing (it may have made the plague more virulent, for example), or that it is a good thing that the function continues.

genetically advantageous marriages and sterilization or extermination of the unfit, would be good for human flourishing. But it surely does not follow that such a eugenic plan is morally good. In fact, Darwin admits as much when he claims that civilization has extended our moral sympathy beyond our social instincts. While our instinctive sympathy "is directed solely towards members of the same community … [and] not to all members of the same species," (Darwin 1998: 109–10) it can be progressively widened:

> [A]s man gradually advanced in intellectual power, and was able to trace the more remote consequences of his actions; as he acquired sufficient knowledge to reject baneful customs and superstitions; as he regarded more and more, not only the welfare, but the happiness of his fellow-men; as from habit, following on beneficial experience, instruction and example, his sympathies became more tender and widely diffused, extending to men of all races, to the imbecile, maimed and other useless members of society and finally to the lower animals,--so would the standard of his morality rise higher and higher. (Darwin 1998: 128–9)

Here Darwin makes it clear that in his considered view, the biologically "general good" previously defined is not the same as the moral good discernible by "knowledge … experience, instruction and example," so that even if the biological good would be supported by eugenics, it can still be opposed on moral grounds, ensuring the moral protection of "the imbecile, maimed and other useless members of society."

While this speaks well of Darwin's moral sensibilities, it does not help the proponent of Strong EE, because Darwin appeals to sources of moral knowledge (such as reason and experience) which transcend those which derive strictly from biological inheritance, allowing "the standard of his morality [to] rise higher and higher." Once reason is in play, it is possible for a single woman to discern that there is no morally significant difference between herself and her brother, and given her understanding of the worth of her own life, to conclude that fratricide is wrong, even if she has been raised as a hive-bee. Using reason, moral universals are discernible which make the details of natural history irrelevant. In Kantian terms, the problem for Strong EE is that there are moral norms which apply to rational beings as such, so how these beings became embodied as they are is at best of secondary significance.[4]

4 Our mode of embodiment does limit the practical means by which we can pursue moral norms, so that, although we have a duty to preserve life, we cannot do so by flying, etc., and we must be concerned with physical resources necessary for our bodies to live, such as oxygen, water and food; but this is not the basis for the duty itself. This can be seen from the fact that conceivable rational beings without bodies, such as angels, still fall under the moral demand.

The Scope of Morality

Further problems for Strong EE center on its claim that the general good can be defined in terms of *human* flourishing. One concern is that it is not clear from an evolutionary perspective why human beings should enjoy the protection of special rights not belonging to other creatures. In Richard Dawkins's memorable phrase, natural selection is a blind watchmaker, with no goals or purposes in mind. From the perspective of naturalistic evolution, human beings are not here for a reason, and if the environment had been different, they would not be here at all. True, extant humans are adapted to their environment, and in that sense are "functional"; but as James Rachels points out, the same can be said for the humble cockroach: "we are not entitled—not on evolutionary grounds, at any rate—to regard our own adaptive behavior as 'better' or 'higher' than that of a cockroach, who, after all, is adapted equally well to life in its own environmental niche" (Rachels 1990: 70). So, on evolutionary grounds, it is pure "species-ism" to suppose that natural selection has conferred greater value on us than on any other creature.

On the other hand, if, like Albert Schweitzer and other biocentric environmental philosophers, one claims that all life has value, there will still be no basis for *distinctively* human rights that cannot be overridden by the case for preserving many other creatures. Even if we appeal to the fact that humans in general have more highly developed capacities than other creatures, not only does this not show that these capacities are more valuable (creatures with more modest abilities may be just as well adapted), it is also not true that *all* human beings have capacities higher than *all* other creatures. It is precisely on this basis that the animal rights activist and utilitarian philosopher Peter Singer argues that "If we must choose between saving an intelligent, fully developed pig or the Down Syndrome baby … we should opt for the pig" (Gage 2010: 191).

The same problem arises even within the human population. For, as J.P. Moreland points out, human rights presuppose that at some level, human beings have equal worth, but from the perspective of naturalistic evolution, natural advantages (like intelligence and strength) are not uniformly distributed and they are degreed properties (some are smarter or stronger than others), so "Why should we treat all people equally in any respect in the face of manifest inequalities among them?" (Moreland 2009: 144) On a naturalistic view, it is very hard to avoid the Orwellian conclusion that some animals [or people] are more equal than others.

Second, and more fundamentally, any attempt to base moral rights on biological history commits the is-ought fallacy, of moving from descriptions of natural fact to prescriptions guiding moral behavior. David Hume first identified the fallacy:

> In every system of morality, which I have hitherto met with, I have always remark'd, that the author proceeds for some time in the ordinary way of reasoning … when of a sudden I am surpriz'd to find, that instead of the usual copulations of propositions, *is*, and *is not*, I meet with no proposition that is not connected with an *ought*, or an *ought not* … [A]s this *ought*, or *ought not*,

> expresses some new relation or affirmation, 'tis necessary that it shou'd be observ'd and explain'd; and at the same time that a reason should be given, for what seems altogether inconceivable, how this new relation can be a deduction from others, which are entirely different from it. (Hume 1984: 521)

Since Strong EE bases its account of the origin of moral demands ("oughts" and "ought nots") on the facts of biological history, it certainly seems to fall foul of Hume's objection. And as we have seen, even if a Darwinian account can license our speaking of the biological good of human beings, this is still far short of what we mean by the moral good.

This case is strengthened by noting that naturalism seems incapable of locating intrinsic prescriptivity (action-guiding moral directives) in a world of undirected cause and effect. The processes studied by natural science are not trying to achieve any goals, nor, being impersonal, can they offer any instructions concerning the best way to live: in our experience, it is only persons, such as physicians, who are capable of issuing prescriptions. Thus, as the great atheist philosopher J.L. Mackie conceded, "objective intrinsically prescriptive features … constitute so odd a cluster of qualities and relations that they are most unlikely to have arisen in the ordinary course of events, without an all-powerful god to create them" (Mackie 1983: 115). But without prescriptivity, there can be no human rights that we ought to protect, and hence no basis for saying that humans have special dignity and worth. Indeed, there is no basis for saying that anything has value, for to say that something has value implies an obligation to protect it.

Third, even if naturalism can explain why the world has some sort of value, it does not tell us *what* to value, or *how much* we should value it. As Holmes Rolston III argues, even a complete scientific account of the natural world, will not tell us what is morally important:

> But what ought we to desire? Our enlightened self-interest? Our genetic self-interest? More children? More science? The conservation of biodiversity? Sustainable development? A sustainable biosphere? The love of neighbor? The love of God? Justice? Equity? Charity? … After science, we still need help deciding what to value; what is right and wrong, good and evil, how to behave as we cope. The end of life still lies in its meaning, the domain of religion and ethics. (Rolston 1999: 161–2)

That this is a serious issue is shown by the bewildering variety of views on the locus of moral value found in the literature on environmental ethics (for example see the wide range of views in Pojman and Pojman 2008). Some, like Peter Singer, privilege sentient creatures; others, like Albert Schweitzer, uphold the value of all life, sentient or not; and still others, like Aldo Leopold, defend the value of ecosystems, including living and non-living components. It is hard to see how naturalism can adjudicate between these positions, and it is also hard to refute a moral skeptic who says that on strictly Darwinian grounds, might is right, and that no particular form of life enjoys special protection. From a Darwinian perspective, the most plausible locus of value is DNA, but this provides no reason to privilege human DNA over any other. To the extent that the propagation of human DNA thwarts the propagation of other creatures' DNA (via destruction of their habitats), it is not clear that human flourishing is an unqualified good.

A fourth concern (parallel to a classic objection to utilitarianism) is that what is good for human flourishing as a whole may be achieved by violating the human rights of a minority. This objection does not require appeal to counterfactual examples, like humans raised as hive-bees. As Darwinist philosopher Larry Arnhart points out, Darwin "stressed the importance of tribal warfare in the development of morality: such contests spurred the development of the intellectual and moral capacities that allow individuals to cooperate within groups so as to compete successfully against other groups" (Arnhart 2005: 36). Apparently, a certain amount of tribal warfare is good for the biological flourishing of humans as a whole, and if so, it can hardly matter whether the war meets the requirements of just war theory (*jus ad bello* and *jus in bellum*). Should civilized countries become too individualistic, it seems to follow that arbitrary, unjustified wars involving major human rights abuses would be morally justified on the grounds of increased intra-tribal cooperation and its benefits for human survival and reproduction.

A fifth concern is that while an evolutionary account might explain the appearance of moral instincts, there is a large gap between moral instincts and moral demands. This is shown by the simple fact that instincts conflict, as Darwin realized. The conflict in instincts can arise (a) between different species, (b) in the same species under different conditions and (c) in the same creature at the same time. As an example of (a), Darwin claims both that many creatures have an instinct for parental and filial affection, but also that others have an instinct for "the unusual and opposite feeling of hatred between the nearest relations, as with the worker-bees which kill their brother-drones, and with the queen-bees which kill their daughter-queens; the desire to destroy their nearest relatives having been in this case of service to the community" (Darwin 1998: 109). Most of us cannot take seriously the idea that a moral demand applies to bees, for as Kant argued, they are not under the moral law, having neither an understanding of moral rules, nor the free will to obey or disobey them.[5] But if some other creatures are under the moral law (for example intelligent aliens), then we have a kind of *inter-species relativism*, according to which different rational beings have different rights and human rights could be abridged by the competing moral demands of these other creatures. Case (b) illustrates *intra-species historical relativism*, for example, some human rights that exist in one era might be abridged because, for example, we start to live like hive-bees. And in case (c), *subjectivism* looms, because the same creature, as Darwin realizes, experiences conflicts between his social instincts and the more urgent instincts of self-preservation, feeding and reproduction.

5 For discussion, see Holly Wilson, The Green Kant: Kant's Treatment of Animals, in Louis and Paul Pojman, *Environmental Ethics*, 65–72, 67.

As we saw in section 2, in this last case, Darwin thought that we could rank the instincts, and creatures would feel guilty for acting against their more enduring social and maternal instincts by caving in to their more transient urges. However, the claim that facts about instincts (such as their relative longevity or urgency) imply anything about their moral force commits the is-ought fallacy. And an account of why we may feel guilty falls short of showing that we actually are: sensitive children often blame themselves for their parents' divorce when they are not responsible for it. Darwin assumes the moral superiority of the more enduring social instinct, but one might just as well (or just as illogically) argue that more short-lived urges should be acted on (*carpe diem*!): perhaps we should feel guilty for passing up these opportunities.

Further, as C.S. Lewis long ago pointed out, even if instincts do have moral force, if two instincts conflict, the only morally decisive tie-breaker will be something other than the instincts themselves. Thus if a hand grenade lands in a foxhole and a marine experiences a conflict between the "herd" instinct to preserve the life of others (by diving on the grenade) and the instinct of self-preservation, he must decide which instinct he should side with:

> Now this thing that judges between two instincts, that decides which should be encouraged, cannot be either of them. You might as well say the sheet of music which tells you, at any given moment, to play one note on the piano and not another, is itself one of the notes on the keyboard. The Moral Law tells us the tune we have to play: our instincts are merely the notes. (Lewis 1952: 22)

Of course Darwin might reply that sympathy for one's fellow man can also be taught by reason and experience, which goes beyond mere instinct, but this opens the possibility that humans are discerning objective moral values which are not limited by the contingencies of their biological history, so it does not help Strong EE. This possibility can only be foreclosed by assuming a moral non-cognitivism, which denies the existence of mind-independent truth-makers for moral statements; but this begs the question against objectivist ethical theories.

The Problem of Human Nature

Some Darwinist philosophers think they can overcome many of the above objections by showing how a Darwinian account explains the appearance of a human nature capable of grasping the moral demand. Thus, for Larry Arnhart, "human beings can learn morality because they have moral instincts that prepare them to learn certain kinds of moral norms" (Arnhart 2005: 41). But can such an account explain why we have an obligation to protect human rights? In his sophisticated study of our moral sense, James Q. Wilson is aware that evolutionary accounts have a hard time explaining why we have a moral obligation to *all* human beings. At first sight, it seems that humans only have an interest in preserving their own genes, limiting their moral obligations to their own family.[6] However, William Hamilton extended the range of genetic interest via the notion of "inclusive fitness":

> An individual is reproductively successful to the extent that his genes occur in the next generation, and he can assure that occurrence not only by reproducing himself but also by assisting in the reproduction of individuals who have some of his genes. The more closely related the first individual is to the second, the greater the number of the first's genes will appear in the next generation if the second individual produces offspring. (Wilson 1993: 41)

Yet, Wilson realizes, this still does not explain the moral obligation we have to *genetic strangers*, those who are not kin, which is vital to our recognition that all human beings have rights. Even factoring in inclusive fitness, the Darwinian account seems at best capable of defending tribalism, according to which our primary moral obligations are limited to a genetically related tribe. Yet, Wilson notes, studies of adoptive families show that human beings can be at least as loving and protective of non-kin as they are of their biological families (Wilson 1993: 42–3):

> Humans may not sacrifice as much for their own kin as do ants, but they sacrifice more than do ants for nonkin—adopted children, friends, neighbors, and countrymen ... they even make sacrifices for other species ... Sympathy for persons who are not offspring and creatures that are not human is a characteristic of almost all humans. (Wilson 1993: 43–4)

This is closely connected to the classic problem of altruism for EE, which points out that during major disasters like 9/11, heroic individuals risked their lives to save genetic strangers from many nations. Wilson attempts to square these facts about human nature with EE by suggesting that our sympathy is attuned to features of kin shared by non-kin:

> If sympathy is widespread, it must have been adaptive, but what was selected for was not a simple desire for reproductive success; what has been selected for is a generalized trait that both encourages reproductive fitness and stimulates sympathetic behavior. That trait, or adaptive mechanism, is *attachment* or *affiliative behavior* ... [H]umans are biologically disposed to care for their young, but, unlike other species, what people find attractive in their own young are traits that, to some degree, are also present in other people (and even other species). (Wilson 1993: 44)

---

6 Actually, not even all of those, since those past child-bearing age no longer have genetic potential.

There is, however, an obvious logical problem with this proposal. The fact that human beings feel an obligation to non-kin is made contingent on the fact that evolution did not develop emotional faculties capable of discriminating between kin and non-kin. For one thing, this is not obviously true, since there are highly tribal and ethnocentric societies which seem to have done just that. But even supposing it is true, it will not show that we actually do have a moral obligation to non-kin. For surely we can imagine counterfactual creatures that develop emotional faculties which do distinguish kin from non-kin. Since it remains a fact that it is in our genetic interest only to be concerned about kin, we cannot say *on evolutionary grounds* that these counterfactual creatures are being immoral for favoring their own kin. In fact, they could accuse us of being immoral, of being deceived by our frail faculties into neglecting our own kin for the sake of non-kin, to whom we have no moral obligation. While Darwin and many other evolutionary ethicists believe that we have moral obligations to all humans, it is not at all clear how this can be justified in purely evolutionary terms: the committed tribalist seems on at least as firm ground.

But there is a much deeper problem for Strong EE. Regardless of how persuasive we find evolutionary explanations of moral sympathy, all of them presuppose that naturalistic processes can ground an account of human nature. G.K. Chesterton realized that this was a highly problematic claim, arguing that "Evolution … does not especially deny the existence of God; what it does deny is the existence of man" (Chesterton 1989: 196). Chesterton's point is that Darwinian metaphysics undermines the idea that there is a determinate human nature, which might ground universal rights and responsibilities. As Logan Gage points out, before Darwin, our understanding of human nature was dominated by the Aristotelian/Thomistic paradigm, according to which each organism shares a stable nature or essence (Gage 2010). On this basis one could understand why there was an objective answer to the question, "How do humans flourish?" and one could see why, if any human being is valuable, they all are.

However, on Darwin's view, the natural world is in a constant state of flux and transition between forms. If we are defined by the organization of matter, and that organization is malleable, there is no sharp boundary between one kind of creature and another. For this reason, Darwin saw "the term species as one arbitrarily given, for the sake of convenience, to a set of individuals closely resembling each other …" (Darwin 1993: 78–9). On this view, there is no such thing as a human essence, shared by all and only human beings, a conclusion explicitly drawn by the great evolutionary biologist Ernst Mayr: "the essentialist philosophies of Aristotle and Plato are incompatible with evolutionary thinking" (Mayr 1970: 4). So one cannot talk with any confidence of the human rights of future generations (or even of human rights abuses in the remote past), since the term "human" may apply to quite different creatures who do not share our characteristics. This creates a *diachronic* problem of human rights: how can we confidently legislate for the future protection of creatures related to, but not like, us? But worse, at a purely material level, there are also marked genetic differences between human beings *at* a given time. Natural selection has seen fit to allow the existence of mentally and physically defective humans and also of psychopaths and rapists. Shall we argue that since there is no such thing as a human essence, and since the defective humans are very unlike us, we have no reason to extend the rights we enjoy to them? And shall we conclude that individuals genetically disposed to murder and rape others without compassion are so unlike us, that we cannot say that the moral demand to refrain from murder and rape applies to them? This creates a *synchronic* problem of human rights: why say that all extant creatures we call "human" have anything sufficiently in common to ground the claims (a) that they *all* have fundamental rights deserving protection and (b) that they *all* have an obligation to respect the rights of others? Once the ground of moral value is tied to contingently distributed physical and mental characteristics, there is no longer a sound basis for distinctively human rights. As Peter Singer has noticed, whatever characteristic we pick will be shared by some non-human animals and absent in some humans (Singer 1976).

In conclusion, Strong EE is incapable of accounting for the kind of moral norms required to support human rights. This is because (1) there are no inalienable rights, since any right could be suspended by natural or artificial changes in social organization; (2) we can speak of what is contingently good for the human species at a time but not of what is morally required, since there is no normative necessity; (3) there is nothing special about humans and no reason why we should care about *all* of them (rather than care only about our kin or a tribe); and (4) there is no such thing as human nature, which makes it arbitrary and chauvinistic to speak of human rights in the first place.

The Epistemological Problem for Weak EE

Many proponents of EE find Strong EE implausible. They are aware that explaining the emotional responses of approval or disapproval we have for certain actions is not the same as showing that those responses are justified. Weak EE, which only claims to account for the origin of human moral psychology, is certainly consistent with the *existence* of human rights. Weak EE is also consistent with two views about humanity's moral sense. The first, Ambitious Weak EE, claims that humanity's instinctive moral sense is a generally reliable guide to moral reality. The second, Modest Weak EE, acknowledges that humanity's moral instincts are an unreliable guide to moral reality, but argues that once humans develop faculties like reason, imagination and intuition, they can discern grounds for criticizing the instincts and impulses implanted in them by evolution, and advance toward a recognition of moral truth.

In what follows, I will offer three arguments to show that Ambitious Weak EE is incompatible with our knowledge of human rights. Modest Weak EE does not strictly require a response, because it concedes that EE is irrelevant to how we know moral truth.

The Unreliability of Humanity's Moral Sense

In his treatment of humanity's moral sense, Darwin relied heavily on Adam Smith's account of sympathy (Smith 1976). According to Smith, when a spectator observes another person act, if the latter's "passions … are in perfect concord with the sympathetic emotions of the spectator, they necessarily appear suitable, and proper to their objects; and, on the contrary, when … they do not coincide with what he feels, they necessarily appear to him unjust and improper" (Smith 1976: 58). Thus, as Arnhart explains, "The virtuousness or viciousness of conduct is determined by whether our sentiment of sympathy leads us to approve or disapprove of the conduct" (Arnhart 2005: 36). Our reaction is dependent on whether or not we sympathize with the motives of the agent (were they kind or cruel?) or with the reactions of those affected (did they express gratitude or resentment?). The idea is that "We then derive the rules of morality by generalizing from these moral sentiments of approval or disapproval" (Arnhart 2005: 36). So the kindness of a nurse is a virtue because we can sympathize with her motive to care for the patient and with the gratitude of the patient, but the cruelty of the torturer is a vice because we cannot sympathize with the motives of the torturer and can sympathize with the resentment of the person tortured. Smith goes further, claiming that the rules are generalized by imagining an impartial spectator, because we care about how others see our conduct.

It is rather obvious, however, that sympathy is inadequate as a guide to moral reality. For one thing, it is not clear why the mere feeling of sympathy has normative force. One can sympathize with the plight of fictional characters (even computer generated or cartoon characters), and even favorite stuffed animals, but one surely cannot have any direct moral obligation to them. And through attachment, it is possible for human beings to sympathize with the most morally abhorrent actions (consider the spouses of "misunderstood" tyrants). Further, even where sympathy is appropriate, it comes in degrees. As Wilson notes, when a person is suffering in public, some react by trying to help the person, but many will move away to relieve the distress they feel (Wilson 1993: 35). Certainly both groups care about the suffering person, but if we assume our moral sense is a reliable guide to moral reality, we will have to espouse the relativistic position that only those moved to help the suffering person had an obligation to do so. Moral obligations, however, surely have a normative necessity that is not dependent on whether we feel like complying with them (for otherwise, few wealthy Americans would file tax returns!).

The same problem arises when we consider the scope of sympathy. As a civilized Victorian, Darwin defended the extension of sympathy to all humans, including the infirm and "useless," and even to non-humans. But there always have been people who feel sympathy only for smaller groups. The Mafia and similar organizations restrict sympathy to the family or the gang, slaughtering without mercy those who obstruct their criminal schemes. Ethnic and religious conflicts, such as those in Bosnia, Rwanda, Sudan and the Middle East, are often marked by a restriction of sympathy to a favored group, and may coexist with genocidal indifference to excluded groups. But the most extreme problem is posed by the existence of psychopaths. As Wilson explains, the problem is that:

> Psychopaths … do not feel, or do not feel very deeply, the social emotions necessary for living as a social animal … they do not feel moral emotions such as guilt, shame, pity, and love, and thus they can deceive, injure, and even brutally torture and murder their fellow human beings without any moral feelings. (Wilson 1993: 44)

True, not everyone shares the moral sensibilities of the Mafia, the genocidal tyrant, or the psychopath.[7] But if humanity's moral sense is a reliable guide to moral reality, what resources does EE have for saying that our perception of moral reality is more accurate than theirs? The easiest way out of this would be some form of relativism, according to which people have value to those who are sympathetic to them, but this allows mobs, dictators and psychopaths a free pass to violate human rights which they do not (and do not have to) recognize.

Matters are no better at the opposite end of the moral spectrum, the realm of saints and heroes: there are people, like Mother Teresa, who are unusually sympathetic to the plight of others. Since most people find it psychologically impossible to match Mother Teresa's sympathy for the poor of Calcutta, should we say that she had a duty to expend enormous effort to save them, while we do not? And suppose that someone invented pills which could expand or contract our moral sensibilities (sympathetic "uppers" and "downers"), could we then increase or decrease the moral demand simply by manipulating our sympathies?[8] If so, we are not far from the abyss of relativism suggested by Shakespeare's Hamlet: "there is nothing either good or bad, but thinking [in this case, feeling] makes it so" (Act II, scene ii).

Finally, there are many issues on which even "normal" people have remarkable divergences of moral sympathy, as evidenced by the ongoing debates about abortion and euthanasia. Those who are "pro-life" strongly sympathize with the plight of the unborn and terminally ill, but at least some who are "pro-choice" do not.

For all of these reasons, we cannot hope to make the protections implied by human rights dependent on anything so fickle and inconsistent as human moral sympathy. It makes no sense to say that you have full dignity and worth as a human being because many people sympathize with you, but that, on the other hand, it is OK for you to be murdered by a psychopath at any time because he does not share that feeling. This is because human rights are inalienable (inviolable),

---

7 It is another example of the is-ought fallacy to argue that because the psychopath's attitudes are not statistically normal, therefore they lack normative force, or that because more compassionate responses are statistically normal, they do have normative force.

8 Such variation of sentiment is also evident in news coverage of disasters: the right picture, the right rhetorical appeal, and the right music, make a huge difference to our emotional response.

which implies that the moral protections of a human right cannot be withdrawn simply because they are not recognized by other people.

The Contingency of Humanity's Moral Sense

But there is another problem here, which arises even if it happens to be true that the moral sense which most normal human beings have is a reliable guide to moral reality. That is the central problem of contingency. Let us suppose that most normal human beings are capable of seeing that all human beings have fundamental rights, and that their perception of these rights is largely accurate. Still, if we had been raised like hive-bees, or if we are so raised in the future (by natural or artificial means), then it would seem to us that fratricide and female infanticide were right, and so the human rights protections currently enjoyed by brothers and daughters could be withdrawn. But if so, then even though our current perception that brothers and daughters do have these rights happens to be correct, we cannot claim to know it. For on any plausible theory of knowledge, one cannot claim to know that a proposition *p* is true unless it is no accident that one is right in believing that *p*. Plato gives a famous illustration of this requirement for knowledge in his *Theaetetus* (201 a-c). Suppose a lawyer uses rhetorical tricks to convince the jury that the defendant is guilty and he actually is; yet, using the same tricks, the lawyer could equally well have persuaded the jury that the defendant was innocent. Then although the jury's belief that the defendant is guilty is true, it is not knowledge. Likewise, even if our beliefs about human rights happen to be true, since they result from the contingencies of our biological history, the same evolutionary processes could just as well have instilled false moral beliefs in us. So even if our moral beliefs about these rights are correct, we cannot claim to have moral knowledge.

Matters are made worse by the fact that we do not really know which position we are in. On what grounds can we say that those humans raised like hive-bees have a deficient moral sense, while our own is reliable? If we reversed the situation (suppose we had been raised like hive-bees and these other humans had been raised like us), then basing our moral beliefs on our actual moral sense and actual history, we would be just as convinced that those defending human rights were guilty of unfounded sentimentality or superstition, and we would no doubt be strenuous in our efforts to help them overcome their irrational inhibitions about fratricide and infanticide. This naturally leads us to our last problem for Ambitious Weak EE, namely, that the consistent proponent of EE should embrace moral skepticism, according to which our evolutionary history undercuts any reason for believing that moral truths exist.[9]

---

9 A possible way out here is moral anti-realism, which allows that moral truths exist but claims they do depend on our evaluative attitudes. As we noted earlier, however, this will not allow us to defend the idea of inalienable human rights, since on this view, those

Moral Skepticism

Michael Ruse and E.O. Wilson are well-known for giving the most striking statement of the moral skepticism which, they claim, is an inevitable consequence of human evolution. "Human beings function better if they are deceived by their genes into thinking that there is a disinterested objective morality binding upon them, which all should obey" (Ruse and Wilson 1986: 179). They link their skepticism explicitly to the contingent connection between our moral sense and our biological history, noting that it is "easy to conceive of an alien intelligent species evolving rules its members consider highly moral but which are repugnant to human beings, such as cannibalism, incest and love of darkness and decay" (Ruse and Wilson 1986: 186). The conclusion that they draw is that there is no reason for any species, including humans, to think that its moral principles are universal truths.

In his meticulous study, *The Evolution of Morality*, Richard Joyce shows that the connection between EE and moral skepticism is very strong. What evolutionary theory was designed to explain is the emergence of useful adaptations to the environment. On this view, it is natural to suppose that moral sensibilities and rules are genetically useful adaptations. For example, an inclination to cooperation facilitates human survival and reproduction. But, as Joyce argues, the claim that moral feelings and beliefs are useful is consistent with their being either false or without epistemic justification (neither self-evident nor demonstrable, nor founded in external evidence). The fact that it was "systematically useful for our ancestors to form beliefs about moral rightness and wrongness," does not imply "that any actual moral rightness or wrongness existed in the ancestral environment" (Joyce 2007: 183)—or that it exists in our own. Even if no moral values existed or even if it were objectively true that we should all be ethical egoists who doggedly pursue self-interest, it would remain a fact that cooperation would be genetically useful. So it seems that what EE actually does is gives an explanation of why we believe in morality without requiring (or providing evidence) that our beliefs have any foundation in reality. The account implies that we would have the same moral beliefs even if moral reality were wildly different, or even if there were no moral reality. As Joyce concludes:

> [O]n no epistemological theory worth its salt should the justificatory status of a belief remain unaffected by the discovery of an empirically supported theory that provides a complete explanation of why we have the belief while nowhere presupposing its truth. We should reject or modify any theory that would render us epistemic slaves to the baby-bearing capacity of our ancestors. (Joyce 2007: 219)

---

attitudes and moral truth itself are dependent on the contingencies of natural (or artificial) selection.

Matters are made worse by the fact that naturalistic evolution can only operate on physical responses to physical features of the environment. Yet, as J.P. Moreland points out, "value properties are not empirically detectable nor are they the sorts of properties whose instances can stand in physical causal relations with the brain" (Moreland 2009: 149). So even if there are non-empirical normative features in the world, natural selection is insensitive to their presence, and cannot build a faculty capable of reliably detecting them. In other words, from the perspective of naturalistic evolution, it could not be the case that we developed moral faculties *because* we causally interacted with moral values, so we cannot claim that natural selection might have honed the reliability of these faculties, as we might with ordinary faculties of physical perception like sight or hearing.

The defender of EE might claim that we can "see" there is an objective connection between cooperation and human flourishing, and that this is why cooperation is morally right. The trouble is, we would think we could just "see" this even if cooperation were wrong or had no moral value. Further, even if naturalistic evolution does explain how we can know that cooperation is right, this is no comfort for the defender of human rights. This is because the same theory also explains tribal warfare—as a way of promoting cooperation!—so our cooperative instincts do not imply a recognition of the value of all human beings; if anything, they depend on denying that fact, whenever cooperation is enhanced by attacking other tribes.

So it seems that for defenders of human rights, the only defensible version of EE left is Modest Weak EE, which admits the unreliability of humanity's moral sense but claims that evolution has provided other faculties such as reason and intuition that allow access to moral truth. However, since reason and intuition can contact non-contingent universals, they clearly provide access to truths (such as the necessary truths of logic and practical reason) which are in no way dependent on our natural history. Even if humans were raised like hive-bees, 2+2 = 4, and if Kant is right, they should so act that their maxim is a universal law for all people.

Conclusion

We have examined two main versions of Evolutionary Ethics, and shown that they both undermine the project of defending universal human rights. According to Strong EE, naturalistic evolution somehow explains the emergence of beings under the moral demand, but we have seen that naturalistic evolution makes it unreasonable to believe both that moral prescriptions exist and that human beings have any special worth or dignity which distinguishes their moral status from other creatures. According to Weak EE, all naturalistic evolution does is explain the emergence of beings capable of recognizing the moral demand (which demand can have a different source). For Ambitious Weak EE, our instinctive moral sense is expected to be generally reliable, but we saw that the processes which generated our moral sense would have worked in just the same way if there were no moral values, or if those values were wildly different. For Modest Weak EE, our instinctive moral sense is not expected to be reliable, but can be corrected through reason. However, reason grants access to non-contingent universal truths which make the accidents of natural history, and hence EE, irrelevant to how we know moral truth.

The most reasonable conclusion from all this is that if naturalistic evolution is the complete explanation of human faculties, then our moral sense is simply a useful delusion: a false belief in an independent moral order which fosters behaviors, such as cooperation (and tribal warfare!) which happen to be beneficial to our genes. So, those of us who believe that there are genuine obligations to protect human rights, and that we are capable of knowing this, have good reason to go elsewhere to explain these apparent facts. If human rights cannot be made contingent on the accidents of natural history, and if all other attempts to ground human rights outside revelation have ended in failure, we are surely justified in reconsidering the case for a transcendent word as the proper justification for human rights.

Bibliography

Arnhart, L. 1998. *Darwinian Natural Right*. Albany, NY: State University of New York Press.

Arnhart, L. 2005. *Darwinian Conservatism*. Exeter: Imprint Academic.

Behe, M. 2007. *The Edge of Evolution: The Search for the Limits of Darwinism*. New York: The Free Press.

Chesterton, G.K. 1989. *G.K. Chesterton: Collected Works*. Volume XV. San Francisco, CA: Ignatius Press.

Darwin, C. 1993. *The Origin of Species*. New York: The Modern Library.

Darwin, C. 1998. *The Descent of Man*. Amherst, NY: Prometheus Books.

De Waal, F. 2009. *Primates and Philosophers: How Morality Evolved*. Princeton, NJ: Princeton University Press.

Gage, L.P. 2010. Can a Thomist be a Darwinist? In *God and Evolution*, edited by J. Richards. Seattle, WA: Discovery Institute Press.

Hume, D. 1984. *Treatise of Human Nature*. London: Penguin Classics.

Joyce, R. 2007. *The Evolution of Morality*. Cambridge, MA: MIT Press.

Katz, L. (ed.) 2000. *Evolutionary Origins of Morality*. Exeter: Imprint Academic.

Lewis, C. 1952. *Mere Christianity*. New York: Macmillan.

Mackie, J. 1983. *The Miracle of Theism*. New York: Oxford University Press.

Mayr, E. 1970. *Population, Species, and Evolution*. Cambridge, MA: Harvard University Press.

Montgomery, J.W. 1986. *Human Rights and Human Dignity*. Dallas, TX: Probe Books.

Moreland, J.P. 2009. *The Recalcitrant Imago Dei: Human Persons and the Failure of Naturalism*. London: SCM Press.

Pojman, L. and Pojman, P. (eds) 2008. *Environmental Ethics*, 5th edn. Belmont, CA: Thomson.
Rachels, J. 1990. *Created From Animals*. Oxford: Oxford University Press.
Rolston III, H. 1999. *Genes, Genesis, and God*. New York: Cambridge University Press.
Ruse, M. and Wilson, E. 1986. Moral Philosophy as Applied Science. *Philosophy*, 61(236), 173–92.
Singer, P. 1976. *Animal Rights and Human Obligations*. Englewood Cliffs, NJ: Prentice-Hall.
Smith, A. 1976. *The Theory of Moral Sentiments*. Indianapolis, IN: Liberty Classics.
Sober, E. and Wilson, D.S. 1998. *Unto Others: The Evolution and Psychology of Unselfish Behavior*. Cambridge, MA: Harvard University Press.
Street, S. 2006. A Darwinian Dilemma for Realist Theories of Value. *Philosophical Studies*, 127(1), 109–66.
Wilson, J. 1993. *The Moral Sense*. New York: The Free Press.

Chapter 4
Human Rights as Legal Rights

Friedrich Toepel

The Problem

Is it harmless to recognize human rights in accordance with a popular view in Western legal culture even when they are not institutionalized in a (international) legal system? To my mind, acceptance of human rights which are not institutionalized is bound to cause innumerable problems of understanding between different moral worldviews. Confining the use of the term "human rights" to institutionalized rights is the obvious solution to such problems of understanding.

Probably, my suggestion will be labeled as "positivism" by some for whom this is a negative catch-word. However, I wish to show in this chapter that the fears of these people are ungrounded. Apart from that, I do not wish to convey the idea that institutionalized rights possess a particular quality which would make them in any way superior to positions which are only worth being protected according to certain moral views. Neither is it my intention to endorse a moral relativism which would exclude the possibility that one of the worldviews swirling through modern multicultural society may be the correct one. To the contrary, I merely would like to emphasize that we always judge these issues from a perspective and that none of us is immune against making mistakes. One might call such a position a combination of positivism and constructivism or—rather pompously—constructo-positivism (Totaro 2007/2008: 721–2). I think that confining oneself to the recognition of institutionalized rights in a forum whose participants are adherents of different moral views is the most just and most honest solution and the one most apt to further the understanding between peoples.

With this chapter, I wish to express my concerns regarding the above-mentioned popular view in Western legal culture that human rights ought to be enforceable as claim-rights without being institutionalized in a (international) legal system. Surprisingly, such a view is not held by religious fundamentalists alone but also by liberals, indeed by a whole spectrum of diverse opinions. It is usually born from a strong conviction that a certain transcendental basis for human rights is unquestionably the only right one and that this basis is universally recognized by all peoples at all times and places.

Usually, holders of such an opinion are shocked by documents like the Cairo Declaration on Human Rights in Islam of August 5, 1990, particularly by clauses like Art. 2 (a) of the Cairo Declaration that "… it is prohibited to take away life except for a shari'ah prescribed reason." The religious fundamentalists and the liberalists do not see that their own human rights concepts are precisely what makes documents like the Cairo Declaration on Human Rights possible. If a transcendental basis is invoked as sufficient not only for the creation of human rights but also for their enforceability, then a good Muslim cannot help thinking of the Qu'ran or the Shari'ah as being such a basis. I do not want to exclude that it may be possible to prove such a view to be wrong objectively. But it is a fact that Muslims at least do not agree that they are wrong. It may even be the case that they negligently hold wrong opinions. However, the definition of negligence causes trouble here. Negligent is he who fails to exercise due care. It must be determined in relation to a system of norms what would count as exercising due care. If no legal institution is available to define the standards, only a moral system of norms can fill the gap. But who could reproach someone for choosing one moral system over another? In any way, it is natural for a practicing Muslim to revert to the Qu'ran or the Shari'ah as the most reliable source of norms.

I am aware that the afore-mentioned Western view has a long tradition. John Locke explained that when faced with the problem of deposing a tyrant, we should appeal to heaven and derive our rights to use violence against the tyrant from there (Locke 1993: ch. XIV section 169). More recently, Ronald Dworkin has endorsed a view according to which human rights are rights that the "treaties should protect, the rights no nation should be permitted to violate even for reasons of security" (Dworkin 2006: 29).

To my mind, this traditional view did fit in a relatively homogeneous society in which one moral system was nearly universally recognized. This is true of the times of Aquinas and even Locke in which the Christian world view was not seriously disputed. There may even have been a time in which a relatively neutral liberal system corresponded with widespread beliefs. However, we do not find this situation in our modern world in which we constantly come into contact with people who do not share our own worldviews. If it is true that one true moral system is still recognizable even today, it is at least covered by thick layers heaped up by various religions or other worldviews. It is therefore not any longer possible to make a remaining feeble awareness of objectivity the unquestionable basis of a system of human rights. That does not mean that a homogeneous moral basis would not be desirable. We have only to become aware of the fact that it does not already exist. We have to take one step back and to enter into moral discussions with the aim of convincing each other and thus creating the missing moral basis. While we have not accomplished our aim, we need a temporary solution which enables us to solve conflicts not merely with our fists as long as we have not succeeded in convincing each other.

To my mind, it can be harmful to imagine that we have reached a stage in history in which we are able to presuppose universal agreement at least with respect to the most fundamental issues. In practice that can only mean that either we elbow out minorities which we as the majority believe or wish to be negligible, or we are a weak minority ourselves in which case our opinion will be of no consequence whatsoever.

Two Possible Ways Out of the Dilemma

To my mind, the difficulty with the traditional view described in the last section is that according to it human rights may be plain moral rights[1] which are not institutionalized in a legal system. Moral rights cannot be justified like legal rights by merely pointing out that they belong to a legal system. They are rather in need of some other legitimation which can only be found in relation to a system of norms, for an argument can only be built on a normative foundation which is itself well-founded, that is, supported by a structure of norms and arguments connecting these norms. However, the only systems of norms left after we have excluded legal systems are moral systems, and moral systems are precisely those troublesome constructions characterized by widespread disagreement.

Seen in this way, there are only two solutions available to avoid pre-empting moral discourse and slighting minorities: Either we define human rights in a very narrow sense so that all moral views on the globe can accept the definition—henceforth the "*narrow definition solution*," or we give up any pretensions of universal moral justification and confine the use of the term human rights to rights institutionalized and listed as part of systems of international law—henceforth the "*instutionalization solution*."

I think that it is usual to attempt to define human rights in a very narrow sense, but then the problem arises how to determine in a universally acceptable way when all moral views "can" accept a human right.

Traditionally, this issue is not answered by consulting the moral views held in fact, but by determining with the help of standards of a particular moral system whether a certain result *should* be acceptable to all moral views. Particularly Christians are tempted to pursue such a solution, keeping in mind St Paul's allegation that "Since the creation of the world His invisible attributes are clearly seen, being understood by the things that are made, even His eternal power and Godhead, so that they are without excuse" (Romans 1:20). Seen from this perspective, Art. 2 of the Cairo Declaration that "… it is prohibited to take away life except for a shari'ah prescribed reason" may be thought to be wrong. If a woman, for example, has been condemned to death by stoning in accordance with Shari'ah law for having committed adultery, a Christian may be tempted to think that this woman still has a human right not be stoned. A Muslim, however, would disagree from his perspective. Here, to my mind, it cannot be determined by a moral view what should be acceptable for another moral view. For by what

1 See Gardner (2008: 1, 7).

authority should one moral view prevail over another, given the fact that there is no international institution supporting the solution?[2]

But if our answer is in the negative, the only alternative which remains is that each proponent of a moral view must determine himself whether he can accept a certain human right. Yet, this solution in turn renders the concept of human rights altogether useless. We could try to avoid the acceptance of all morally relevant utterances by defining the term "moral view." But how should we do that without introducing evaluations which are not universally accepted? We could at least demand a certain degree of sophistication and the attempt to build a moral system. However, most of the oppressive states of the past have tried to systemize their oppressive views—even the Nazis did that. Following this line of thought, we would end up with human rights which are human rights as long as everybody agrees. They cease to be human rights as soon as conflict arises and each side of the conflict is able to state reasons which express a moral view. Moral views change, and therefore what is accepted as human rights would change also.

Having come so far, we have to recognize that there is not really much difference in practice between the two solutions offered at the beginning of the section. If—according to the "narrow definition solution"—different human rights are accepted as human rights at different times, we may at each time insist that the human right we are endorsing at the moment has always been a human right and will always be a human right. But how can that approach be distinguished from confining the term "human rights" to rights institutionalized and listed as part of systems of international law? The only difference discernible is that what counts as eternal human rights may change more quickly when it is not institutionalized, for then changing one's mind may already suffice to change general acceptance of something as a human right, while derogation of existing human rights requires at least going through the appropriate procedures.

One might object that the "narrow definition solution" leaves open the possibility that one of the moral views stated at a certain time is really correct eternally. The proponents of the other moral views simply do not recognize this. But this may also be the case when according to the "institutionalization solution," acceptance of human rights is confined to rights institutionalized in international law. We merely are not able to speak about human rights in a universe of discourse

2 I have deliberately omitted a discussion of Kant in this chapter. His criteria for international law are more sophisticated than other theories and deserve special attention. However, I believe that in the end Kant's criteria face the same problems as religious views, for example, because they to a large extent rest on equality considerations (cf. Gierhake 2004: 109, 223, 230) which are only plausible against the backdrop of further value judgments. For Kant, this may not have been a difficulty since he presupposed the values of a Christian worldview. However, in a modern pluralistic society such values may not any longer just be taken for granted. I do not feel myself obliged to show in detail that my conjecture concerning Kant is correct, but would be grateful if someone would one day make an effort.

to which proponents of each moral view have access, and that is the case whether we agree that human rights are universally accepted moral rights or whether we hold that human rights are institutionalized rights (perhaps) not universally recognized as such.

Therefore, the right use of the term "human rights" is an issue concerning the appropriate language at a certain place and time. Even if it is not appropriate to use their particular human rights concept in a forum to which proponents of all moral views have access, the proponent of one moral view may still use the term in that sense in discussions with adherents of the same moral view.

In my opinion, this issue is to be handled exactly parallel to the general problem of making oneself understood by a foreigner. I may be perfectly justified to address a Chinese person in Chinese in China, I may encounter some difficulties when addressing a Japanese in Chinese in Japan, but with a high probability I would run into difficulties when trying to argue about my hotel bill in London in Chinese. In the same way talk about the human rights of fetuses presupposing Roman Catholic social doctrine may be in order at a Roman Catholic bishops' conference, but may sound slightly odd at a corresponding Protestant event and may be like Chinese at a meeting of American Feminists.

Seen like that, the main difference between the two solutions discussed here is that the "narrow definition solution" prefers a disorganized coincidental overlapping consensus between moral views concerning human rights, while the "institutionalization solution" prefers the conscious creation of a public sphere of talking about human rights and suggests that possible deviating uses of the term human rights should be restricted to forums in which adherents of the same moral view discuss human rights issues.

I am convinced that experience has shown the failure of the "narrow definition solution." Quarrels among worldviews reveal that problem-solving is practically impossible when relying on a coincidental overlapping consensus, and enforcing rights which are not institutionalized can never be effectively guaranteed. I even wish to encourage adherents of strong moral views which feel themselves well-established to drop human rights language altogether and to be content to decide what is morally right or wrong. Only weak moral views should have to compensate their lack of rationality with loud proclamations of human rights.

It is necessary for me therefore to endorse the "institutionalization solution" as the only practically possible way, and I shall devote the rest of the chapter to show to skeptics that this way can also be satisfactory in theory. But before I do that, I have to guard against a possible misunderstanding of the result I have reached so far.

A Linguistic Recommendation Only

I wish to emphasize that I do not want to dispute that human rights used in a certain way different from the one recommended here are "really" rights nor do I want to doubt that human rights as seen from a certain moral perspective do exist. I only recommend restricting talk about human rights to institutionalized rights. If you do not want to follow that recommendation, fine. However, if people with persisting differences of opinion intend to reach a solution and an effective protection against human rights violations, they in my opinion would be compelled to follow my advice. Further, if they feel strongly enough that they can afford to be honest and to defend their moral views with arguments, then I think it would be necessary to enter into a moral discourse with people disagreeing and only use the term "human rights" when an authoritatively secured agreement has been reached. I do not deny that if you feel weak or wish to cheat, it may be more effective just to cry out that human rights have been violated than to bother yourself with complicated moral arguments. However, those are special situations demanding special treatment.

I not only wish to confine myself to a linguistic recommendation. I also believe the linguistic question to be the central issue behind discussions about the term "human rights" and that questions whether human rights are really rights or whether human rights exist only arise because the fact is concealed that the one term "human rights" may be defined by different linguistic conventions. Thus I can only follow John Gardner up to a point when he finds it hard to raise the question whether human rights are really rights with a straight face (Gardner 2008: 1). I would agree as long as it is ensured that the criteria for human rights and for plain rights are taken from the same moral or legal system with which the speaker himself is acquainted. There might, for example, be the question on the agenda of a Roman Catholic bishops' conference what to do to promote the human rights of fetuses. If in this situation, one member of the conference would object "Wait a minute, before we do anything, we should clarify whether human rights are really rights," I could well imagine that the objection would be a rare occasion for hilarity for the illustrious assembly. However, if it would be discussed at the same conference how to comment on a new right (for example a right to same-sex marriage) included in a list of human rights by a body of international law, I can well imagine that the gentlemen present would be able to ask without twitching lips whether human rights according to international law are really (moral) rights (in accordance with Roman Catholic social doctrine, for example).

Further, in my opinion, all moral views which have developed human rights concepts presuppose the existence of human rights. In this respect, human rights are different from, say, unicorns (see Gardner 2008: 1, 2–3). That is the case because the use of human rights language has a different function than the use of the term "unicorn." Human rights language aims at an agreement among all moral views to reduce human suffering. Human rights violations are taken to be actually perceived. It is also not difficult to determine which human rights exist from a certain moral point of view. The difficulties start only when we try to reconcile the different moral views with each other. Unicorns, in contrast, are contrived to make fairy tales more interesting. You can go around and test things as to whether they might not be unicorns, but the result is fairly predictable. Nothing in reality will answer your test in the positive.

This difference also determines our attitude towards human rights. While we would not dream to change the concept of unicorns because we find none, we may well be induced to change our concept of human rights when we find that it only yields an empty set.

Appropriateness of the Term "Human Rights" for Controversial Institutionalized Rights

The question concerning the right use of the term "human rights" is not a legal issue because positive international law has its own mechanisms to deal with human rights which, as I see it, are not different in kind from the mechanisms of domestic positive laws. It is true that the effective enforcement of human rights depends on the will of some sovereign states to consider themselves bound by the relevant provisions of international law. But if international institutions have been founded which are able to conduct judicial proceedings concerning breaches of human rights, a realistic possibility of enforcing the institution's verdicts, however weak it may be, suffices to my mind to view those verdicts as parts of a genuine legal system of international law and the human rights recognized by such institutions as genuine legal rights. Contrary to Jeremy Bentham (Bentham 1907: 25 note 1) and Herbert L. Hart (Hart 1994: 237), I think that it is not necessary to treat international law as only analogous in content to domestic positive law. Law enforcement officials enforcing domestic laws may face the same temptation as officials enforcing international law to ignore law protecting individual persons if enforcement clashes with the authorities' own interest. The domestic official may only feel more secure when breaching international law than when breaching domestic law because he thinks that the arm of international law is not as long as the arm of domestic law. However, that means that there is only a difference of degree, not of principle between the two.

To my mind, it is obvious that the decision of a competent institution of international law granting an enforceable human right generally or in a particular situation must be taken into account. To ignore such a decision would be foolish. Therefore, the use of the term human rights in this context is a legitimate use. The remaining problem is whether there exists a legitimate use over and above the one warranted by international law. If freedom of speech is taken for granted, this problem concerns only the appropriateness of the assumption of human rights, provided this assumption is not supported by institutions of international law. I think that such an issue is a moral, not a legal issue. Nonetheless, it is important to see clearly in this respect because the misleading use of the term "human rights" may create wrong expectations for uncritical minds and obscure the discussion.

Restriction to institutionalized rights ensures maximum clarity for the concept of human rights. Talk of rights merely in the sense of "what is good and right" may have been legitimate in medieval times where the notion of rights was not confined to entitlements. A somewhat loose talk of rights as a program for future entitlements may also have been tolerable in the age of enlightenment. Thus, it may have been possible to sign the American Declaration of Independence in 1776 according to which "all men … are endowed by their Creator with certain unalienable Rights …" while being a slave owner. Today, people would see such talk of human rights without entitlements as hypocrisy because our thinking has become dominated by legal concepts. To my mind, it is not possible to turn back the clock.

The Legitimation of a Right on the Domestic Level

If we therefore endorse the "institutionalization solution," then human rights have the same structure as legal rights on the domestic level. In order to understand how problems of legitimacy are solved within the context of human rights, let us therefore recapitulate first how the problem is solved on the domestic level.

When it is intended to bind people with many conflicting moral views by the law, none of these views is directly suitable as a source of law because moral views without any law enforcement authorities supporting them can only bind by the insight into their merit, and people with different views precisely do not all have this insight. Modern multicultural societies cannot be ruled by simple moral discourse. There is not enough common ground to support stable social systems by the different moral views. This insight has deeply impressed itself on Western democracies. The horrors of the religious wars before their eyes, people have shaped the structures of modern liberal states to give expression to their deep mistrust in the moral views of individual persons. Therefore it is not only attempted to purge the law of moral concepts wherever they can be avoided, but also to create mechanisms which make the law enforceable independently of its correspondence with moral views. Mistrust leads also to the creation of authoritative positions (Lagerspetz 1995: 153) for each citizen in order to be able to participate in the political process and to initiate legal proceedings which will result in coercing other people to do what the citizen can demand of them. Such entitlements are called (subjective) rights in a modern state. These rights bear the second characteristic of the Hohfeldian definition of rights.[3] Particularly, modern legal rights are not thinkable without the second of Hohfeld's basic elements that each right involves a claim.[4]

Modern states carefully detach claim-rights granted within their systems from the question of legitimacy. All the different moral views present may influence the laws enacted by the legislative power. But once the laws are enacted, moral discussions about the existence of entitlements cease entirely. There is no room for dispute anymore whether a particular entitlement exists. There can only be dispute whether it is "right" in the sense of fair and good that the legal system grants the title.

Whether a right exists and whether it is good and fair that it exists are different issues as long as the disputant regards the legal system as a relevant entity. If he does not do that, it is still possible that it would be reasonable for him to take the existence of the legal system into account because others respect it. Only if no substantial minority remains which would regard the legal system as a non-negligible entity, then the questions of the existence of an entitlement and of its legitimacy will become one and the same issue again. Philosophers have named such a situation the state of nature and painted it, if not with dark colors, at least as an unstable situation.

Here we see a strange relationship between a legal system and the moral views of its members. While the existence of the legal system does not depend on any particular view, it also cannot wholly free itself from its members' support. Being a social construction, it ceases to exist if nobody follows its patterns anymore. Thus, a sufficient quantity of persons must respect the construction in order to ensure its continued existence. These persons will typically have reasons for their views, but it is not directly relevant what these reasons are. That is only indirectly

---

3 See Hohfeld (1919: 36): "In the strictest sense, all rights are claims." It has been maintained that some rights may only be liberty rights or rights conferring a power without the correlate of a claim-right. However, within a legal system the meaning of the concept of right quickly evaporates if the holder of the right has no claim to demand that corresponding duty-bearers have to refrain from actions interfering with the right. Similarly, an official may have a power-right to appoint another person to an office while not having a corresponding claim-right personally to demand not to be obstructed when exercising that right. But such examples to my mind can be easily reconciled with the view that all rights are claim-rights. One just has to be reminded that the official does not act as a private person when he appoints the other person. He rather represents the state. Therefore, only the state needs to have a corresponding claim-right not to be obstructed when the person is appointed. Without such claim-right it is difficult to comprehend that there should be a right at all. See also Hart 1973: 179–82, approvingly cited by Finnis 2011: 227.

4 In contrast, for example, to medieval concepts of rights, such as Aquinas' *ius* which is a primarily objective notion though John Finnis has argued that Aquinas also uses *ius* in a subjective sense, Finnis 2002: 407–10; Finnis 2011: 423–4.

relevant because persons endorsing certain beliefs which are firmly established are less likely to change their views than persons whose beliefs are only supported by weak arguments or by no reason at all. However, the state cannot guarantee that the support in people's minds on which it depends is well-founded. Therefore, it has been aptly expressed by the German constitutional judge Böckenförde that the state depends on something it cannot guarantee itself (Böckenförde 1976: 60).

If the state cannot guarantee the solidity of its citizens' beliefs or even its citizens' continued existence, it still can encourage the continuation of respect and support. It does this by creating institutions and proceedings which make the continued existence of the state and its statutes visible, which pronounce the law and which offer arguments for the statutes consistent with the moral systems of its citizens or at least of most of its citizens.[5]

The state accomplishes this task by creating higher order norms, that is norms which refer to other lower order norms in such a way that they create authorities competent to watch over the fulfillment of the lower order norms—the judicative function—and to impose and execute sanctions provided for violations of lower order norms in the higher order norms—the judicative and the executive functions (Hart 1994: 79–99). Finally they also create authorities which have the power to create more authorities or sanctions if need be—the legislative function.[6] The interplay of these functions enabled by the network of higher order norms makes the state a system of norms which continually creates and sustains itself. I think therefore that Niklas Luhmann has rightly termed such a system a self-creating or autopoietic system (Luhmann 1993: 44; Luhmann 1995: 12–13).

The strength of the system rests on two stabilizing factors. The network of higher order norms makes it possible to judge the citizen's behavior and enforce the lower order norms irrespective of the citizen's continued belief in the underlying moral principles, and by requiring the system's authorities to give reasons for their actions it at the same time is able to strengthen confidence in the system. A system becomes a legal system only by this unique stability added to it by the network of higher order norms. Without it, talk of a legal system is misleading. A system

5 I only wish to describe here how a state works in fact on the domestic level. However, even this part of my presentation has been criticized as "positivistic." It would not be clear how I could avoid "cultural relativism." I can only answer that it is not possible to avoid "cultural relativism" if that just means that not all legal systems are identical. But even a non-positivist could not avoid this. States are run by human beings, and not all human beings have the same mindset. Therefore, necessarily legal systems will differ. If the term "cultural relativism" should be meant as the endorsement of the view that there is no right answer to some moral questions, however, such an accusation would be unfounded. I am not compelled at all to embrace such a view because I differentiate between legal and moral issues. Legally many questions will necessarily be answered differently because of the different moral backgrounds of the deciders, but this leaves unaffected the possibility that morally there may only be one right answer.

6 Which does not have to be fulfilled by a parliament: a precedent-creating panel of common law judges also creates law and insofar is a legislator.

of first order norms not supported by authorities cannot be distinguished from a motley collection of moral norms or systems.

Rights defined as that which is due to a person by just claim only become rights within the system because the system's norm stating the right is supported by the network of higher order norms which guarantee enforcement of the right. Invoking "rights" which are not supported by this network before one of the system's authorities will only meet deaf ears and lead to nothing. Who may say that norms laying down "rights" within a system can exist without the support of the system's authorities? Nobody. The authorities of a system are its eyes, ears and hands. Who within the system will see if the authorities do not see? Who within the system will act if the authorities do not act?

If systems need the self-supporting structure of higher order norms to be rightly called legal systems, then the insight may be generalized: there cannot exist legal rights which are not recognized as such by a legal system's authorities.

The Specificity of Human Rights

General Features

It is widely acknowledged that human rights are characterized by the following general criteria: they are rights people simply have by virtue of being human, they are equal rights for all, they are inalienable and they are universal, that is apply to all human beings in all countries.

However, if we examine these criteria more closely, we recognize that they say practically nothing: if you have a right by virtue of being human, it is still possible to limit the right by so many express or implied exceptions that practically nothing certain remains. Each human being has a right to life, except as a soldier in combat, except when killed in self-defense, except when executed upon the judgment of a competent court and after a fair trial, etc.

In the same way it is easy to find a way to undermine equality. Human rights are enjoyed by all human beings alike, yes, but always with respect to a *tertium comparationis*. That exception enables us to justify each differentiation for a good reason. Yet, what is a good reason? Who shall be the judge? *Quis iudicabit?* In the end, everything short of sheer arbitrariness may be justified.

Nor does inalienability or universality help us much if we recognize the host of exceptions and differentiations around. Human rights therefore cannot be found merely by subsumption under abstract terms. If we want to discover what people mean by human rights we must look at their application of the term in reality. But we will not fare much better with this endeavor than we did with our attempt to bring the meaning to light with the help of abstract terms. All that seems to be certain is that human rights ought to be high-priority norms ensuring minimal standards, avoiding the terrible rather than achieving the best (Nickel 2010). But people's ideas about human rights seem to be as diverse as their moral background.

Agreement about Human Rights

In order to understand how the institutionalization of human rights can help in this situation, let us examine in detail how far people would be able to agree about human rights according to the tradition of those who regard human rights primarily as moral rights (Fagan 2005; Lyons 2009; Nickel 2010). James Nickel, for example, defines a human right as a shared norm of actual human moralities or a justified moral norm supported by strong reasons (Nickel 2010).

When endorsing such a definition, we leave the field of law entirely and enter the field of morality. The trouble with moral discussions is that it is never secure to talk about the details of morality before a common background structure has been accepted. Nonetheless, talk about moral rights, that is about what is morally right, refers to such common background structure. If I say that I have a moral right not to be tortured, I claim that according to a specific moral view it is wrong for someone to torture me. What is morally right can only be understood in relation to a specific moral view because a moral right can only be derived from a specific moral view. Therefore, what James Nickel calls a shared norm of actual human moralities will either presuppose a very superficial form of agreement without understanding or a detailed knowledge and acceptance of each other's moral views. If there is only a superficial agreement that it is wrong to torture, then it does make sense to say to someone who accepts another moral view than oneself: it is wrong to torture. But it is not possible to say meaningfully to one another "You know that I have a moral right not to be tortured" unless we at least know each other's moral views so well that we are able to talk correctly about them in a hypothetical way. Even if we have such basic mutual knowledge, talk about moral rights will remain complicated and hypothetical. Spelled out in full, "You know that I have a moral right not to be tortured" may mean:

1. Given what you believe, according to that moral system, it is wrong to torture. You are violating your own rules if you act contrary to your beliefs. I would be justified in expecting you to refrain from torturing me if I would share your beliefs.

or

2. Given what I believe, according to that moral system, it is wrong to torture. You are violating rules belonging to a system in which I believe. I would be justified in expecting you to refrain from torturing me if you would share my beliefs.

Note that I may neither in (1) nor in (2) expect categorically that you act according to your or my beliefs unless we not only share the beliefs that torture is wrong, but also share the derivation of the norm, that is at least the partial moral systems which are necessary to derive the norm not to torture in each case respectively. For it is a poor sort of argument to say "I am justified to expect you to act in this way because this conclusion is compelled by such and such background assumptions which you believe—I think it's a rotten conclusion, by the way, because I do not share your background assumptions." This just means building up the argument and then destroying it with your own hands. Argument (2) is no better because showing someone how he would have to act if he would share my background assumptions does not sound very convincing if we both know that he does not share my background assumptions.

We are also no better off if we combine (1) and (2). Not being able to share the background assumptions, the arguments do not become more convincing. Therefore, the situation is really not much better than if we would not understand each other at all and would only agree in a superficial way. If we understand each other well enough to go through the arguments without accepting each other's reasons, we are just able to acknowledge mutually: "The poor fool really believes this. Fortunately, we come to the same conclusion, and therefore his dreams are harmless. Let's hope they do not develop into something less pleasant."

The problem becomes worse if we apply such a notion of moral rights to the realm of human rights. If human rights are moral rights in the sense of "shared norms of actual human moralities" (Nickel 2010), this means together with the characteristic of universality that they must be the shared norms of *all* actual human moralities. Given the situation of many diverse human moral views, it is impossible to know each other's moral view well. There can only be superficial acceptance, and thus mere "moral rights" on the level of human rights are an—if not theoretical, at least practical—impossibility. In the same way, human rights cannot be "justified moral norms supported by strong reasons" (Nickel 2010), for strong reasons are only strong by virtue of being understood as strong.

The situation of merely moral rights lacks stability precisely because the common higher order structure of a legal system is missing which guarantees stability of the superficial content of a norm without the necessity to refer to a moral background structure.

When I pointed out above that it is not possible to say meaningfully to one another "You know that I have a moral right not to be tortured" unless we at least know each other's moral views, I referred to communication between persons who respect each other as such. To be precise, it has to be mentioned that of course it is always possible to emphasize something in the hope that it will be taken over by the listener. When I say to a torturer who does not at all understand my beliefs that it is wrong to torture, "I have a right not to be tortured," this may be the last attempt to teach him something as one shouts at a child or dog in the hope that he or it will somehow get the message. I do not deny that there may be situations in which there is an acute need for such use of the term "moral right" or "human right" in the sense of mere moral rights. There may be no time to suggest to your torturer to have a cup of tea together and thoroughly to discuss the moral questions involved in what he is about to do. However, such situations are exceptional where mere moral rights are invoked between people who adhere to different moral views. Such talk is not justified when cultivated philosophers or honest politicians meet. It would be a circumvention of a diligent investigation of moral questions in which each participant must be able to articulate his point of view. It would be wrong to insist that the other participant must begin such investigation by blindly taking over his opponent's point of view before he thoroughly understands it. But such is the effect of an invocation of human rights as merely moral rights among people who do not share each other's moral views.

The conclusion of this analysis must be that the moral rights aspect does not help to deal adequately with the issue of human rights. Moral discussions of rights are as necessary for human rights as they are for other legal rights because moral arguments provide the ties by which people feel bound to human rights. But such moral discussions cannot be cut short by reference to moral rights because such rights—unlike legal rights—would not be independent from the different moral views.

The Relevance of Legal Human Rights

What solution remains for the recognition of human rights? They must be instituted within a framework of higher order norms with authoritative positions to judge, enforce and legislate if need be. Such frameworks are provided by states which guarantee protection of the human rights in their constitutions and by international systems which are powerful enough to break the power of particular states which violate human rights themselves or which tolerate violations of human rights within their boundaries. Within such frameworks a stable existence of human rights at least as parts of an international legal system and thus as legal rights is possible. Rights here may be invoked regardless of the different moral views which support the concrete legal norms because the rights are part of the higher order framework, not because of the differing moral systems. The moral arguments supporting the conclusions are able to function within this context because each member or beneficiary of the international order is invited to support the legal norms categorically. He is invited to say:

1. "I may expect compliance with this norm because it belongs to the international framework. I myself support that framework for the sake of the moral system to which I adhere."

He also may still think in his heart: "My neighbor who endorses another moral system than I is an old fool. But thankfully, because of the higher order framework I am entitled to expect him to comply with the norms regardless of his weird beliefs." Yet this thought no longer destroys his argument which entitles him to expect compliance with the norms, and his neighbor may likewise think the same of this man. Thus the different moral views are able to strengthen the whole structure like beams of a saddle roof without destroying each other, provided of course that they are supporting the legal norm at all. The latter cannot be guaranteed.[7]

Apart from that, there lurk problems under the stable surface. If questions of interpretation arise and the text of the norm does not provide any clear guidance, then the different moral views may gain relevance for the solution. Likewise, people who belong to the legislative body may try to gain influence to the advantage of the moral view they endorse. The legislative body is the right place for such political power struggle. However, honest men do discuss such influence openly and do not try to hide it or introduce changes stealthily as did Sir Edward Coke in his struggle with James I (Presser and Zainaldin 2009: 1–8). No invocation of moral rights may be of assistance in an honest debate, only the investigation of the strengths and weaknesses of arguments seen from the majority's point of view.

Prospective and Retrospective Use of Human Rights

It has been unjustly alleged that for legal positivism the task of ascertaining the existence of human rights is "too easy" and that a legal positivist account of human rights cannot deal with obviously accepted uses of human rights outside legal systems. That is not true.

There rather remains room enough for a prospective and retrospective use of the term "human rights." My rejection of the term moral rights does not preclude this, for it is still possible to use the term human rights with respect to a future recognition of legal rights if no legal right exists at present. Equally, it may be possible for an international institution to treat a person as if a right existed already in the past at a time at which the person acted contrary to the right.

It may be, for example, that the country in which I am living has not signed a treaty which would prohibit torturing the country's subjects. While it does not help me to point to a mere moral right which is not accepted by the addressee, it can make sense to let him bear in mind that one day the country could join the treaty and then my position at the present moment would be retrospectively regarded as one in which I have a right vis-à-vis the addressee not to be tortured.

Besides, when the country does indeed sign the treaty prohibiting torture, nothing hinders a stipulation of retrospective validity of the treaty. If a legislative

7 In particular, some states may agree on a protection of human rights they do not wholly endorse. A Muslim state may sign an international treaty protecting the religious freedom of "infidels" because it also protects the Muslim faith, for example. The members signing the treaty can only be invited to wholly endorse its content, they cannot be compelled to do that, but this is irrelevant for the validity of the signed treaty.

body agrees that a human right has always existed though it was not laid down in any statute, it may define the validity of the right with retrospective effect.[8] If the legislative body is part of a legal system which has the power to enforce its norms, then the right existed already in the past. Who may judge to the contrary? I therefore, in contrast to many criminal and international law scholars do not believe that the Nuremberg Trials unjustifiably stipulated the existence of norms which the Nazis had violated.[9] True, this may be called victors' justice, but who may justly criticize such definition? Only a system which would have to be strong enough to void the effect of the victors' systems of international law.

What is Left of the Universality and Inalienability of Human Rights?

Not so easily to be dismissed is the objection that not much is left of the universality and inalienability of human rights. If my account is correct that the existence of human rights may vary with the relevance of a perspective, then different human rights will emerge when the relevant perspective changes. This statement seems not to be in accordance with the inalienable rights referred to in the preambles of the Universal Declaration of Human Rights of 1948, the United Nations International Covenant on Civil and Political Rights of 1966 and the European Convention for the Protection of Human Rights and Fundamental Freedoms of 1952 which in turn refers to the Universal Declaration of 1948.

However, to my mind the solution to this problem is found in the concept of the relevant perspective. While the existence of human rights may vary with the relevant perspective, a particular perspective may view the rights it endorses as eternal and inalienable. That does not at all change the insight that from another perspective these eternal and inalienable rights can be observed to emerge only with the increase of relevance of the former perspective.[10] The Universal

8 Of course, it may be prudent not to make too extensive use of such a stipulation and not to distance oneself too much from the people's common sense. However, one should be reminded that current domestic laws already contain far-reaching fiction like the old institution of annulment of marriage which makes a marriage that may have already lasted for some years null and void from the beginning.

9 I do not refer to the problem of jurisdiction here but to the retroactive introduction of crimes against humanity.

10 Contrary to Searle 2011: 177, 182, I believe that there is a genuine contradiction between the statement that people have lost their (institutionalized) rights and the statement that they have retained these rights because they are eternal and inalienable. Seen from a clearly defined perspective, there is a correct or incorrect use of the term "right" in such a context. The contradiction does not vanish if it is explained that when we say people have lost their rights "we are recognizing that the functioning of the Y status function requires recognition, and hence, in the absence of that recognition we can deny that it exists," while when we say that people have retained their rights we are identifying the satisfaction of the X condition as sufficient for the possession of the Y status function" (Searle 2011: 182). It

Declaration of Human Rights itself seems to recognize that there may be difficulties of interpretation concerning particular human rights because it concedes in its preamble that "a common understanding of these rights and freedoms is of the greatest importance for the full realization of this pledge." This suggests that the framers of the Declaration knew such common understanding could not be taken for granted.

An even less naïve mind will notice that eternal and inalienable rights cannot be fitted into a coherent picture of history. There are too many unanswerable questions: It may be that one should regard the U.S.A. of 1776 as a rogue state because it held that all men are created equal and that they are endowed by their creator with certain unalienable rights, but at the same time tolerated slavery. But should the U.S.A. of 1776 also be regarded as a rogue state because women were not allowed to vote? Or should one rather deny even today that the right to vote is a human right? I think that neither question should be answered in the affirmative. On the one hand, a woman in 1776 could well be regarded as not suffering an infringement of her human rights even if she did not have the right to vote. On the other hand, it can hardly be denied that the right to free and equal suffrage is a human right today (Art. 21 Universal Declaration of Human Rights). However, a plausible explanation of the different situation today can only be that a new perspective has gained relevance between 1776 and the present time and that therefore new rights have come into existence which did not exist before.

Even those who purport to identify a core of absolute human claim-rights are not able to lay to rest doubts about the existence of eternal and unalienable human rights. Finnis for example contends that there are absolute human rights where it is always unreasonable to choose against the basic values expressed by such rights. Among those are the right not to have one's life taken directly as a means to an end (Finnis 2011: 225). However, this does not prevent him from suggesting that the death penalty may be justifiable because he who violates the order of fairness forfeits certain of his own rights.[11] Here, it becomes obvious that a right may be

---

is much clearer if we distinguish two perspectives which nonetheless are able to contradict each other. Mere positivism needs to be complemented by constructivism.

11 Finnis 1983: 129–30; contra Wright 2000: 558. In Finnis 1983: 130 he shifts his opinion a bit by saying that capital punishment would not need to be regarded as treating the criminal "as a *mere* means" instead of "a means to a further end." The difference between the formulations in Finnis 2011: 225 and Finnis 1983: 130 becomes clear when we look at the reason Finnis gives for his view in Finnis 1983. He thinks that the deprivation of rights connected with punishment would be intended neither for its own sake nor as a means to any further state of affairs. Rather it would be intended as itself a good, namely the good of restoring the order of justice, Finnis 1983: 129. Hereby, Finnis has indeed left open the possibility that a criminal may not *only* be treated as a means when he is executed. However, this argument in no way excludes the fact that capital punishment is at least in part a means to a further end. The execution may itself be regarded as part of the good of restoring the order of justice. But it is not identical with restoring the order of justice because restoring the order of justice may require more than punishing the criminal in this particular instance.

made absolute by including the exceptions in the formulation of rights. The citizen no longer has an absolute human right not to have one's life taken, but an absolute right not to have one's life taken subject to whatever conditions one wishes to include in the definition of the right. Applying such method of restriction, it is always possible to "discover" new restrictions of the right and to include them in the definition of the right, always maintaining that these restrictions have been tacitly presupposed at all times.

To my mind, it is more plausible to concede that there are no absolute human rights which the law has to take into account, except those rights which according to the mechanisms of the legal system have been made (absolute) human rights and have not been abolished. In a democracy, inevitably the majority of the people will decide what these human rights are.[12]

Infinite Regress?

A formal objection against the view set out here is the regress argument known as the Hobbesian regress of legitimation (Hobbes 1968: 367; Lagerspetz 1995: 110) which has often been used to discredit the older legal positivist theories by Kelsen and Hart. An authoritative position must be created by norms, these norms must be created by other authoritative positions etc. ad infinitum. If a legal system is seen as a hierarchical structure, this infinite regress destroys the possibility of a satisfactory legitimation of the officials acting for the state. The legal positivist theories of Kelsen and Hart were thought to succumb to the infinite regress argument because they relied on hierarchical structures. Kelsen cut off the regress by positing a Grundnorm as the highest norm (Kelsen 2000: 198–202; Kelsen 2008: 73–6). Hart posited a rule of recognition (Hart 1994: 100–10) to deal with the problem of the infinite regress. I do not wish to decide whether the objection against these older legal positivist theories was justified or not. At any rate, I believe that the problem has been finally solved by functionalism as follows.

The victim may have to be compensated, for example. Therefore, the partial action can be regarded as a means of contributing to the further and more comprehensive task of restoring the order of justice.

12 Insofar, I am sympathetic with Scalia 2004: 136. He was asked how he would comment on the thesis that there is a natural law of reason which obliges governments to obey certain laws of reason derived from man's nature. Scalia answered: "It just seems to me incompatible with democratic theory that it's good and right for the state to do something that the majority of the people do not want done." Asked whether it would be possible that some common fundamental ethics can give something to the positive law, he answered: "Yes, of course, and it must. But that process is achieved not within the context of government, but outside the context of government with free men and women persuading one another … "

If we see a legal system as an autopoietic (self-creating) system (Luhmann 1997: 92–3), then it is characterized by a circular structure. However, the circles are not vicious circles, but virtuous circles because the authoritative positions which are part of the system make use of their discretion and therefore ensure that an official acting within the system does not just legitimize his own actions. If for example, a legislative body enacts a law, the legislative body is legitimized by the election proceedings conducted by officials which are legitimized by laws which may have been enacted by the same legislative body. As long as the system works, no reference to a Grundnorm or rule of recognition is necessary. When the system's members no longer believe in the system and therefore the system breaks down, the system just ceases to exist and consequently cannot continue to legitimize any actions.

Such a circular structure is only capable of legitimizing actions within the system from an internal legal perspective. It cannot legitimize these actions from an external perspective because all persons acting as members of the system are required to assume the system's perspective. If these persons take another (perhaps critical)[13] perspective, they no longer assess the world from the system's point of view. The system cannot process such views. From the system's perspective, such views assume a non-legal external perspective. The external perspective could also be called a moral perspective.

Conclusion

I plead for an understanding of human rights as primarily legal rights. It is possible to see these rights as eternal and inalienable from a certain moral perspective once they have been recognized by a system of international law. History teaches us, however, that human rights have come to be recognized which were not always recognized as such (for example the women's right to vote). Legal positivism makes the clearest understanding of human rights possible. Other views which treat human rights as moral rights are dangerous insofar as they foster unrealistic expectations. Rights are nowadays predominantly understood as Hohfeldian claim-rights, and it is not realistic to expect the enforcement of a claim based merely on a moral right which is not supported by institutions of international law. Moral rights are not necessary concepts of moral discourse. It should be sufficient to determine whether it is morally right or wrong for someone to have something instead of determining whether someone has a moral right to it.

Legal positivism combined with constructivism can also allow for a legal perspective which introduces human rights retroactively. Moreover, if legal

13 It goes without saying that I only mean criticism here which is not allowed by the legal system. If a country grants its citizens freedom of speech, and the citizens make use of it, they keep their internal perspective. They then do not exchange it for an external perspective.

positivism treats the legal system as an autopoietic system, it can escape the Hobbesian legitimation regress argument.

Acknowledgements

I hereby wish to thank the audiences at the 25th IVR World Congress on August 16, 2011 (workshop chaired by Angus J.L. Menuge), and at Ulfrid Neumann's seminar in Frankfurt on January 17, 2013, for helpful comments.

Bibliography

Bentham, J. 1907 (reprint; first publication date 1789). *An Introduction to the Principles of Morals and Legislation*. Oxford: Clarendon.

Böckenförde, E.W. 1976. *Staat, Gesellschaft, Freiheit*. Frankfurt am Main: Suhrkamp.

Dworkin, R. 2006. *Is Democracy Possible?* Princeton, NJ: Princeton University Press.

Fagan, A. 2005. Article on Human Rights, *Internet Encyclopedia of Philosophy*. Available at: http//:iep.utm.edu/hum-rts [accessed: June 16, 2012].

Finnis, J.M. 1983. *Fundamentals of Ethics*. Washington: Georgetown University Press.

Finnis, J.M. 2002. Aquinas on ius and Hart on rights: A response to Tierney. *The Review of Politics*, 64, 407–10.

Finnis, J.M. 2011. *Natural Law and Natural Rights*, 2nd edn. Oxford: Oxford University Press.

Gardner, J. 2008. Simply in virtue of being human: The whos and whys of human rights. *Journal of Ethics and Social Philosophy*, 2, 1–22.

Gierhake, K. 2004. *Begruendung des Voelkerstrafrechts auf der Grundlage der Kantischen Rechtslehre*. Berlin: Duncker & Humblot.

Hart, H.L.A. 1973. Bentham on legal rights, in *Oxford Essays in Jurisprudence*, 2nd series, edited by A.L. Simpson. Oxford: Clarendon, 171–201.

Hart, H.L.A. 1994. *The Concept of Law*, 2nd edn. Oxford: Clarendon.

Hobbes, T. 1968. *Leviathan*, edited by C.B. MacPherson. Harmondsworth: Penguin.

Hohfeld, W.N. 1919. *Fundamental Legal Conceptions as Applied to Judicial Reasoning: And Other Legal Essays*. New Haven: Yale University Press.

Kelsen, H. 2000. Reine Rechtslehre (reprint of the 2nd edn; first publication date 1960).Vienna: Verlag Oesterreich.

Kelsen, H. 2008. Reine Rechtslehre (reprint of the 1st edn; first publication date 1934), edited by M. Jestaedt. Tuebingen: Mohr Siebeck.

Lagerspetz, E. 1995. *The Opposite Mirrors: An Essay on the Conventionalist Theory of Institutions*. Dordrecht: Kluwer Academic Publishers.

Locke, J. 1993. *Two Treatises on Government*. London: Everyman Paperbacks.
Luhmann, N. 1993. *Das Recht der Gesellschaft*. Frankfurt am Main: Suhrkamp.
Luhmann, N. 1995. *Soziologische Aufklärung 6 – Die Soziologie und der Mensch*. Opladen: Westdeutscher Verlag.
Luhmann, N. 1997. *Die Gesellschaft der Gesellschaft*. Frankfurt am Main: Suhrkamp.
Lyons, D. 2009. Article on Legal and Moral Rights. *IVR-Encyclopedia of Jurisprudence, Legal Theory and Philosophy of Law*. Available at: http://ivr-enc.info/index/php?title=Legal_and_Moral_Rights [accessed: June 16, 2012].
Nickel, J. 2010. Article on Human Rights. *Stanford Encyclopedia of Philosophy*. Available at: http//:plato.stanford.edu/entries/rights-human/ [accessed: June 16, 2012].
Presser, S.B. and Zainaldin, J.S. 2009. *Law and Jurisprudence in American History*, 7th edn. Rochester, NY: West.
Rachels, J. 2011. The challenge of cultural relativism. *Homepage of Norman R. Schultz*. Available at: http://normanrschultz.org/ethics/Rachels_challengeofcultural relativism.pdf [accessed: June 16, 2012].
Scalia, A. 2004. Of democracy, morality and the majority, in *The American Constitutional Order, History, Cases and Philosophy*, edited by D.W. Kmiec, S.B. Presser, J.C. Eastman, R.B. Marcin. Newark, NJ: LexisNexis, 136–8.
Searle, J.R. 2011. Making the social world: the structure of human civilization. Oxford: Oxford University Press.
Totaro, M.V. 2007/2008. Legal positivism, constructivism and human rights law: The case of participatory development. *Virginia Journal of International Law*, 48, 719–65.
Wright, R. 2000. The Death Penalty and the Way We Think Now. *Loyola of Los Angeles Law Review*, 33, 533–84.

PART II
Religious Liberty and the Secular State

Chapter 5
Human Rights in a Secular State Will Depend on its Legal Definition of Religion

John H. Calvert

Introduction

This chapter notes that the human rights recognized by any given jurisdiction or "state" depend on the laws of the state that establish and then secure the rights. It then argues that the human rights that a state does establish and secure will be significantly influenced by the religious bias of the state. This is because our concepts about the rights of humans turn on our answers to ultimate religious questions like: *Where do we come from? What is the nature of human life? What is the purpose of life and how should it be lived, individually and collectively from a moral and ethical standpoint?* Since religions provide answers to all of these questions, they tend to define the scope and extent of human rights. Accordingly, the particular religious bias of a state will tend to determine the human rights it allows for its citizens.

As an example, a theocracy like Iran will define the human rights of its citizens consistent with the religion of Islam. Similarly, an atheocracy like Marxist Russia defined human rights consistent with the religious ideas of Atheism.

But what about a secular state? What religious rights might one expect from a "secular" state, one which commits to having no religious bias at all? This chapter argues that the religious rights of a citizen of a secular state will depend on how the state defines the word "religion." It further contends that an inclusive definition of religion is necessary to maximize and secure those rights.

The Defining Characteristic of a Secular State is that it is not Religious

A Secular State Cannot be Secular until it Defines what is Religious

The most important question a secular state must answer is the meaning of the word "religion." This is because "secular" means "not religious" (Webster's 2003, Random House 2005). Since a secular state commits to being not religious, it must know what is religious so that it can avoid being religious. Once the state knows what is within the religious sphere, then it may logically infer that all else is secular. That secular or "all else" then defines the scope of activities with which the secular government may be concerned. Secular or *all else* content is sometimes described as "mundane," such as "human affairs, concerns, and activities that are often practical, immediate, transitory, and ordinary" (Webster's 2003). For example, in *Lemon v. Kurtzman* (S.Ct. 1971: 430 U.S. 602, 610), the Court considered a statute that classified the following subjects as "secular": "mathematics, modern foreign languages, physical science, and physical education."

Demarcating the Religious from the Secular

Once the concept of mutually exclusive spheres is understood, the inquiry turns to defining the boundary that separates the two. Where does the religious sphere end and where does the secular sphere begin? In a sense there is no outside boundary to the secular. It is just everything not within the religious sphere. As an analogy, one might think of the earth as like the religious and everything outside as like the secular. The analogy is imperfect, however. In the case of the earth it is relatively easy to mark the physical boundary between it and everything else once you define the limits of its atmosphere. By contrast, the religious sphere is a concept that describes the essential attributes of a class of belief systems which also affect non-religious or secular beliefs. So a key task of the secular state is to identify the boundary between the religious and the secular. It is important. If the boundary is not drawn with clarity then government may cross it and thereby deprive its citizens of their religious rights.

The division between the religious and the secular is almost irrelevant in a non-secular or a religious state. In a state driven by a particular religion, human rights are defined by the tenets of that religion. Accordingly, whether a particular activity is permitted or proscribed will depend on the tenets of the governing religion. For example, the religious and other rights of a woman in Iran will be limited to those permitted by the Koran, the Sharia Law and Islamic religious customs. Similarly, in an atheistic state that promotes non-theistic religion while suppressing theistic religion, conduct consistent with atheistic ideas may be permitted while contradictory behavior directed by theistic religions may be outlawed. In an atheistic state, it may be permissible to require citizens to worship the world and the state rather than a creator of both. Thus, in a religious state, there is no essential need to demarcate the religious from the secular as the state can operate freely within both spheres.

Religious Neutrality is the Goal of the Secular State

A truly secular state does not seek to unify its citizens around a single religious view. Rather it recognizes that its citizens have diverse religious beliefs. Accordingly, the constitutional mandate of a secular state is to not interfere with any religious activity while being neutral as to all. This idea requires the state to promote harmony among diverse and competing religions and religious beliefs. It is a challenging task, as it is very difficult to remove religious bias from the agents of the state. Neutrality in an absolute sense is an impossibility. However, it is an impossibility that a truly secular state seeks to achieve. As the state strives for that neutral goal it perhaps comes closer to its attainment. Neutral metaphors that come to mind are judges, juries, umpires and football leagues that promote competition between rival teams while favoring none.

In the US the Constitutional provisions which require the state to be secular are the First and Fourteenth Amendments. Together, these have been held to preclude any Federal, state or local government or agency, including a public school, from enacting a law or adopting a policy "respecting an establishment of religion or abridging the free exercise thereof" (*Cantwell*, S.Ct. 1940 and *McCollum*, S.Ct. 1948).

The idea is that not only is the government banned from abridging or interfering with the exercise of religion, but neither may government endorse or support a competing religion. Thus, a secular state guarantees religious neutrality rather than the imposition of a religious orthodoxy. This idea of neutrality was succinctly explained by Justice Marshall in writing for the majority in *Gillette v. U.S.*:

> [W]hen government activities *touch on the religious sphere*, they must be *secular in purpose*, evenhanded in operation, and neutral in primary impact. (*Gillette*, S.Ct.1971: 401 U.S. 437, 450, emphasis added)

But What is Included in the "Religious Sphere"?

Notice the importance of defining the boundaries of the "religious sphere." If government activities "touch it," then the government must go into a neutral mode. The idea of defining the boundaries of the religious sphere might be aided by a metaphor.

Suppose the secular state defines religion as being limited to the worship of chocolate cake. Since a secular state may not be religious then it may not abridge one's right to make, consume and otherwise worship chocolate cake. Nor may it endorse or support the consumption of chocolate cake in its public schools. During a classroom birthday party for a child the school may serve white cake, but not chocolate cake. Since the worship of white cake is not included within the definition of religion, its consumption in public schools is secular and therefore permitted. The school may also cause children to worship veggies, as the worship of veggies, not involving the worship of chocolate cake, is not religious. Also, under this narrow definition of religion, the state may provide for the exclusive worship of no-God or even of God, as neither of these concepts fall within the definition of religion.

This metaphor illustrates how the definition of religion profoundly affects the scope of a secular state's authority, which is confined to the secular sphere. As the scope of the definition of religion changes the scope of the secular sphere varies inversely. Thus, as the scope of the religious sphere expands, the scope of the secular governmental sphere shrinks.

So the question becomes: what is logically and legally the scope of the religious sphere? To address this question, we will explore the content of recognized religions based on the observations of two religious scholars. Then we will compare those observations with the conclusions of US Courts about the content of the religious sphere from a legal perspective.

The Views of Felix Frankfurter, Roy Clouser and Stephen Prothero about Religion

This section deals with the conclusions of a few religious authorities and scholars about the nature of religion. We start with the conclusion of Justice Felix Frankfurter in *McGowan v. Maryland.* Atheists sought to enjoin Sunday closing laws as they were claimed to be offensive to their religious belief that God does not exist. The court denied the injunction on the ground that the laws did not intrude into the religious sphere, as they merely provided a day of rest to both theists and atheists. In reaching this conclusion, Justice Frankfurter defined religion as an activity that deals with subjects more profound than chocolate cake or labor laws:

> By its nature, religion – in the comprehensive sense in which the Constitution uses that word – is *an aspect of human thought and action which profoundly relates the life of man to the world in which he lives.*" (*McGowan*, S.Ct. 1961: 366 U.S. 420, 461, emphasis added)

Because the Sunday closing laws do not profoundly relate the lives of workers to the world in which they live, they do not fall within the religious sphere.

If we allow *McGowan* to guide our search for the scope of the religious sphere, we then ask what kinds of issues and what kinds of subject matter have that effect—the effect of profoundly relating human life to the world in which it is lived?

Roy Clouser, a professor of philosophy and religion, addresses this question in *The Myth of Religious Neutrality*. Based on 50 years of investigation Clouser sought to "define the nature of religious belief by seeking common features among the central beliefs of the world's religious traditions … we are trying to arrive at an understanding of what religion – any religion – *is*" (Clouser 2005: 9). In seeking to answer this question he included in his survey recognized religions such as Judaism, Christianity, Islam, Hinduism, Buddhism, Taoism, as well as ancient religions such as Epicureanism, Druidism, Zoroastrianism, and Shintoism "and a host of other candidates."

In his search for the common elements of all of these diverse belief systems, Clouser first eliminated elements that *are not common* to all religions. Not all religions have rituals, worship, worship of a creator or superhuman controlling power, or a specific code of morality and ethics (Clouser 2005: 10–12). After excluding common elements one often associates with religion, he then turned to the key question—what *is common* among all of these religious belief systems? What subjects or issues do all religions address?

Clouser concludes that all religious beliefs *begin* with a belief about what is the "unconditional non-dependent reality."

> A religious belief is a belief in something as divine per se no matter how that is further described, where "divine per se" means having *unconditionally non-dependent reality*. (Clouser 2005: 23, emphasis added)

For the traditional theist the ultimate or unconditional non-dependent reality is a self-existing Creator God who created the world *ex nihilo* and then created life for a purpose. However, for the Atheist, the unconditional non-dependent reality is a self-existing universe that reduces to nothing more than matter, energy and the forces. Life just emerges via unguided evolutionary processes, not by the intellect of a supernatural entity.

In simpler terms, the unconditional non-dependent reality is the answer to this question: "*Where do we come from?*" What is the ultimate cause of life?

Clouser then recognizes that "although this definition captures the essential core of religious belief in its primary sense," it does not "cover still other beliefs in realities thought to be *divine dependent* rather than *divine per se*." Nor does it "cover still other beliefs that also deserve to be called 'religious' in yet other secondary senses." So to complete his definition of religious belief he contends that:

> A belief is a religious belief provided that:
>
> (1) It is a belief in something as divine per se no matter how that is further described, or
> (2) it is a belief about how the non-divine depends upon the divine per se, or
> (3) it is a belief about how humans come to stand in proper relation to the divine per se; and
> (4) where the central core of divinity per se is to have the status of unconditional non-dependent reality (Clouser 2005: 24).

Based on this definition of religious belief, Clouser then classifies religions into three broad categories: the traditional theistic, the materialistic/naturalistic/atheistic or "pagan," and the pantheistic. In many respects the pantheistic and materialistic/atheistic are harmonious, as they do not depend on a Creator God that intervenes in the universe to make life for a specific purpose.

We note that Clouser's definition of religious belief addresses three "ultimate questions" that are commonly associated with all religious beliefs:

1. Where do we come from – what is the origin of life and the universe?
2. What is the nature of life and what happens when it ends?
3. What is the meaning or purpose of life, if any? How should it be lived?

Answers to these three questions will identify the unconditional non-dependent reality, how the non-divine life depends on that reality and how it may come to stand in proper relationship to it. Thus, Clouser's definition of religious belief identifies a hierarchy of ultimate religious questions that all religions address: what is the cause, nature and purpose of life and how should it be lived?

The hierarchy of religious inquiry starts with this question:

1. Where do we come from – What is the origin of life?

There are a variety of answers to this ultimate question. However, principal competing explanations are theistic and atheistic. For the traditional theist, life comes from a God that created the universe and life for a purpose. A Creator God is the unconditional non-dependent reality that generates and transcends the physical world. For the Atheist, life just "emerges" from matter via unguided evolutionary mechanisms over seemingly infinite stretches of time. Life arises from matter, not mind. The unconditional non-dependent reality is a self-existing material universe.

Once one forms a belief about the origin of life the hierarchy naturally leads us to the next ultimate question, which is:

2. What is the nature of life and what happens when we die?

For the Atheist life is just an occurrence. It just happens. By faith, an Atheist believes life emerges from unguided natural or material causes. Per the laws of entropy, it ends on death. Life is finite, not eternal. This would not be true for many pantheists who believe life has a spiritual dimension that is reincarnated after death into another physical being.

The traditional theist believes that life is a creation, not just an occurrence. As a creation it has an inherent purpose. Most theists believe that life does not end on death, but continues in a spiritual realm, which is often divided into heaven or hell. The final destination may depend on how the individual fulfills the purpose for which he or she was created during life. In this sense life has both a physical and spiritual dimension, including a "soul."

Having formed a belief regarding the cause and nature of life, the hierarchy leads us to ask the third key question:

3. What is the inherent purpose of life if any? How should life be lived?

An atheistic faith logically entails that life has no inherent purpose. This is because it is an occurrence, not a creation. Purpose only derives from an active mind or some form of intelligence that has made a "choice" for a purpose. Often the choices made are manifested by the output generated by the mind. This chapter reflects innumerable choices made by the mind of its author. Hopefully, the purpose is clearly manifested.

Since life is not imbued with an inherent purpose, the Atheist is logically left to human reason to define the purpose of life. Reason led atheistic Epicureans to logically define the purpose of a finite life as one that avoids pain and disturbance while seeking pleasure or happiness (Wiker 2002: 10). Epicureanism is the precursor to the more modern Religious ("Secular") Humanism. Religious

Humanists look to materialistic science in its comprehensive sense and human reason to inform decisions about how life should be lived (Calvert 2009: 234–6).

For the theist, life has an inherent purpose. Hence, it is to be led to achieve that purpose. Typically, the theist informs his view of the purpose of life from a mix of subjective, logical, experiential and scientific inputs, guided by scriptural and natural revelations about God's intentions. Scriptural revelations include commands, like the Ten Commandments, and teachings such as those of Jesus in the Gospels.

The Christian religion defines the purpose of life very subjectively with each individual being created differently to satisfy a unique purpose. Rick Warren's popular book, *The Purpose Driven Life: What on Earth Am I Here for?* (Warren 2002) explains that the specific purpose depends on a personal experience with the Holy Spirit of Jesus, who said: "If anyone would come after me, *he must deny himself* and take up his cross daily and follow me" (Luke 9:23, emphasis added).

Thus, our particular religious beliefs will depend on how we each answer a hierarchy of ultimate religious questions. The first question, where do we come from, actually is the root of a profound decision tree that will influence all of the rest of our decisions of life. An example of this idea is roughly diagramed in the illustration in Figure 5.1.

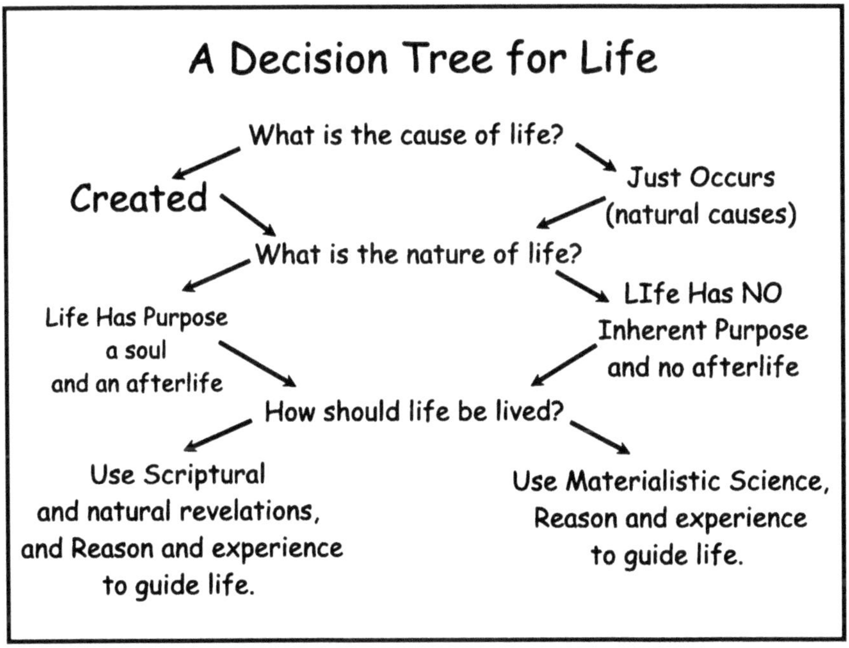

Figure 5.1 A decision tree for life

Accordingly, our lives will be informed and guided by our conscious and subconscious answers to these ultimate religious questions. One who trusts Jesus as a guide will likely have a profoundly different idea about how life should be lived, than one who places his trust in one's self or in the opinions of other humans who might control one's self.

Stephen Prothero, a professor of Religion at Boston University comes to a conclusion similar to that of Clouser. In *God is not One* Prothero compares and contrasts nine religions of the world, including Atheism. He argues that the common denominator of all religions is that they identify a core problem of life. They then identify a solution to the problem, techniques for reaching the solution and exemplars for charting the path from problem to solution (Prothero 2010: 14).

For example, Prothero argues that "in Christianity … the problem is sin … the solution (or goal) is salvation; the technique for achieving salvation is some combination of faith and good works; and the exemplars who chart this path are the saints in Roman Catholicism and Orthodoxy and ordinary people of faith in Protestantism"; whereas "[I]n Buddhism … the problem is suffering, the solution (or goal) is nirvana, the technique for achieving nirvana is the Noble Eightfold Path, which includes such classic Buddhist practices as meditation and chanting, and the exemplars … are *arhats* (for Theravada Buddhists), *bodhisattvas* (for Mahayana Buddhists), or *lamas* (for Vajrayana Buddhists)" (Prothero 2010: 14–15).

Prothero describes Atheism as a religion which holds that:

> [theistic] religion is itself the problem. [Theistic] religious belief is man-made and murderous—irrational, superstitious, and hazardous to our health. The solution is to flush this poison out of our system—to follow the courageous examples of heroic unbelievers from Diagoras to Freud to the patron saints of the New Atheism: American writer Sam Harris, American philosopher Daniel Dennett, British evolutionary biologist Richard Dawkins, British journalist Christopher Hitchens, and French philosopher Michel Onfray. And where will this cleansing lead? To a postreligious utopia. Without the foolishness of faith, all will be well, and all manner of things will be well. (Prothero 2010: 318)

The atheistic technique for getting from the problem to the solution is to use "reason over revelation, logic over faith, and scientific experimentation over magical thinking" (Prothero 2010: 318). Thus Atheism enshrines reason and materialistic science over reasoned and rational applications of the "wisdom of God."

Prothero's idea that all religions seeks to solve an ultimate problem of life addresses the third key question—how should one live life? His analysis assumes that the religion in question has already answered the first two questions—where do we come from and what is the nature of life? Thus the core problem, once the first two questions are answered, deals with how life should be led from an ethical and moral standpoint.

Although dictionaries are not dispositive, they often tend to succinctly summarize collective viewpoints. Interestingly, the first listed definition in a popular dictionary is consistent with the foregoing conclusions about the meaning of the word "religion." It defines religion in terms of the three ultimate questions and their hierarchy as follows:

> Religion: 1. a set of beliefs *concerning the cause, nature, and purpose of [life and] the universe*, esp. when considered as the creation of a superhuman agency or agencies, usu. involving devotional and ritual observances, and often containing a moral code for the conduct of human affairs. (Random House 2005, emphasis added)

This chapter argues that a definition of religion that captures the essence of all religions and that "profoundly relates the life of man to the world in which he lives" is:

> Religion: an organized set of beliefs concerning ultimate questions such as the cause, nature and purpose of life and how it should be lived.

The Views of US Courts about Religion

Since the word "religion" is not defined in the US Constitution, its legal meaning is found in the opinions of US Courts.

The US Supreme Court has yet to provide a definitive definition of religion. However, it has held that certain beliefs are properly classified as religious and has adopted and announced religious tests which may be applied to determine whether a particular subject falls within the religious sphere. The Court has also expressed its views about religion in persuasive but non-binding "dicta" or judicial assertions. The body of these opinions and consistent rulings of subordinate US Courts have shown that the religious sphere in the secular US is a comprehensive and inclusive sphere that has fuzzy edges.

Because the definition of religion is a matter of interpretation, it has evolved over time as cases dealing with different issues have been decided. Since each interpretation affects subsequent interpretations, it is helpful to study the evolution of the legal meaning of "religion" chronologically.

One of the first US cases about the meaning of the word is found in the 1890 Supreme Court case of *Davis v. Beason*. The issue in Davis involved a religious tenet regarding human sexuality in the context of a polygamy statute that made it a crime. The court held that the free exercise clause does not exempt a religious exercise of polygamy from generally applicable criminal laws that prohibit it.

In reaching its decision the *Davis* Court explained in *dicta* that "'religion' has reference to one's views of his relations to his Creator, and to the obligations they impose of reverence for his being and character, and of obedience to his will" (*Davis v. Beason*, S.Ct. 1890: 133 U.S. 333, 342). This definition arguably limits religion to beliefs in a Creator God because it implicitly assumes that there is one.

The assumption was common as 95 percent of the population in the US in 1890 were likely traditional theists.

However, since the formation of the country, the mix of its population has changed enormously and the Courts have uniformly recognized that the US is populated by a large plurality of differing religious perspectives, many of which are not theistic (*Malnak v. Yogi*, 3rd Cir. 1979: 592 F.2d 197, 207; and *Lee v. Weisman*, S.Ct. 1992: 505 U.S. 577, 617). This recognition has caused many non-theists to assert religious rights and Courts to recognize and uphold them.

The popular idea that religion is limited to theistic beliefs was first tested in 1957 in the case of *Fellowship of Humanity v. County of Alameda* (*Fellowship*, Cal. App. 1957). The question in *Fellowship* was whether a belief system called "Religious Humanism" (now sometimes called "Secular Humanism") was a religion. Religious Humanism was proclaimed as a religion in 1933 through the publication of the first of three Manifestos. The Manifestos trace the roots of Religious Humanism to Epicureanism developed in the third and fourth centuries BC and Jainism, an East Asian analogue, both of which deny a Creator God. Religious Humanism was developed in the first half of the twentieth century by John Dewey, Charles Potter and others to insert into public schools (Potter 1930). The first Manifesto declared it to be a new religion designed to replace traditional religions that "have lost their significance and which are powerless to solve the problem of human living in the Twentieth Century … [T]he time has passed for theism" (*Humanist Manifesto I* 1933).

The key tenets of this atheistic religion, as set out in its Manifestos, are (1) there is no "supernatural" or God; (2) the unconditional non-dependent reality is "a self-existing and not created" physical universe; (3) "[Man] has *emerged* as a result of a continuous" "unguided evolutionary process," (Humanist Manifesto III 2003); (4) humans should use reason and materialistic science to guide life; *and* (5) it should have as its "purpose and program" the "transformation, control, and direction of [all associations and institutions]" by Religious Humanism "with a view to the enhancement of human life" (Humanist Manifesto I 1933).

Manifesto II explains: "Humanism can provide the purpose and inspiration that so many seek; it can give personal meaning and significance to human life … *Free thought, atheism, agnosticism, skepticism, deism, rationalism, ethical culture, and liberal religion all claim to be heir to the humanist tradition …*" (Humanist Manifesto II 1973, emphasis added).

By the 1950s Oakland, CA was the home of 14 Humanist churches which sought tax exemptions for real property used to promote their religion. The County of Alameda denied the exemption on the grounds that the property was not used "exclusively for religious worship," since Humanists do not worship a God. The California Court of Appeals, per the opinion of Judge Peters, rejected the idea that religion is limited to a belief in God.

According to Judge Peters, a belief system is religious if it functions in the lives of its adherents in the same manner as recognized religions function in the lives of their adherents. By using a functional definition the court caused the state to avoid the discriminatory and non-neutral effect of providing tax relief for those who promote belief in God while withholding it from those who promote disbelief (*Fellowship*, Cal. Ct. App. 1957: 315 P.2d 394; 405).

In using this functional approach to include non-theistic religion, Judge Peters concluded that all religions share certain common attributes:

> Religion simply includes: (1) a belief, not necessarily referring to supernatural powers; (2) a cult, involving a gregarious association openly expressing the belief; (3) a system of moral practice directly resulting from an adherence to the belief; and (4) an organization within the cult designed to observe the tenets of belief.
>
> The content of the belief is of no moment (*Fellowship*, Cal. Ct. App. 1957: 315 P.2d 394; 406).

This definition identifies religion with "a system of moral practice directly resulting from" a belief *about* but not necessarily *in* "supernatural powers." Thus, the Peters definition is consistent with the idea that religion is an organized set of beliefs about ultimate questions, such as the cause, nature and purpose of life and the idea of Justices Frankfurter and Harlan in *McGowan* that religion profoundly relates life to the world in which it is lived.

Fellowship is important because Judge Peters' functional test for determining whether a belief system is religious was adopted by the US Supreme Court eight years later (*U.S. v. Seeger*, S.Ct. 1965: 380 U.S. 163, 176). In finding that a professed non-theistic belief was religious, the Supreme Court held that a belief is religious if it is "a sincere and meaningful belief which occupies in the life of its possessor a place parallel to that filled by the God of those admittedly qualifying" as religious.

Justice Peters' 1957 holding that Religious Humanism is a religion was embraced one month later by a Federal Circuit Court of Appeals (*Washington Ethical Society*, DC Cir. 1957: 249 F.2d 127), 30 years later by an Alabama Federal District Court (*Smith*, D. Ala 1987: 655 F. Supp. 939) and 46 years later by the Texas Court of Appeals (*Strayhorn*, Tex App. 2003: 110 S.W. 3d 458).

In 1961 the US Supreme Court held that Atheism is a religion under the free exercise clause of the First Amendment, citing Fellowship of Humanity and Washington Ethical society as examples of non-theistic religions (*Torcaso*, S.Ct. 1961: 367 U.S. 488, 495 note 11).

The boundaries of the religious sphere were again tested in the previously mentioned 1961 case of *McGowan v. Maryland* where Sunday closing laws were not deemed to promote theistic over atheistic beliefs as they did not have the effect of profoundly relating the life of man to the world in which he lives.

In 1965 the religious sphere was further expanded by the US Supreme Court in *U.S. v. Seeger* with respect to a sanctity of life law that provides a religious exemption from mandatory military service that might require the taking of another's life. Those who disbelieved in the taking of another's life were entitled to an exemption, but only if their religious belief was based on a belief in a Supreme Being. Mr. Seeger failed to check the "belief in a Supreme Being" box on his application, so the exemption was denied. The court held that religious beliefs were not confined to beliefs in a Supreme Being. Justice Clark, writing for the majority, concluded that religious belief includes belief in a power or faith upon which all else is ultimately dependent:

> Within [the phrase "religious training and belief"] would come all sincere religious beliefs which are based upon a power or being, *or upon a faith*, to which all else is subordinate *or upon which all else is ultimately dependent* (*U.S. v. Seeger*, S.Ct. 1965: 380 U.S. 163, 176; emphasis added).

Thus what one believes about the sanctity of life falls within the religious sphere, while beliefs about appropriate employment regulations do not. The court's view that religion describes a "*faith*, to which all else is subordinate *or upon which all else is ultimately dependent*," is consistent with Clouser's conclusion that all religions are first based on a belief in an unconditional non-dependent reality upon which all else is ultimately dependent.

In 1979 and 1981 Judge Adams of the Third Circuit Court of appeals decided two cases showing that religion is about "ultimate" rather than mundane questions. In *Malnak v. Yogi* (1979: 592 F.2d 197) the Court held that a public school course in a pantheistic "Science of Transcendental Meditation" involved religious subject matter while an ad hoc belief system about diet developed by prisoners was not (*Africa v. Pennsylvania*, 3rd Cir. 1981: *Africa v. Pennsylvania*, 662 F.2d 1025).

In *Africa* Judge Adams summarized the Court's conclusions regarding the scope of the religious sphere in a manner consistent with the views articulated by Judge Peters in Fellowship in 1957. Adams listed three criteria for determining whether a belief system amounted to a religion:

> *First*, a religion addresses *fundamental and ultimate questions* having to do with deep and imponderable matters.
>
> *Second*, a religion is comprehensive in nature; it consists of a belief-system as opposed to an isolated teaching.
>
> *Third*, a religion often can be recognized by the presence of certain formal and external signs (*Africa*, 3rd Cir. 1981: 662 F.2d 1025, 1032–3; emphasis added).

The subject matter of the belief system is listed in the first criteria—"fundamental and ultimate question." Adams further explained "fundamental and ultimate questions" as follows:

> *Fundamental and ultimate questions.* Traditional religions consider and attempt to come to terms with what could best be described as "ultimate" questions-*questions having to do with, among other things, life and death, right and wrong, and good and evil.* Not every tenet of an established theology need focus upon such elemental matters, of course; still, it is difficult to conceive of a religion that does not address these larger concerns. For, above all else, religions are characterized by their adherence to and promotion of certain "*underlying theories of man's nature or his place in the Universe*" (*Africa*, 3rd Cir. 1981: 662 F.2d 1025, 1032–3; emphasis added).

The last sentence again captures the idea of Clouser and the Supreme Court in *U.S. v. Seeger* that all religions take a position on the unconditional non-dependent reality. Based on that position it then seeks to provide answers to other "ultimate questions" or, as Prothero explains, solutions to ultimate problems, about life and death, right and wrong, and good and evil. This is consistent with Judge Peters' definition that religions take a position on unconditional non-dependent reality and then develops "a system of moral practice," "directly resulting from an adherence to [that] belief."

A definition very much like the Random House definition and consistent with the Peters and Adams definitions was adopted by Judge Hand in 1987 in *Smith v. Board* after extensive testimony from a variety of experts. Judge Hand's holding that Religious ("Secular") Humanism is a religion under the Establishment Clause of the First Amendment was based on his conclusion that:

> [all religions] may be classified *by the questions they raise and issues they address*. Some of these matters overlap with non-religious governmental concerns. A religion, however, approaches them on the basis of *certain fundamental assumptions with which governments are unconcerned.* These assumptions may be grouped as *about*:
>
> 1) the existence of supernatural and/or transcendent reality;
>
> 2) the nature of man;
>
> 3) the ultimate end, or goal or purpose of man's existence, both individually and collectively;
>
> 4) the purpose and nature of the universe. (*Smith*, SD Ala 1987: 655 F. Supp. 939, 979; emphasis added)

Notice that each of these "fundamental assumptions" all "profoundly relate the life of man to the world in which he lives." The assumptions provide answers to ultimate questions about the cause, nature and purpose of life. According to Justice Frankfurter this concept describes the nature of religion in the "comprehensive sense in which the Constitution uses that word" (*McGowan v. Maryland*, S.Ct. 1961: 366 U.S. 420, 461).

Consistent with the above, a number of cases have held that Atheism is a First Amendment religion. These include those previously mentioned that have found Religious Humanism to be a religion, as that religion is explicitly atheistic in its denial of a supernatural. Others include *Torcaso v. Watkins* (S.Ct. 1961: 367 U.S. 488), holding that the free exercise rights of an Atheist were abridged by requiring him to take an oath to God, *Lee v. Weisman* (S.Ct. 1992: 505 U.S. 577), holding under the Establishment Clause that a so-called "nonpreferential" or "nonsectarian" prayer to an unnamed God, was in fact preferential and sectarian as it preferred "theistic over *nontheistic religion*;" and *Kaufman v. McCaughtry* (7th Cir. 2005: 419 F.3d 678), holding that prison regulations denying religious status to Atheists violated the Establishment Clause.

The organized and evangelistic nature of Atheism is reflected in a series of advertisements published by the *Freedom from Religion Foundation* and other atheistic organizations during the Christmas season in 2010. Each advertisement promoted a core tenet of the religion. The tenet that there is no supernatural or God was proclaimed by a display stating: "YES VIRGINIA, THERE IS NO GOD"; the tenet that life is not created as it emerges from unguided evolutionary processes was promoted by an ad that urged one to "PRAISE DARWIN: EVOLVE BEYOND BELIEF." The idea that because life reduces to matter, there is no afterlife, was promoted by the slogan: "ENJOY LIFE NOW. THERE IS NO AFTERLIFE," and the idea that we should rely on human reason rather than the wisdom of God, was promoted by ads urging the public to celebrate reason: "YOU KNOW IT'S A MYTH: THIS SEASON CELEBRATE REASON;" and "SLEEP IN ON SUNDAYS: I HAVE FAITH IN PEOPLE, NOT IN A GOD" (*Freedom* 2010).

Other non-theistic belief systems found to be religions include Buddhism and Taoism (*Torcaso*, S.Ct. 1961: 367 U.S. 488, 495 note 11), Scientology (*Founding Church*, DC Cir. 1969: 409 F.2d 1146), Wicca (*Dettmer*, 4th Cir. 1986: 799 F.2d 929), and an atheistic White Supremacist religion based on survival of the fittest and natural selection (*Peterson*, ED Wis 2002: 205 F. Supp. 2d 1014).

In conclusion the cases support the idea that "an establishment of religion" within the meaning of the First Amendment is an organized set of beliefs about ultimate questions. The cases also show that ultimate questions deal with issues like *Where do we come from? What is the nature of life—is it a creation made for a purpose or a purposeless occurrence that has emerged from matter from an unguided evolutionary process? Does life have a soul or spirit which continues after death or does it end on death? Given the answers to these questions, then how should one live life from a moral and ethical standpoint?*

Implementing the State's Commitment to Secularity

The Benefits and Detriments of a Religious Classification in a Secular State

The First Amendment defines two religious rights. One is the right of non-interference. The state may not adopt a policy that would "abridge the free exercise" of one's religious beliefs. This right is a benefit, although it may be somewhat attenuated if it conflicts with a law of general applicability that is deemed religiously neutral (*Emp. Div ... v. Smith*, S.Ct. 1990: 494 U.S. 872, 879).

The other is the right of a citizen to a state that is neutral with respect to religion so that it does not support or endorse a particular religious viewpoint that may compete with yours. This right of non-support and non-endorsement is embodied in the Establishment Clause—the state may not adopt a policy "respecting an establishment of religion." The Courts have construed this provision as requiring the state to be neutral with respect to conflicting religious views.

This right of neutrality can be a detriment rather than a benefit. If one's belief system is classified as "religious," then it may not receive support or endorsement from the state. For example, the state may not lead a prayer to God at a high school graduation ceremony as this would prefer "theistic over non-theistic religion" (*Lee v. Weisman*, S.Ct. 1992: 505 U.S. 577, 617).

The detriment becomes quite severe, if the views which compete with the views religiously classified, are not also classified as religious. This then allows the functionally competing view to be classified as "secular," as it is, by definition, not religious. The state may then endorse that secular view exclusively to the detriment of the adherent of the view given a religious classification. Thus if religion is defined as limited to chocolate cake worship, then public schools may ban all chocolate cake, and serve exclusively white cake. Similarly, if religion is limited to theistic beliefs then the school may ban theistic viewpoints and promote exclusively atheistic views.

The Two Ways a Truly Secular State May Achieve Neutrality

The case of *Epperson v. Arkansas* (S.Ct. 1968: 393 U.S. 97, 109) reflects the two ways a secular state may achieve neutrality. One is to simply tailor its activities so that they never touch the religious sphere. This achieves neutrality by way of exclusion. The other is to include the religious subject for a secular purpose and then treat it objectively so that the inclusion has a religiously neutral effect. For example, suppose a public debate is to be held between theists and atheists. The state may decline to sponsor the event or, if it chooses to do so, it may serve as a neutral moderator, but not as a contestant. It may not take a position as to the validity of the competing views (*U.S. v. Ballard*, S.Ct. 1944: 322 U.S. 78, 87), but it can promote the contest itself.

In *Epperson*, the State of Arkansas had adopted a law banning the teaching of evolution, but not all teachings about the origin of man. The Court said that if the law had banned all teachings about origins, it would have been constitutional. Thus by excluding the religious subject of origins, the curricula would remain secular. The court also explained that the alternative would be to address the religious subject but to do so objectively. Banning one of the competing views would not be objective, but would promote the religious viewpoint not excluded.

The Detrimental Effect of Classifying Religion as Limited to the Theistic

It should become apparent that a narrow definition of religion that divides functionally competing religious views into different classes itself has a profoundly discriminatory rather than a neutral effect. The belief excluded from the religious class that now is deemed "secular" may be supported in all forums touched by a tax dollar while competing theistic views may be systematically excluded.

The classification problem today inheres in institutions of science and education, as they typically use a narrow definition of religion that confines it to beliefs *in* a Supreme Being or God. Other competing beliefs, including atheistic ones, by default become "secular," while actually being functionally religious. This allows public schools and venues to systematically exclude from the classroom discussion or mention of the theistic views. The vacuum is then filled by atheistic and other non-theistic views.

In the US the narrow classification is seldom challenged because many traditional theists continue to use the narrow theistic definition. This may be because, until 1940 most states were functional theocracies that were not required to be neutral. When the Constitution and bill of rights were adopted in 1791 only the Federal government was required to be religiously neutral as most states had established theistic state religions. It was not until 1940 that the constitutional requirement of secularity was imposed on state and local governments and agencies by Supreme Court rulings (*Cantwell*, S.Ct. 1940: 310 U.S. 296: and *McCollum*, S.Ct. 1948: 333 U.S. 203).

Gerrymandering the Definition of Religion to Effect Religious Discrimination

The definition of religion can be manipulated in a variety of ways to effect religious discrimination. One may simply ignore judicial decisions that have defined religion inclusively and implicitly employ a narrow theistic definition. If no one objects, the illegality of the effect becomes moot. Another is to classify non-theistic religious views as something other than religion, such as "science." If the view in question is scientific, then it cannot be religious. A third way, is to admit that certain non-theistic views are religious, but seek to limit that classification to the free exercise clause so that the state may in any event support them under the Establishment Clause.

A subtle method of achieving a religiously discriminatory classification is to use the word "religion" without a modifier. For example The Freedom from Religion Foundation explicitly promotes the religions of Atheism and Religious Humanism as shown in its Christmas advertisements mentioned above. The Foundation does not actually seek freedom from all religions, it seeks only freedom from theistic religion. Since it evangelizes for Atheism, its name should use a modifier before the word religion. It should be named "The Freedom from *Theistic* Religion Foundation." By omitting the modifier the label misleads as to its actual goal and the meaning of religion.

The popular theistic definition of religion is widely used, by theists and non-theists alike. As a consequence, when a judge or government official uses the theistic definition to achieve a non-neutral religious effect, the misclassification is often ignored. This then encourages public officials to systematically exclude theistic ideas while embracing their atheistic competitors.

Even in the face of an inclusive definition of religion, a religiously discriminatory effect may be achieved if the competing view is classified as something other than religion, like "science." Examples of this discriminatory strategy are found in *Malnak, Smith* and *Kitzmiller*.

In *Malnak v. Yogi*, a course in "The Science of Transcendental Meditation" (SC/TM) was being taught in a public school. SC/TM promotes various aspects of a Hindu religion. The Court found evidence in the record that it had been relabeled as "science" so that it could be included in the public school curriculum. The court saw through the label holding that the course promoted a religion in violation of the Establishment Clause (*Malnak*, 3rd Cir. 1979: 592 F.2d 197, 215).

The same labeling tactic was used to remove Religious Humanism from a religious classification. That belief system was specifically proclaimed as a religion in the 1933 Manifesto, with the view of promoting it in public schools, as was Christianity at the time. In 1940 the Supreme Court held that the Fourteenth Amendment made the First Amendment applicable not only to laws adopted by congress but also to laws and policies adopted by state and local governments and agencies, thereby requiring state schools to abandon religious preferences. To avoid having its belief system removed from the schools, Humanists revised their Manifestos to remove the "Religious" modifier to the word "Humanism." They replaced the modifier in their common discourse with the word "Secular." Paul Kurtz, a co-author of *Manifesto II*, explained that the belief system is really "science," not religion. According to Kurtz, Religious Humanists had just made a mistake in the first Manifesto. However, Judge Hand did not find any mistake, as he found that Secular Humanism is religion and not science "because it makes statements on faith-assumptions" about the cause, nature and purpose of life (*Smith*, SD Ala 1987: 655 F. Supp. 939, 982).

A third strategy is to argue that the word "religion" has two different meanings. For purposes of abridgment or interference it has been argued that it is permissible to use a broad definition that includes Atheism. The idea is that government should not adopt laws or policies that might abridge the free exercise of the tenets of Atheism to worship materialistic science and reason rather than the wisdom of God. However, for purposes of the Establishment Clause, non-theists have argued that the word religion should be confined to traditional theistic beliefs. In this way, government may support and endorse Atheism as secular, but not theism. This self-contradictory argument for a dual definition was rejected by Judge Adams in *Malnak*, because it is inherently discriminatory and because the grammatical construction of the religion clauses shows that only one meaning was intended (*Malnak*, 3rd Cir 1979: 592 F.2d 197, 211–13).

Securing Religious Rights in Secular Public Education

As explained above the law of the secular US generally requires that "[W]hen government activities *touch on the religious sphere*, they must be *secular in purpose*, evenhanded in operation, and neutral in primary impact" (*Gillette v. U.S.*, S.Ct. 1971: 401 U.S. 437, 450; emphasis added).

The area of government activity that requires particular vigilance is in the public schools. Parents have the religious right to direct the religious education of their children. However, they are also required to provide their children with a secular education specified by the state. Public schools are the only means available to many parents. Accordingly the Supreme Court views public schools as having a public trust to not interfere with the rights of parents when they gain access to the minds of their children eight hours a day, five days a week, and 270 days out of the year:

> The Court has been particularly vigilant in monitoring compliance with the Establishment Clause in elementary and secondary schools. Families entrust public schools with the education of their children, but condition their trust on the understanding that the classroom will not purposely be used to advance religious views that may conflict with the private beliefs of the student and his or her family. Students in such institutions are impressionable and their attendance is involuntary. (*Edwards*, S.Ct. 1987: 482 U.S. 578, 583–4)

This trust protects not only the rights of parents but also the rights of the captive child. Children have the right to be free from a program that may indoctrinate them to accept a particular religious view (*Mitchell v. Helms*, S.Ct. 2000: 530 U.S. 793, 844).

To execute this trust with an inclusive definition of religion requires the school to first identify school curricula that address religious subjects, such as curricula that tend to answer ultimate questions about where we come from, the nature of a child's life and how it should it be lived. These subjects routinely arise in origins science and courses that deal with human sexuality as is the case with sex education.

Once the religious subject is identified, the state must then ascertain whether there is a secular purpose for teaching it. If so, the state must then decide if the subject is age appropriate. Can a child with a first grade level of knowledge and mental capacity be expected to have the ability to make an informed choice about the issue? If not, then the state actually has no choice, as it may not teach the religious subject unless it does so objectively so that it has a neutral effect. One cannot expect a neutral effect from a mind lacking the requisite mental maturity or capacity. Legally, children are deemed to lack the capacity to consent to a number of acts until they attain a certain age, as is the case with sexual activities, the right to vote, the right to drive a motor vehicle and the right to enter into an enforceable contract. The same logic applies to teachings about highly controversial religious concepts that may interfere with a parent's religious teachings and profoundly affect the way the children decide to vote and to live the rest of their lives.

If the subject is age appropriate, then the requirement of objectivity would necessitate that the body of knowledge about the subject be carefully analyzed to identify the principle competing evidence and views that the child must understand in order to be able to reach an informed decision about the matter. The state must then determine whether the curriculum presents those views objectively so that the state does not effectively endorse one religious view over another. If the curriculum is not objective, then the holding in *Epperson* would necessitate its removal or a revision that would achieve the required neutral effect.

A necessity for the implementation of this law is that all involved in the educational process must themselves employ the inclusive legal definition of religion. If a teacher, school administrator or textbook publisher defines religion as just theistic, then they will view the religious sphere as consisting only of theistic ideas. They may then carefully exclude from the curriculum matter supporting theistic views while presenting only the atheistic viewpoint, thinking it to be "secular." Because they use a non-neutral definition of religion they may unwittingly produce a non-neutral religious effect, thereby violating the religious rights of parents, students and taxpayers.

The educational problem is significant as many within the educational and scientific communities define religion as just theistic. As a consequence curriculum often systematically suppresses theistic views while providing only atheistic friendly ones. An example of the error is reflected in the decision of the court in *Kitzmiller v. Dover Area School District* (MD. Pa 2005: 400 F. Supp. 2d 707). In that case the court defined religion as just theistic. This caused it to classify a policy that would objectively inform students about origins to be religious and therefore illegal. Under an inclusive definition of religion, the policy was actually necessary rather than illegal (Calvert 2009).

The Problem of Methodological Naturalism in Science Education

Securing the religious rights of parents and students becomes difficult in science education about cosmological, chemical and biological evolution. These branches of science address the ultimate of ultimate religious questions—"Where do we come from?" and "What is the nature of life?"

Furthermore, science has not provided definitive answers to the big questions. We do not know the origin of (a) the universe, (b) the genetic codes, (c) the first living cell, (d) the initial messages needed to get life started, (e) the Cambrian explosion, (f) biological convergence, (g) orphan genes, (h) human consciousness, and a variety of other things. These are all mysteries and are likely to remain mysteries and "unanswered" questions due to their singular occurrences billions of years ago and their unobservable historical character.

Two competing hypotheses about origins logically arise from the data (Calvert 2009). One supports theistic religion while the other supports non-theistic religions like Atheism and Religious Humanism.

The theistic friendly hypothesis that certain natural phenomena may be the product of an intelligent cause is based on two key observations. The universe itself appears to be "fine-tuned" or designed for life (Davies 1983: 189; Rees 2001: 146–8; Calvert 2009: 225 note 48). Vary by a smidgen any of a number of key values that inhere in matter, energy and the forces and life would not exist. Statistically, chance is not a plausible explanation, unless our universe is merely one of an infinite number of unobservable but imagined parallel universes. The second observation is that living systems operate on the basis of organized or functional information of the kind found in human designed information processing systems. No one has ever observed or plausibly imagined how an information processing system can self-organize without a mind. The mystery is that life runs on them. Each cell is a sophisticated information storage and processing system (Monod 1971: 95–6; Johnson 2010: vii-viii; Calvert 2009: 226–34).

The atheistic hypothesis is that the "programming" of life just emerges from matter over long periods of time without any guiding intelligence. Life is an occurrence, not a design or a creation. The critical issue for this hypothesis is whether a combination of random mutation, natural selection and other undirected processes can plausibly and adequately explain the exceedingly complex and integrated information processing systems of life within the finite time frames permitted by our universe. Everyone agrees that living systems look designed. Even Richard Dawkins acknowledges that "biology is the study of complicated things that give the appearance of having been designed for a purpose" (Dawkins 1996: 1). The question then becomes whether that appearance of design is an illusion. In fact, science has yet to show the apparent design is an illusion.

If students were carefully shown the evidence and arguments on both sides of this issue, then the effect could be religiously neutral. However, that objective method is currently precluded by a "Rule" that is employed by institutions of science which does not permit an objective explanation about the origin of life and its diversity. The "Rule" is called "methodological naturalism," or "scientific materialism." That Rule requires scientists to explain the cause of events with only unintelligent "material" or "natural" causes. Thus, the Rule permits only a functionally atheistic answer to these unanswered ultimate questions which happen to be the core questions of all religions.

When the Rule is employed regarding the origin of life and its diversity, life is necessarily explained as not being created and as arising from a mix of unguided random processes and natural sorting called natural "selection." Mention of the design hypothesis or criticisms of the natural cause explanations are forbidden by the Rule. This was the effect of the Court's ruling in *Kitzmiller v. Dover Area School District* (MD. Pa. 2005). This case and methodological naturalism are discussed extensively in *Kitzmiller's Error* (Calvert 2009).

Use of the Rule has the effect of a religious dogma in the context of an inclusive definition of religion. However, when a theistic definition is employed, the atheistic dogma achieves a secular classification as a "rule of science." Using this definition of religion, the design hypothesis and its critiques of natural/material cause explanations are classified as religion while the atheistic explanation is classified as science. This false dichotomy often causes schools to promote non-theistic religions over theistic religions.

An application of the First Amendment to science education should eliminate the use of the Rule to suppress curricula that informs students of the competing evidence and ideas. It should also require the educator to explain that the Rule has been and is being used and that most modern explanations of origins depend on it. Students should then be shown the evidence suppressed by the Rule and how that suppression affects the plausibility of the atheistic explanations provided. *The Rule* is a one-act play describing how the process might work (Schwabauer 2002).

A truly secular state will also delay the teaching of origins until students have attained the age, mental maturity and appropriate level of scientific knowledge about geology, chemistry, physics and information theory to be able to understand and make their own independent judgments about what to believe. Thus, it would not seem appropriate to begin the teaching of origins science in Kindergarten, as has been recently proposed by the National Academy of Sciences in a *Framework for K-12 Science Education* (*Framework* 2011).

Conclusion

In seeking to know the scope of human rights in an abstract sense, the noted Jurist Felix S. Cohen asked this question:

> What rights, if any, can a man claim of me not because he is my brother or my neighbor or my colleague or co-religionist or fellow-citizen, but just because he's human? (Cohen 1953: 617–22)

The question is profound for it argues that our human rights turn on what it means to be human. But to answer that question, one must ask and answer the three religious questions we have been discussing in this chapter—*What is the cause, nature and purpose of life?* Once we have answered those questions we will have developed a concept of what it means to be human, and in the process we will have described a religious belief system. Thus, our human rights ultimately depend on the religious bias of the state which grants them by law and then seeks to secure them.

A secular state like the US has made a commitment to be neutral with respect to the competing religious views of its pluralistic culture. To execute this commitment in a manner that is functionally neutral, it must define religion so that it includes functionally competing belief systems. The US Courts and recognized non-judicial authorities show that functionally competitive religious beliefs include not only Catholic and Protestant, but also atheistic and pantheistic. Unfortunately, many involved in securing the human and religious rights of US citizens often employ a narrow theistic definition of religion. This has caused the state to endorse competing non-theistic religious views as secular when they are in fact religious. In the context of public schools, this can effectively deprive parents, children and taxpayers of their right to a religiously neutral public education.

To secure those human and religious rights public schools should carefully develop curricula that address religious issues to ensure that they are objective and age appropriate so that their presentation will have a religiously neutral effect. Particular care is needed in origins science education as it addresses the ultimate of religious questions about the cause and nature of life while often using a rule that permits only functionally atheistic explanations.

Bibliography

Africa v. Pennsylvania [1981] 3rd Cir. 662 F.2d 1025.

Clouser, R. 2005. *The Myth of Religious Neutrality: An Essay on the Hidden Role of Religious Belief in Theories*. Notre Dame, IN: Notre Dame Press.

Calvert, J. 2009. *Kitzmiller's Error: Using an Exclusive rather than Inclusive Definition of Religion. Liberty University Law Review*, 3(2), 213–328. Available at: http://www.intelligentdesignnetwork.org/Kitzmiller%27s_Error.pdf [accessed: September 22, 2012].

Cantwell v. Connecticut [1940] 310 U.S. 296.

Church of Scientology v.CIR [1987] 9th Cir. 823 F2d 1310.

Cohen, F. 1953. Human Rights: An Appeal to Philosophers. *The Review of Metaphysics*, 6(4), 617–22.

Dawkins, R. 1996. *The Blind Watchmaker: Why The Evidence of Evolution Reveals A Universe Without Design*. New York: W.W. Norton.

Davies, P. 1983. *God and the New Physics*. New York: Simon and Schuster.

Davis v. Beason [1890] 133 U.S. 333.

Dettmer v. Landon [1986] 4th Cir. 799 F.2d 929.

Edwards v. Aguillard [1987] 482 U.S. 578.

Emp. Div., Ore. Dept. of Human Res. v. Smith [1990] 494 U.S. 872.

Epperson v. Arkansas [1968] 393 U.S. 97.

Fellowship of Humanity v. County of Alameda [1957] Cal. Ct. App. 315 P.2d 394.

Founding Church of Scientology v. U.S. [1969] DC Cir. 409 F.2d 1146.

Framework for K-12 Science Education. 2011. National Academy of Sciences.

Freedom from Religion Foundation advertisements. Available at: http://www.intelligentdesignnetwork.org/Tenets_of_Atheism.jpgg [accessed: September 22, 2012].

Gillette v. U.S. [1971] 401 U.S. 437.

Humanist Manifesto I. 1933. Available at: http://www.americanhumanist.org/Humanism/Humanist_Manifesto_I [accessed: September 22, 2012].

Humanist Manifesto II. 1973. Available at: http://www.americanhumanist.org/Humanism/Humanist_Manifesto_II [accessed: September 22, 2012].

Humanist Manifesto III. 2003. Available at: http://www.americanhumanist.org/humanism/Humanist_Manifesto_III [accessed: September 22, 2012].

Johnson, D. 2010. *Programming of Life*. Kingston, TN: Big Mac Publishers.

Kaufman v. McCaughtry [2005] 7th Cir. 419 F.3d 678.

Kitzmiller v. Dover Area School Dist. [2005] MD. Pa. 400 F. Supp. 2d 707.

Lee v. Weisman [1992] 505 U.S. 577.

Lemon v. Kurtzman [1971] 403 U.S. 602.

Malnak v. Yogi [1979] 3d Cir. 592 F.2d 197.

McCollum v. Bd. of Educ. [1948] 333 U.S. 203.

McGowan v. Maryland [1961] 366 U.S. 420.

Monod, J. 1971. *Chance and Necessity*. Translated by A. Wainhouse. New York: Vintage Books.

Potter, C. 1930. *Humanism: A New Religion*. New York: Simon & Schuster.

Mitchell v. Helms [2000] 530 U.S. 793.

Peterson v. Wilmur Communications, Inc. [2002] E.D. Wisc. 205 F. Supp. 2d 1014.

Prothero, S. 2010. *God is not One: The Eight Rival Religions that Run the World and Why Their Differences Matter*. New York: HarperOne.

Random House Webster's College Dictionary. 2005.

Rees, M. 2000. *Just Six Numbers: The Deep Forces that Shape the Universe*. New York: Basic Books.

Schwabauer, D. and Calvert, J. 2002. *The Rule*. Intelligent Design Network. Available at: http://intelligentdesignnetwork.org/TheRule.PDF [accessed: September 22, 2012].

Smith v. Bd. of Sch. Comm'rs of Mobile County [1987] S.D. Ala. 655 F. Supp. 939, *rev'd on other grounds* [1987] 11th Cir. 827 F.2d 684.

Strayhorn v. Ethical Society of Austin [2003] Tex. App. - Austin 110 S.W. 3d 458.

Torcaso v. Watkins [1961] 367 U.S. 488.

U.S. v. Seeger [1965] 380 U.S. 163.

United States v. Ballard [1944] 322 U.S. 78, 87.

Warren, R. 2002. *The Purpose Driven Life: What on Earth Am I Here for?* Grand Rapids, MI: Zondervan.

Washington Ethical Soc'y v. District of Columbia [1957] D.C. Cir. 249 F.2d 127

Webster's Third New International Dictionary of the English Language. 2003.

West Virginia Bd. of Educ. v. Barnette [1943] 319 U.S. 624.

Wiker, B. 2002. *Moral Darwinism: How We Became Hedonists*. Downers Grove, IL: InterVarsity Press.

Chapter 6

Balancing Secularism with Religious Freedom: In *Lautsi v. Italy*, the European Court of Human Rights Evolved

Vito Breda

Until recently, the principles of secularism, religious pluralism and state neutrality have been perceived in the jurisprudence of the European Court of Human Rights (ECtHR) as partially overlapping concepts. However, in *Lautsi and others v. Italy*, the Grand Chamber of the ECtHR has—in a landmark decision—qualified the interplay between these ideas. This chapter will argue that *Lautsi v. Italy* signals a turning point in the previous ECtHR jurisprudence, which often associated secularism with the protection of pluralism and democracy.

There are two main consequences of the decision. Firstly, the ECtHR recognized that a state's neutrality cannot be deductively constructed as a logical manifestation of secularism. In this context secularism means "a secular view of a lay public sphere as the only solution to ensuring genuine equality between members of majority and minority churches, agnostics, atheists or non-theists and eliminating religious and anti-religious tensions" (McGoldrick 2011: 454). For instance, in *Sahin v. Turkey*, the Grand Chamber explicitly embraced the narrative of the Turkish Constitutional Court that allied secularism with a defense of pluralism.

Secondly, in *Lautsi v. Italy*, the ECtHR recognized the epistemic implications of pluralism. Pluralism as a legal concept demands the recognition of diversity and the acceptance of a dialogue that transforms a multitude of legal orders (and a plurality of perceptions of the good life represented by such a multitude), in procedures aimed at accommodating concurring individual rights. Concurring rights are granted to all (for example the right given to parents to choose the type of education for their children) but they might generate competing claims over public resources. The multiplicity of calls for recognition of individual rights makes it inappropriate and impractical for a state to favor one group over the other, leading instead to an open-ended dialogue in which institutions are, by default, receptive of all demands. McGoldrick calls this pluralist approach to faith based demands: "positively secular" (2011: 455)

I argue that the recognition of pluralism and the democratic practices that qualify that pluralism should be a point of departure for the jurisprudence of the ECtHR in areas such as the display of religious symbols in classrooms. This approach serves as an alternative to the practice of balancing rights, which greatly restricts the breadth of religious freedom and *de jure* imposes a monist conception of rational thinking.

The chapter will be divided into three sections. The first part will discuss how the antagonistic relationship between theism and secularism in Italy has shaped the issues of religious symbols in the schoolroom. I will argue that concurring views of the significance of symbols have historically been part of Italy's cultural heritage and that there are strong indications that such a democratic dialogue will continue without a definitive solution being reached.

In the second section, I will explain the benefits of accepting pluralism as a criterion for assessing the extent of religious freedom in signatory states. A short third section will suggest a procedure that democratically accommodates concurrent rights.

Introduction

The case of *Lautsi v. Italy* reinvigorated a debate over the role of religious symbols in public schools in a way that is unprecedented in the modern history of Europe. In 2002, Mrs Lautsi complained about the Italian school policy of hanging crucifixes in her children's school classes. She probably would not have expected that, by the time her complaint against the school governors of a school in Abano Terme reached the Grand Chamber of the ECtHR, her legal team would have had to plead against Italy and another 21 signatory states. At the time of her initial complaint, Mrs Lautsi's children were in a middle school (normally attended by children from 11 to 13 years old). The school was located in the small town of Abano Terme, on the outskirts of Padua and in the middle of the Venetian region.

Following a secret ballot, the Council of School Governors (composed of an equal number of teachers and parents) refused Mrs Lautsi's request. The council's deliberation was, subsequently, challenged by Mrs Lautsi at the first-instance administrative tribunal in Venice (Tribunale Aministrativo del Veneto). Italy, as is the case in many other European states, has a system of special jurisdictions that deal respectively with civil, administrative and labor law litigation with different final appellate courts (Walker 2010). However, questions concerning constitutional compatibility may be raised to the Italian Constitutions Court at any stage of the judicial process. Mrs Lautsi's counselors did indeed question the constitutional admissibility of the crucifixes in her children's school classes.

More specifically, Lautsi's legal team asked the Italian Constitutional Court, via the incidental procedure, whether the two articles of two Royal Decrees (RDs) from the 1920s (Art 118 RD 965 of April 30, 1924, and Art 119 of RD 1297 of April 26, 1928), that by default imposed the display of crucifixes in school classes, were compatible with the secular principles adopted by the 1948 Italian Constitution (Panara 2011, Ronchi 2011). It was unfortunate that such a request was dismissed by the Italian Constitutional Court because both decrees were considered as secondary legislation (Order 389 2004). The Italian Constitutional Court could decide only on the constitutional compatibility of primary legislation and the two Royal Decrees were secondary legislation.

Following the refusal by the Constitutional Court to evaluate the legitimacy of the two RDs via the incidental procedure, Lautsi's case reached the final appeal jurisdiction in administrative law matters (Consiglio di Stato). In 2006, the Consiglio di Stato also rejected Mrs Lautsi's complaint but, in that instance, the court discussed the significance of the crucifix within the school room (Order 556 2006). Ronchi provides a detailed analysis of the argumentation delivered by the Italian administrative courts (2011). For a statutory analysis of the constitutional case, see Panara (2011: 141). Having exhausted all internal remedies, Mrs Lautsi's team brought her application to the ECtHR.

In 2009, the first instance of the second section of the ECtHR court ruled in favor of Lautsi (Weiler 2010). One of the arguments provided by the court was that having a crucifix hung in a classroom could be perceived by pupils as an attempt to direct their learning towards a particular faith (2009: 55). However, in the appeal stage in the Grand Chamber, the ECtHR accepted the Italian submission.

In Lautsi, the Grand Chamber of the ECtHR agreed (by a large majority) that the Italian state did not breach Art 2 of the First Protocol European Convention on Human Rights (ECHR) by imposing a duty on schools to display a crucifix on the classroom wall. Art 2 (in the First Protocol) safeguards the right of parents to have their children educated in accordance with their philosophical and religious beliefs. The court explicitly said on page 26 of the official ECtHR typescript that Art 2 of the First Protocol has to be read in relation to the second comma of Art 9 ECHR (2011: 60), which gives a certain level of discretion to signatory states in setting the limits of freedom of thought, conscience and religion.

The ECtHR argued that whilst a signatory state cannot set educational policies that indoctrinate pupils, Italy had a 'margin of appreciation' in setting policies such as the one that allows the hanging of religious symbols in school classes. The range of analyses that followed the Crucifix Case engaged the plurality of theoretical, legal and pragmatic aspects raised by the decision. The verdict also divided the already polarized debate. Zucca, for instance, who welcomed the first-instance decision (of the ECtHR that ruled in favor of Mrs Lautsi) was not persuaded by the reasoning provided by the Grand Chamber that favored Italy (2011).

It is outside the remit of this chapter to provide a comprehensive summary of the reactions that followed *Lautsi v. Italy*. My aim is, instead, to show the enrichment brought by the Lautsi decision to the debate over religious pluralism. In particular, I would argue that by recognizing a member state's discretion in setting a policy that accommodates concurring rights, the ECtHR accepted the pragmatic limits of imposing secularism as the default neutral stance of a modern pluralistic society. Before I articulate my argument, a series of methodological and contextual analyses are necessary as a preliminary aid to the discussion.

First, in this chapter I will use the term "belief-based political claims" to describe both theist and secular reasons for supporting an argument for or against the display of religious symbols in public institutions. Even if, in a debate over the historical development of human rights doctrine, a distinction can be made between assertions based on religious and secular narratives, in modern pluralistic societies, both groups of demands have to be considered as representative of a distinctive democratic political stance. In particular, it is a diminution of the democratic dimension of the debate over religious symbols to assume that secularism is not a belief-based set of assumptions (which might not be able to be rationally verified). In other words, secularism is no more able than theism to establish that all of its assumptions are self-evident and therefore neutral (Clouser 2005: 9).

The logic of such an approach would automatically impose secularism as a default position for any political system (and for the ECtHR), instead of giving a polity the possibility of being able to retrieve the pragmatic accommodation of claims made by two different political stances. I will also use the term "belief-based symbols" as inclusive of both the argument for the hanging of the crucifix and for the empty wall argument. Clouser explains, I think in a very persuasive narrative, the close relation between the epistemic structure of non-secular and secular beliefs (2005: 35–41)

Second, the Lautsi case discusses a signatory state's prerogative to accommodate in practice the concurring rights given to parents in Art 2 of the ECHR to decide on the religious education of their children. The debate over religious symbols in public space is inclusive of two typologies of debates (Mancini 2009). The first debate concerns whether the signatory state has the prerogative to display belief-based symbols in classrooms. A second typology of debates engages the dilemma as to whether a signatory state can impose a policy that prevents pupils, teachers and students from wearing garments that display a religious affiliation.

As an example of the latter typology, in *Sahin v. Turkey*, a Turkish medical student wearing an Islamic headscarf was refused entry to one of her exams by the exam invigilators. In the case that followed, the ECtHR accepted the Turkish state submission that justified the ban of headscarves on the basis, among other arguments, of reasoned protection of public order (2005). In the same category as Sahin, we might include decisions over the wearing of the veil in French schools (1995) and cases over school uniforms in England and Wales. These cases are the end points of a multifaceted debate over the limits of the rights allocated to *individuals* by the ECHR (Art 9) to manifest religious beliefs by wearing a garment with religious significance in a public space.

However, the case of Lautsi fits squarely into the first group of debates (Mancini 2009). In Lautsi, the ECtHR was asked whether a state policy that accommodates concurring rights (that is, the right of parents to choose a type of education fitting their beliefs) was set in a way that imposes religious indoctrination. Both dilemmas (the one raised in Sahin and the one in Lautsi) might engage Art 9 of the ECHR and the obligation of the state to be neutral, but the answer relating to their accommodation can be distinguished from the state's stance in terms of neutrality. The first dilemma focuses on an assessment of whether a right granted to individuals by the ECHR has been infringed by a state policy; the second concerns whether a member state's procedure is adequate for individuals to accommodate their concurring stances based on the same right.

Aggressive Secularism in Catholic Italy: Not as Odd as You Might Think

Italy, along with many other European countries, is experiencing the effect of what McGoldrick calls aggressive secularism. There is a plethora of reasons for the expansion of secularization. Some are well articulated in debates such as the one between Ratzinger and Habermas, which explores the philosophical genesis of the debate (2005). Other analyses focus, instead, on the specific issues generated by the expansion of secular visions generated in European societies (McGoldrick 2011).

Perhaps one of the persuasive explanations of the increasing polarization of views relating to the role of theist and secular stances occurs in Bauman's analysis. Bauman argues, for instance, that one of the side effects of a globalized society is the anxiety of belonging to an identity group. The identity group gives shelter from the instability of a fast-flowing society, but it demands, in exchange, a periodic re-assertion of commitment by its members. The display of belligerence against aliens, or even better, against a rival group, is one of the ways in which individuals reassert their commitment to the community (Bauman 1999). However, the same level of animosity may also be found in the theist/secular debate and in the literature that seeks to explain it. In this section, I will argue that such a method of analysis is sterile and a manifestation of the antagonism it seeks to explain. In particular, I would like to argue that a richer understanding of Lautsi's case can be obtained by considering an acknowledgement of pluralism and of the democratic limits of the jurisdictional accommodation of concurring belief-based claims.

Bauman's globalized society is a leviathan of polarized communities, which struggle for the recognition of their creeds and/or to retrieve resources. Parliaments and final appellate jurisdictions in Europe try to cope with the whirlpool of claims to the best of their abilities, worried that they too might be perceived as aliens and be the object of criticism by the losing faction (Benhabib 1996, Breda 2007). At first sight, Mrs Lautsi's claims also appear to be a manifestation of a belligerent member of a minority group of atheists seeking an unreasonable recognition in a deeply Catholic state. The description is misleading.

The media and the great majority of polarized commentaries engaging the ECtHR decision dwelled on that set of assumptions. For instance, articles quickly referred to the fact that Mrs Lautsi held a Finnish passport and lived in a strongly Catholic region (Lamb 2011: 754, McGoldrick 2011: 464, Panara 2011: 143). The first assertion is irrelevant. The prerogative to challenge administrative acts by school governors is given to all parents, including those who might be considered immigrants without resident permits, and thus reporting in legal commentaries the fact that Mrs Lautsi was Finnish (with double citizenship) appears, at the very least, odd. Indeed, this would appear to be "normal" procedure to discredit the claims of the "out" group and reaffirm the "in" group. For an analysis of the effect of portraying aliens in Italy, see Calvanese (2011).

The second observation—the reference to Catholic Italy—is misleading. Here, a distinction has to be made between articles that give blatant misdirection to their readers, and analyses taken from erroneous assumptions.

Lamb, for instance, considers Italy to be the successor of the Holy Roman Empire. "It [the ECtHR] decided that the Italian Republic, home of the Vatican and heir to the Holy Empire, was violating the human rights of its citizens by displaying crucifixes in its state schools" (at 752). The Italian Peninsula is where the Vatican (a sovereign, international recognized state) is located, yet that space is shared with the Republic of San Marino and the Italian Republic. Just as the United States of America is not the home of Canada, none of the three states located in the Italian Peninsula is the home of any of the others. Furthermore, the Holy Roman Empire, which is normally associated with the Central European Carolingian Empire, has never included Rome, the Vatican State or the Venetian region, in which the case of Lautsi originated.

The analysis in Lamb's article might be described either as an unwitting display of a lack of research or as a quixotic attempt to inflate his argument for rhetorical effect. However, these types of narrative, which seek to isolate Mrs Lautsi's claim as an unreasonable demand can be found in most of the literature. For instance, McGoldrick uses this wording to describe the case: "Mrs Lautsi is an Italian national who lives in Abano Terme, in the strongly Catholic region of Veneto in Northern Italy" (at 464).

Again, the assertion is unfounded. Venetians—I use the term Venetians to define the residents of Veneto—might be baptized Catholics in 86 percent of cases, but that is not translated into an acceptance of an overlapping role between the state and Church (Istituto di studi politici economici e sociali 2010). Veneto has historically been a pluralist society with one of the largest communities of Jews and of Greek Orthodox Christians in Europe. This point is delicate, so I need to be precise. Jews were discriminated against by the Venetian laws. In medieval Venice, Jews were confined in a heavily polluted area called the "ghetto." The term ghetto has since become synonymous with discriminated communities. However, the point under discussion here is that Veneto cannot be described as strongly Catholic in the sense given by McGoldrick.

Politically, in Albano Terme and in the Venetian Regions, there is a strong representation of leftist political parties (including the Italian Communist Party). In Abano, for instance, depending on the political cycle, the control of the city council alternated between left and conservative coalitions, which were supported by Catholic-inspired political parties such as the Unione dei Democratici Cristiani. However, in the past decade, the political presence of Catholic-inspired parties in Abano Terme and within the Venetian region has been consistently under 15 percent of the voters. Even if considering the politically active Catholics as all being in favor of crucifixes (that is, the entire 15 percent) in schoolrooms, it is a matter of speculation as to whether the remaining 71 percent would think about the issues concerned. It is certain that at least a quarter of all Catholics in the region voted consistently for a coalition that included leftist parties with strong anticlerical views (Direzione Sistema Statistico Regionale 2011).

So much for McGoldrick's perception of a strongly Catholic Venetian region. However, this is a trivial point. The argument here concerns the attempt to polarize the discussion, masking the true role of the debate as a manifestation of pluralism (Mazie 2004). More specifically, I argue that the attempt to mislead people on the significance of the debate (by somehow trivializing it) overlooked the Italian state's serious attempt to find a pragmatic accommodation of the debate over belief-based symbols in classrooms.

It is reasonable to assume that the decision to 'hang the crucifix' in the classroom was not intended as an imposition by a religious majority. A historical analysis might act to clarify this point. The contentious seed that germinated in the Lautsi case was planted on the morning of Friday September 15, 1860. The King of Piedmont, Victor Emmanuel II, signed RD 4336, which, in Art 140, imposed the obligation for all the kingdom's elementary schools to have a crucifix hung to one of their classroom walls. The motivation for RD 4336 and the edict that followed (for example Art 118 RD 965 of April 30, 1924) has been interpreted by the ECtHR, and by the rich literature that followed the controversial decision, as an obvious affirmation of a more general role of the entanglement between Catholicism and Italian institutions.

The representations made by the legal team representing the Italian state did little to clarify the position of the Italian government. The arguments made in the first instance by the Italian legal team suggested a relationship between Italian national identity and the crucifix. What has been left out was that the King who signed RD 4336 was at war with the Papal state and he was about to be excommunicated.

Let me dwell on the contextual aspects of this point with a narrated reconstruction based on historical events taken from Montanelli's analysis (2011) that I hope will bring some light to the contextual reasons that motivated the three decrees. The narrative will explain that in the debate over religious symbols in classrooms, Italy recognized a democratic accommodation of concurring religious beliefs that has been the result of a dialogue (often acrimonious) between leftist anticlerical positions and Catholics. Lautsi is, with some margin of equivocation that is implicit in any sociological narrative, a continuation of that debate between the holder of concurring rights (for example parents and teachers), which cannot be expected to be curtailed by a court.

On the morning of September 15, the King of Piedmont was in his office. Victor Emanuel II (the soon-to-be King of Italy) sat in front of his desk. His closest adviser, Camillo Benso, the Count of Cavour (the soon-to-be first Italian First Minister) stood next to the King's desk. He thought: "If the Kingdom has to be saved, a series of shift actions have to be taken. The most urgent of all these actions is to prevent Garibaldi's army from taking Rome and the Holy Seat."

The report deposited on the King's table said that eight days before (on September 7), Naples had surrendered. Garibaldi's men, an irregular militia of 25,000 men, had defeated the main army of the Kingdom of Naples (roughly 50,000 men). What was left of the Neapolitan troops was encircled and about to surrender. The intelligence memo came from Piedmont agents (planted in Garibaldi's army by the Count of Cavour). The report continued: "… Garibaldi's troops are training on newly captured rifled barrel cannons … and prepare for an assault on fortified walls of (presumably) Rome." Camillo, who read the report earlier, and Victor Emanuel II, knew that an attack on Rome would drag France—perhaps Austria—into a move in defense of the Pope. Foreign troops would descend on the Kingdom of Piedmont, ending its history and perhaps the life of its King.

Early that summer, Victor Emanuel II sponsored (with weapons and logistic support) Garibaldi's quixotic plan to foster a pro-Piedmont revolt in Sicily. The King did not expect that such a small group of individuals could put an end to his kingdom, and possibly to his life. The Count of Cavour was far more cautious. He opposed the initiative wholeheartedly. He thought that Garibaldi was a maverick and that the plan was very risky with few rewards.

The sponsoring of a civil revolt in Sicily was in violation of a secret agreement between the Kingdom of Piedmont and Napoleon III (the King of France). The agreement granted, in exchange for the Region of Milan given to Piedmont the year before, an area of French political influence in the center and south of Italy. Sponsoring an insurrection in the south was a blunt breach of the agreement. Even worse was that Garibaldi could be "too successful." His army could, for instance, conquer Sicily, try to move north to Naples and finally to Rome. All this could make the Kingdom of Piedmont the official enemy of the Catholic Church and France.

This last forecast turned out to be correct. Garibaldi was preparing to take Rome—the last item on his list of objectives. The Papal army was numerically "a match" for Garibaldi's, but in practice, Garibaldi's forces were veterans who were about to meet a band of inexperienced volunteers. Both the King and the First Minister knew that the Papal armies could not stop Garibaldi, and so Piedmont's troops should be placed between Rome and Naples.

By September 15, the preparations for an expeditionary force were already underway. The Papal state divided the Italian Peninsula in two parts. If Piedmont's armies wanted to stop Garibaldi and a French invasion, they would have to march across the Papal state. Thus, two weeks before that meeting, the King ordered two Piedmont armies to start marching to meet Garibaldi's militia. Officially, sending "uninvited" armies across a sovereign state's borders was an act of war, yet the ambassadors to Paris and London were instructed to explain that the troops' main objective was to protect the Pope and his secular power over central Italy (and was not to engage in a military campaign against the Holy Father or the Catholic Church).

In practice, again, a series of memos from Piedmont's military intelligence scattered on the King's desk drew a different picture. Rome was preparing to engage Piedmont's armies in the field. Strengthened by a flow of volunteers from many Catholic countries, Pius IX was planning to attempt to engage Piedmont's expeditionary forces. The Pope did not need to defeat Piedmont; his objective was to escalate the conflict into a religious war that would have drawn France to his side.

A paradoxical situation unfolded. If the Kingdom of Piedmont wanted to prevent Garibaldi from entering Rome (and capturing the Holy Seat), Piedmont would have to go to war against the Papal armies. On Friday September 15, neither Victor Emmanuel II nor the Count of Cavour knew that, but the following Tuesday (September 18, 1860), Piedmont's army would do exactly that. Piedmont "disabled" the Papal army at the Battle of Casterfidardo. The victory would also bring an excommunication on Victor Emmanuel II. By the 1870s and the end of the Italian unification, with the Savoy troops taking Rome, all members of the Savoy Royal Family would be excommunicated (Montanelli 2011).

On that morning, Victor Emanuel II had had enough. He called one of his footmen and told him to prepare for his trip to Naples. He was about to leave the desk when Camillo Benso took a series of Parliament-stamped papers out of a folder. The two men's eyes met for the first time that morning. The King, famously short tempered, was about to explode. The Count perceived the hesitation and turned the pages of RD 4336 till his finger pointed at Art 140 and he said: "Mon Roi, nous ne conduisons pas une guerre contre Dieu … cette foi."[1]

The statutory provisions of RD 4336 were, by way of comparison to previous policies, idiosyncratic, and might have provided little relief to the Kingdom of Piedmont. In the decade that preceded RD 4336, the Piedmont Parliament sought to eliminate the system of medieval privileges granted to the Catholic Church. In particular, statute 978 of April 29,1855, also known as the Anticlerical Laws, promoted by Camillo Benso, disbanded all Catholic religious orders in Piedmont and commanded the expropriation of all their assets that were not beneficial to the state (for example schools and hospitals). In 1873, and despite the small concession of having crosses hung in the schoolrooms, the policy of the expropriation of Catholic orders was extended to all the territories of the newly formed Italian state—including Rome—and those who tried to oppose the measures were arrested. High prelates, including bishops, who preached against the King and his First Minister, were put in prison all over Italy (Montanelli 2011).

The reconstruction of the meeting is partly fictitious. However, the historical events that surrounded it are, within the margin of error of any historical analysis, accurate (Montanelli 2011). The point that I would like to make is that the statutory measures (*ex* RD 4336) that set the seed for the Lautsi case were firstly, hastily drafted by an individual (Camillo Benso), with distinctive anticlerical views, and secondly, adopted by a worried King in a period of war.

---

1 [My Sire, we are not at war against God … this time.]

In addition, and at pragmatic level, the decree made a very small concession to Italian Catholics. Firstly, the Kingdom of Piedmont could not afford to build new schools and would have had to depend on existing facilities. Two decades of war (including a costly expedition in the Crimea as an ally of France and Britain) sent the small state to the edge of bankruptcy. In most urban areas and de facto in all rural provinces, Sunday school classes "doubled up" as elementary schools. It is highly unlikely that the local priests (or those newly graduated from Catholic institutions) would have taken the time, each Monday, to take down the crucifix from the school wall and put it back up on Friday. Secondly, the great majority of elementary schools in the territories annexed after the 1859 Franco-Austrian War (for example Tuscany and the Milan Region) were managed by Jesuits and/or other religious orders. Thirdly, religious orders were also the governors of high schools and universities (spared by the 1855 Anticlerical Laws) that, at that time, trained the large bulk of the elementary and high school teachers. Given the admission process adopted by these educational institutions, it is logical to assume that most individuals were Catholics.

In short, RD 4336 gave to foreign powers (for example France) the impression of a tolerant Christian constitutional monarchy, but it de facto registered the existence of the crucifix on primary school walls (rather than imposing it). The historical situation surrounding RD 4336 also provides the necessary context to understand the Fascist decrees of the 1920s (RD 965 of April 30, 1924, and RD 1297 of April 26, 1928) directly reviewed in the Lautsi case. Fifty years after the unification of Italy, the pragmatic aspects that muddled the role of primary and Sunday schools were reduced. The anticlerical left, supported by Camillo Benso half a century before, had a significant impact on promoting a state-sponsored alphabetization program that included, among other things, a new school-building program and the exclusion of religious teaching from the ministerial curriculum (Primary Education Guidance in RD 5724, September 25, 1888). A policy of separation between state and Church was also extended to the enforcement of common morality. Civil marriage was introduced in 1855, and in 1889, the Italian Parliament decriminalized homosexuality.

Given the historical trajectory taken by the young Italian state, RD 965 of April 30, 1924, and the later decree RD 1297 of April 26, 1928, which extended the crucifix on the walls of middle and high schools, appear incongruous.

However, the insertion of RD 965 might be explained by the attempt of a newly installed Fascist Party as a governing party in the Italian Parliament to reduce the political strength of its opposition by forging an alliance with Catholic-inspired parties (Montanelli and Cervi 1981). The opposition of the "soon-to-be" dictatorship included the anticlerical left, which, in the early years of the kingdom, promoted an open anticlericalism. In 1924, the perceived necessity of a larger political support for the Fascist regime among Catholics motivated Benito Mussolini and Giovanni Gentile (the Minister of Education) to have the King sign a decree that extended the practice of hanging the crucifix in middle and high schools.

It is significant that until 1924, Mussolini had been an active exponent of the anticlerical movement (by writing, for instance, several pamphlets and editorials for the official socialist newspaper) and had worked, albeit quite briefly, as a primary school teacher. It is reasonable to speculate that both Mussolini and Gentile might have been witnessing some of the effects of the new secular school policies in forming the anticlerical teachers. Gentile noted, for instance, that taking the crucifix down from school walls had become common practice (Panara 2011: 140). Again, the reason for the change of heart by Mussolini is a matter of speculation, but there is enough historical evidence to suggest that he was willing to reduce the process of state-sponsored aggressive secular indoctrination in exchange for support for his antidemocratic policies.

To support the speculation that Mussolini's "change of heart" was motivated by pragmatism, there is an articulated literature and also the fact that the U-turn was hidden from the view of the Italian Parliament (Montanelli and Cervi 1981). Indeed, Art 118 of the 1924 RD 965 (as well as Art 119 of RD 1297 of April 26, 1928), which imposed the display of the crucifix in middle and high school classes, was an administrative order (without parliamentary scrutiny) aimed at "reiterating" the statutory measures of the RD 4336 (1860).

After the collapse of the Fascist regime, the debate over the hanging of the crucifix continued in Italian institutions. For instance, in 1950, religious symbols were excluded from the places that were used for elections. It is noteworthy that ballot boxes were often located in schools, and that that created situations in which crucifixes were taken down and not rehung. There are also indications that the measure was not complied with by those to whom it was directed. For instance, it would appear to be impractical to expect that a hospital managed by a Catholic order would take the crucifixes down from its walls if its bedbound patients expressed their intention to vote. For a narrated insight into the election practices in Italy within a hospital managed by a religious order, please read Calvino's *The Watcher* (1975).

The example of a Jesuit hospital might be extreme, but the contentions I make here are that firstly, in Italy, there is a robust debate over the role of the theist and secular, and secondly, that the Italian deliberative institution (the Parliament) has consistently perceived the debate as unsettled. The state-wide lack of a settlement over the issue does not (and did not) prevent a local accommodation of the debate that expressed teachers' and parents' views.

Crucifixes: Symbols of Divided Societies or a Manifestation of Pluralism?

In the previous section, I explained how Italy is a pluralistic democracy with strong belief-based communities, which represent secular and religious groups. The existence of such pluralism is axiomatic and is historically inherited and recognized by the Catholic Church (Hasson 2003). In this section, I would like to argue that an open and ongoing dialogue between theism and secularism is beneficial for developing a richer understanding of the role of symbols in public spaces. In particular, I would argue that a policy of light intervention by the state and by international jurisdictions might foster a democratic debate that dynamically adapts to set the scene for the increased demands of recognition.

At the theoretical level, a polity could generate a sense of solidarity and alliance among its members by discussing their aspirations without any reference to identity, history or faith. Habermas's theory of Constitution Patriotism is one of the latest attempts to set the basis for a post-national state and possibly a post-secular polity (1996). However, human rights principles are implemented by a process of dialectical refinement within a distinctive constituency. In the debate over state-recognized symbols in classrooms, there is reasonable evidence that such a process is ongoing within Italian councils through their school governors and, more generally, in the whole Italian political arena.

Recall, for instance, that with the post-1948 Constitution, which recognized the secular nature of the Italian state, parliaments had several opportunities to engage with the issue, but left it unchanged. The idea of administratively allowing the crucifix in the classroom might be perceived as a sign of institutional bias, even perhaps state indoctrination, but this fear is unproved.

Crucifixes in Italian classrooms are part of an ongoing debate, not an attempt to impose beliefs on others. All parents (Italian or not) can question the role of religious symbols (or the lack of them) in schools and it is the persistence of those symbols in some schools that is the most obvious evidence of the tension that a plurality of a system of beliefs generates in a diversified society. It is important in all democratic dialogues over concurring rights that a decision might have an impact (but, perhaps, it is more important in Italy, which historically has passed through the experience of the struggle for the recognition of a system of beliefs and has learned the hard way that such struggles do not admit a definitive solution).

However, developing a general criterion appears to be what is expected from the ECtHR, even in cases in which it might be unreasonable and undemocratic to assume that this would bring about a beneficial result. For instance, Ronchi points out the limited logical appeal of the idea of consensus as a criterion for a judicial decision (2011: 295). The rejection of the consensus as one of the supporting reasons is also found in Zucca:

> The Court goes on to say that the philosophical convictions of the parents must be respected by the State … Nevertheless, the Court manages to take away with one hand what it gives with the other in the very same paragraph, and in a feast of poor logic holds that this respect … depends on the context and European consensus. (Zucca 2011)

Indeed, the reference to consensus could be further articulated. However, the frustration with the legal reasoning given by the court is a manifestation (based on a combined reading of Art 2 of the First Protocol and Art 9) of the court acknowledging the limits of its jurisdiction.

In particular, the case shows that Mrs Lautsi's demand to the Council of School Governors is part of a struggle for the recognition of her beliefs in a democratic legal system: a legal system that recognizes cultural diversity and that provides a variety of systems of accommodation for that diversity. This accommodation is not imposed, but is part of the democratic debate that has historically also been part of the theist–secular dialogue.

It is axiomatic that such a contemporary dialogue must start from some legal basis (two RDs signed during the dark moments of the history of Italy). It is also unfortunate for Mrs Lautsi that her request did not convince the Council of School Governors of Abano Terme; however, the refusal to have Mrs Lautsi's children taught in a school without crucifixes is part of a larger ongoing democratic process.

Developing this point, in *Lautsi v. Italy*, the existence of a consensus is relevant because the interlocutors (for example the school governors, the Ministry of Education, the Association of Atheists) seek to form an intercultural understanding, which does not presuppose (or impose) a comprehensive solution.

It is noteworthy that *Lautsi v. Italy* might not prevent the ECtHR from going back to the issue of crucifixes in school classes. For instance, if there were suspicions that state religious symbols were aprioristically imposed, it would be reasonable for the court to say that the issue set by concurring rights (*ex* Art 2) had not been democratically settled.

However, in Lautsi, the court recognized that the debate over religious symbols in classrooms was part of a well-established dialogue between political stances. It is crucial that signatory states recognize parental desires (*ex* Art 2) and that the court might demand that state institutions acknowledge the parental claims and respond to them. However, it cannot be expected to impose what is the specific accommodation of those demands.

The ECtHR has the task of upholding the freedom of expressing religious beliefs, which the ECHR lists as one of the fundamental rights of modern democracy. However, the court cannot change the democratic process that accommodates concurring rights such as the right given to a parent to choose the type of education for their children (*ex* Art 2 of the First Protocol). What the court could establish is whether each individual (and the political associations that represent him or her) has the democratic prerogative to initiate the process that might implement his/her rights and freedoms. In the absence of such a process, the entitlement of a convention right such as the one given to parents to choose the type of education for their children would be hollow.

The democratic importance of the procedures that decide concurring rights has been downplayed by commentators who have restricted their accounts of the court recognition of the role of the consensus merely to a debate between a majority and a minority. This creates the false assumption that—in cases where there is an ongoing debate over the qualification of concurring rights—a jurisdiction can provide definitive solutions. This expectation is illogical. For instance, the ECtHR might decide that signatory state policies have denied the enjoyment of the right to property (*ex* Art 1 of the First Protocol), yet we cannot expect the court to decide how the property market is regulated. Similarly, the democratic process that decides on the accommodation of belief-based claims in public schools should be considered outside the court's jurisdiction.

Conclusion

Symbols are important. They are particularly significant in public educational establishments. The Grand Chamber of the ECtHR in *Lautsi v. Italy* decided that signatory states have a margin of discretion when deciding on which symbols can be displayed (or indeed not displayed) in Italian public schools.

In a relatively short motivation, the Grand Chamber acknowledged, perhaps for the first time, the conceptual separation between the task entrusted to the court (that is, the protection of the basic principles that allow for the functioning of a liberal democracy) and the practice of deliberating at the pragmatic level as to how concurring rights are accommodated.

The court decision might lack the argumentative support expected in a seminal decision. The reference to a missing European consensus that justified the decision (combined with an interpretation of Art 2 and Art 9) was perceived as an admission that human rights can be curtailed by the majoritarian principle. Such a position is unfounded. It stretches the reference to consensus to build arguments in which the court appears as a "puppet" at the behest of public opinion and/or the Council of Europe.

A more reasonable interpretation of the case would consider the multiple ECtHR references to the concept of consensus as an acknowledgement of a European-wide ongoing debate over the role of belief-based symbols in public schools. In the case of Lautsi, the right allocated to parents to decide on their children's education in relation to their system of beliefs is unchallenged by Italy's submission. However, at the pragmatic level, the right of Lautsi to select the education for her children has to be accommodated with the concurring demands of other parents.

What is missing in the court's decision is, perhaps, an articulation on how consensus should be formed. In the last section of the chapter, I argue that a parent's demand to change the display of belief-based symbols should be made at the school level. The debate should be open to all individuals and associations that might have an interest in the issue. The openness of the process will provide an indication as to how arguments are considered, and should reduce the effect of decisions based on pre-set alliances.

In conclusion, Lautsi created a turning point in the ECtHR jurisprudence relating to the display of belief-based symbols in classrooms. The decision might, in some areas, lack articulation. This is, however, a minor aspect of the case. In Lautsi, the Grand Chamber moved away from the deductive process that assimilates secularism with state neutrality and acknowledged the practical implications of accommodating conflicts in highly diversified European societies.

Bibliography

Bauman, Z. 1999. *In Search of Politics*. Oxford: Polity.

Benhabib, S. 1996. *Democracy and Difference: Contesting the Boundaries of the Political*. Princeton, NJ: Princeton University Press.

Breda, V. 2007. Constitutional identities in a liquid society, in *Liquid Society and its Law*, edited by J. Priban. Aldershot: Ashgate, 153–73.

Calvanese, E. 2011. *Media e Immigrazione tra Stereotipi e Pregiudizi*. Milan: Franco Angeli.

Calvino, I. 1975. *The Watcher and Other Stories*. New York: Harcourt Brace Jovanovich.

Clouser, R. 2005. *The Myth of Religious Neutrality*. Notre Dame, IN: University of Notre Dame Press.

Conseil d'Etat Français [1995]. Decision of July 10.

Consiglio di Stato [2006] Order 556.

Corte Costituzionale [2004] Order 389.

Direzione Sistema Statistico Regionale 2011. *Rapporto Statistico*. Venice: Direzione Sistema Statistico Regionale.

Habermas, J. 1996. The European nation state. Its achievements and its limitations. On the past and future of sovereignty and citizenship. *Ratio Juris*, 9(2), 125–37.

Habermas, J. and Ratzinger, J. 2005. *The Dialectics of Secularization*. San Francisco, CA: Ignatius Press.

Hasson, K. 2003. Religious liberty and human dignity: A tale of two declarations. *Harvard of Law and Public Policy*, 27(1), 81–92.

Istituto di Studi Politici Economici e Sociali. 2010. *Rapporto Italia 2010*. Rome: Istituto di Studi Politici Economici e Sociali.

Lamb, R. 2011. When human rights have gone too far: Religious tradition and equality in *Lautsi v. Italy*. *International Law*, 36(3), 751.

Lautsi v Italy [2009] 50 *E.H.R.R.* 1051.

Lautsi and Others v. Italy [2011] 54 *E.H.R.R.* 60.

Mancini, S. 2009. The power of symbols and symbols as power: Secularism and religion as guarantors of cultural convergence. *Cardozo Law Review*, 30(6), 629–68.

Mazie, S. 2004. Rethinking religious establishment and liberal democracy: Lessons from Israel. *The Brandywine Review of Faith and International Affairs*, 2(2), 3–12.

McGoldrick, D. 2011. Religion in the European public square and the European public life: Crucifixes in the classroom. *Human Rights Law Review*, 11(3), 451–501.

Montanelli, I. 2011. *L'Italia del Risorgimento* (1831–1861) (Storia d'Italia, Milan: Biblioteca Universale Rizzoli.

Montanelli, I. and Cervi, M. 1981. *Il Fascismo si Consolida* (1925–1933). Milan: Biblioteca Universale Rizzoli.

Mouffe, C. 1999. Deliberative democracy or agonistic pluralism? *Social Research*, 66(3), 745–58.

Panara, C. 2011. *Lautsi v Italy*: The display of religious symbols by the state. *European Public Law*, 17(1), 139–68.

R. (On the Application of Begum) v Headteacher and Governors of Denbigh High School [2006] H.R.L.R. 34.

Ronchi, P. 2011. Crucifixes, margin of appreciation and consensus: The Grand Chamber Ruling in *Lautsi v Italy*, *Ecclesiastical Law Journal*, 13, 287–97.

Royal Decrees 4336 of the 15th of September 1860, Turin.

Royal Decrees 965 of the 30th April 1924, Rome.

Royal Decrees 1297 of the 26th April 1928, Rome.

Sahin v Turkey [2005] 44 E.H.R.R. 99.

Walker, N. 2010. *The Final Appellate Jurisdiction: The Scottish Legal System*. Edinburgh: The Scottish Government, The Legal System Division.

Weiler, J. 2010. Lautsi: Crucifix in the Classroom Redux, *EJIL Talk* [Online]. 12(1). Available at: http://www.ejiltalk.org/lautsi-crucifix-in-the-classroom-redux/ [accessed: July 25, 2012].

Zucca, L. 2011. A Comment on Lautsi. *EJIL Analysis* [Online]. Available at: http://www.ejiltalk.org/a-comment-on-lautsi/ [accessed: July 25, 2012].

Chapter 7
Restrictions on Religious Freedom: When and How Justified?

John Warwick Montgomery

The Dilemma

All major human rights instruments include the freedom of religion. At the same time, they provide for limited but undefined restrictions on that freedom. Thus, to take but the two most important examples:

United Nations Civil and Political Covenant, Art. 18 (paragraphs 1–3):

> 1. Everyone shall have the right to freedom of thought, conscience and religion. This right shall include freedom to have or to adopt a religion or belief of his choice, and freedom, either individually or in community with others and in public or private, to manifest his religion or belief in worship, observance, practice and teaching.
>
> 2. No one shall be subject to coercion which would impair his freedom to have or to adopt a religion or belief of his choice.
>
> 3. Freedom to manifest one's religion or beliefs may be subject only to such limitations as are prescribed by law and are necessary to protect public safety, order, health, or morals or the fundamental rights and freedoms of others.

European Convention on Human Rights, Art. 9 (paragraphs 1–2):

> 1. Everyone has the right to freedom of thought, conscience and religion; this right includes freedom to change his religion or belief, and freedom, either alone or in community with others and in public or private, to manifest his religion or belief, in worship, teaching, practice and observance.
>
> 2. Freedom to manifest one's religion or beliefs shall be subject only to such limitations as are prescribed by law and are necessary in a democratic society in the interests of public safety, for the protection of public order, health or morals, or the protection of the rights and freedoms of others.

It will be noted that paragraph 3 of the ICCPR and paragraph 2 of the ECHR speak in much the same terms: the freedoms guaranteed by the instrument may be restricted in limited terms when to do so is legally necessary for the protection of "public safety, order, health, or morals or the rights and freedoms of others." However, the nature of those restrictions is nowhere set forth; nor do we discover from the treaties what are the "rights and (fundamental) freedoms of others" which can legitimately trump the religious liberties guaranteed by these international instruments.

One of the important religious rights set out in these texts is that of "changing one's religion"—which, by definition, entails the existence of religious alternatives and the right to evangelize (Montgomery 2001a). In Islamic Shari'a law, however, apostasy (conversion from Islam to another faith) is not merely prohibited; it generally carries the death penalty.[1] Understandably, therefore, a number of Islamic states, though members of the United Nations, have refused to ratify the ICCPR; these include, inter alia, Brunei, Malaysia, Myanmar (Burma), Oman, Qatar, Saudi Arabia, Singapore, and the United Arab Emirates.

Whilst ratifying the Covenant, other Islamic states have filed reservations to make clear that they do not consider the guaranteed rights as necessarily applicable in their countries. Bahrain's reservation reads: "The Government of the Kingdom of Bahrain interprets the Provisions of Article 3, (18) and (23) as not affecting in any way the prescriptions of the Islamic Shariah." Likewise Mauritania: "The Mauritanian Government, while accepting the provisions set out in Article 18 concerning freedom of thought, conscience and religion, declares that their application shall be without prejudice to the Islamic Shariah." Pakistan restricted its recent ratification of the Covenant in the following similar terms: "[The] Islamic Republic of Pakistan declares that the provisions of Articles 3, 6, 7, 18 and 19 shall be so applied to the extent that they are not repugnant to the Provisions of the Constitution of Pakistan and the Sharia laws."[2]

---

1 "A woman, however, is not slain (for apostasy), but is to be imprisoned and scourged at times of prayer" (S.C. Sircar, n.d.: II, 284–5). Wael B. Hallaq, in his standard, contemporary treatment, explains the death penalty for apostasy in the following terms: "In a culture whose lynchpin is religion, religious principles and religious morality, apostasy is in some way equivalent to high treason in the modern nation state" (Hallaq 2009: 319).

2 See *UN Treaty Collection: International Covenant on Civil and Political Rights* (available at: http://treaties.un.org/pages/ViewDetails.aspx?src=TREATY&mtdsg_no=IV-4&chapter=4&lang=en), accessed: January 17, 2011. The reservations of Mauritania and Pakistan are available at: http://treaties.un.org/doc/publication/mtdsg/volume%20i/chapter%20iv/iv-4.en.pdf [accessed: August 8, 2012], 9, 31. It is worth noting—*en passant*—that U.S. reservations to the ICCPR are so extensive that many commentators, even within the U.S., have asserted that they make the country's ratification of the instrument of little force or effect. Indeed, in the most general sense, the U.S. has an abysmal record in the area of international cooperation as a result of its refusal to ratify international agreements. But at least the U.S. reservations are not restrictive of religious freedoms.

Interestingly, even in the case of a non-binding UN declaration, the Declaration on the Elimination of All Forms of Intolerance and of Discrimination Based on Religion or Belief (1981), Iraq entered a collective reservation on behalf of the Organization of the Islamic Conference as to the applicability of any provision or wording in the Declaration which might be contrary to Shari'a law or to legislation or acts based on Islamic law, and Syria and Iran endorsed this reservation.

Are such reservations acceptable? If not, why not? Even if we find the Islamic approach—though allowable in public international law—thoroughly obnoxious, what justifiable criteria can we offer for restricting antisocial religious practices?

Utah and Beyond

Conan Doyle (or, as devoted Sherlockians prefer to have it, Dr. Watson), in the very first of his immortal stories featuring Sherlock Holmes, *A Study in Scarlet*, saw the publicity value of bringing Mormons into a featured—though negative—role (see Montgomery 2000). We can hardly do less. We therefore begin with the leading Mormon polygamy case (*Reynolds v. U.S.* 1878).[3]

The presidency of the Church of the Latter-day Saints, in order to improve the Church's poor reputation based on bigamous practices and to clarify any ambiguity as to illegal practices by the faithful, brought a test case using, with his agreement, one George Reynolds, a secretary in the presidential office and an admitted bigamist. Reynolds was successfully prosecuted under the existing anti-bigamy law and the case eventually reached the Supreme Court of the United States. The defense presented a number of technical arguments (Utah at that time was a territory and had not attained statehood) but the most important element in the defense argument was that Reynolds, as a believing male Mormon, held polygamy to be his religious duty; he therefore maintained that his constitutional, First Amendment religious rights were being violated.

The Supreme Court in its decision against Reynolds relied principally on Thomas Jefferson's celebrated "wall of separation" letter to the Danbury Baptist Association:

> Mr. Jefferson afterwards, in reply to an address to him by a committee of the Danbury Baptist Association (8 id. 113), took occasion to say: "Believing with you that religion is a matter which lies solely between man and his God; that he owes account to none other for his faith or his worship; that the legislative powers of the government reach actions only, and not opinions, – I contemplate with sovereign reverence that act of the whole American people which declared that their legislature should 'make no law respecting an establishment of religion or prohibiting the free exercise thereof,' thus building a wall of separation between

3 For a careful scholarly study of Mormon polygamy, yesterday and today, see Howick (2007).

> church and State. Adhering to this expression of the supreme will of the nation in behalf of the rights of conscience, I shall see with sincere satisfaction the progress of those sentiments which tend to restore man to all his natural rights, convinced he has no natural right in opposition to his social duties." Coming as this does from an acknowledged leader of the advocates of the measure, it may be accepted almost as an authoritative declaration of the scope and effect of the amendment thus secured. Congress was deprived of all legislative power over mere opinion, but was left free to reach actions which were in violation of social duties or subversive of good order.

It has been rather nastily pointed out that the text of the Jefferson letter used by the Court was a mistaken transcription, Jefferson's original, handwritten copy reading "the legitimate powers of the government reach actions only, and not opinions." Be that as it may, the Court's point is clear: the First Amendment absolutely protects religious *beliefs* but does not necessarily protect religious *actions*. As for bigamy, Reynolds could certainly not be compelled to give up his belief in it, but by practicing that belief, he was earning a prison sentence.

The *Reynolds* decision leaves much to be desired—not so much on the matter of bigamy as such, even though George Quayle Cannon, the "Mormon Richelieu" and Utah territorial delegate, may well have had a point when he commented after the *Reynolds* decision came down: "Our crime has been: We married women instead of seducing them; we reared children instead of destroying them; we desired to exclude from the land prostitution, bastardy and infanticide" (Cannon 1879: 52; see also Larson 1971: 37–89)—points worth more than passing consideration when today homosexual unions are the law in more than one American jurisdiction and the next step might well be the legal right to marry a hippopotamus (unless the hippopotamus has a good lawyer [Richardson 2011]). But the real problem with the *ratio* in the *Reynolds* case is simply its creation of an invidious comparison between religious belief and religious action.

Very little meaningful religious belief exists unconnected with religious practice. To say that the former is protected as a human right but the latter is not is, to say the least, disingenuous. Such an argument has been a *sine qua non* of totalitarian regimes such as the late, unlamented German Democratic Republic, which legislated away religious education and evangelism, whilst maintaining a facade of religious liberty by permitting church services to be held. The same approach has been employed in Egypt to restrict the Copts to their own church buildings, and in Muslim countries in general where non-Muslims can operate only in ghetto communities, unable to offer their wares in the ideological marketplace.

One can hardly claim that all religious practices should be tolerated: sacramental use of psychedelic drugs, Aztec human sacrifice, suicide cults come immediately to mind. In *Reynolds*, Justice Waite, whilst over-generalizing to argue the constitutional non-protection of religious practices in the large, saw this to be true in relation to faith healing (today one thinks of the Christian Scientists and the Jehovah's Witnesses):

> In *Regina v. Wagstaff* (10 Cox Crim. Cases, 531), the parents of a sick child, who omitted to call in medical attendance because of their religious belief that what they did for its cure would be effective, were held not to be guilty of manslaughter, while it was said the contrary would have been the result if the child had actually been starved to death by the parents, under the notion that it was their religious duty to abstain from giving it food. But when the offence consists of a positive act which is knowingly done, it would be dangerous to hold that the offender might escape punishment because he religiously believed the law which he had broken ought never to have been made. No case, we believe, can be found that has gone so far.

But how to distinguish the wheat from the chaff? What criteria can be justified to separate valid religious practices from those deserving banishment from a civilized society?

That this is not an easy question is well illustrated by a recent article concerning the problem of reconciling work requirements with religious practices in Germany (Philippot 2011). The article observes that Germany "prefers to leave to civil servants and the courts the resolution, on a case-by-case basis, of conflicts between work and religion," thereby handling these conflicts not on a principled basis but "pragmatically." The result is often conflicting decisions and crossed signals. Examples: the Regional Labor Court of Schleswig-Holstein has ruled that, in the case of a Muslim worker in a supermarket who was fired after refusing a post in the liquor department, an employer should make the effort to transfer an employee to a department consistent with his or her conscientious beliefs, but if no such post is reasonably available employment can be legally terminated; and the Labor Tribunal in Baden-Würtemberg in August, 2010, upheld the firing of a kindergarten teacher who refused to remove her veil at work—even though in 2002 the Federal Labor Tribunal (the BAG) recognized the right of a supermarket salesgirl to keep her veil on. A specialist in German labor law, Professor Gregor Thüsing of Bonn University, is quoted on the vague philosophy in operation: "The workplace can be compatible with religious exercise—but the latter must not prevent carrying out the essential requirements of the job."

Two Roads Leading into the Proverbial Bramble Bush[4]—Together with a Safer, Logically Justified Route

Natural Law?

Can we not simply restrict religious liberties when (and only when) the exercise of the right would produce "harm to others"? Is this not a transparent, natural

4 The legally educated will immediately think of Karl Llewellyn's (1930) classic essay.

solution? Hardly. In the first place, there is no single accepted definition of what constitutes "harm." Secondly, who is to decide what is "harmful" to A (the exerciser of the right, B? The society to which A and B belong? A himself?). One thinks of the heart-wrenching account by the late Lord Hailsham of St Marylebone concerning the suicide of his brother—suicide being decriminalized today because it allegedly produces harm only to the victim: Lord Hailsham describes the hurt the suicide caused to all those in the family and potentially to an ever-widening circle of which his brother was a member (Hailsham 1975: 60–1; see also Montgomery 2002a).

More generally: are there not built-in answers to human rights issues through an understanding of "natural law"? Do we not inwardly *know* what are genuine religious rights and what religious practices should not be permitted? Is there not a consensus of "right-thinking" people on the issue? Sadly, the answer is a resounding negative.

Eighteenth-century "Enlightenment" confidence in a universally recognized morality collapsed in the wake of nineteenth-century anthropology. The tremendous diversity of standards, ethical norms, and moral practices in the world's cultures made it virtually impossible to sustain the idea of a common human "conscience" adequate to establish a common standard of religious beliefs. Moreover, even supposing that such a common standard could be demonstrated, would that make it right? In 1903, English philosopher G.E. Moore identified as the "naturalistic fallacy" the assumption that an "is" (here, common ethical beliefs) can be regarded *ipso facto* as the equivalent of an "ought" (here, proper natural law) (see Montgomery 2002b). And the hopeless lack of specificity of natural-law principles renders the viewpoint of little practical utility in the legal field. During the Second World War, the Nazis employed as the motto over the entrance to the death camp at Buchenwald a German translation (*Jedem das Seine*) of one of the defining elements of the Justinian Code's understanding of natural law (Montgomery 1975: 37–45).[5]

If more evidence is needed of the impossibility of establishing human rights standards—including definitions of religious liberty and appropriate limits to those standards—through natural-law theory, one need only cite the deep conflict today between Western nations, who argue that civil liberties should not be subordinated to economic and social rights, and Eastern societies, who maintain that economic and social rights must first be established before civil liberties can be effective (Bauer 1995).[6] Underlying this deep ideological cleavage is the difference in the understanding of rights among peoples of different cultures. This being so, one can

5 The *Digest* of the Justinian Code defines the natural law as "*Honeste vivere, neminem laedere, suum cuique tribuere*"—which, as C.J. Friedrich properly observes, is so "imprecise" that it does little more than to underscore the need for "some kind of equity" (Friedrich 1963: 22). The Nazis used the Code's third defining element at Buchenwald.

6 The eastern stress on the primacy of social harmony over individual civil liberties may well connect with Taoist and especially Confucian thought, where "natural law" and

hardly expect religious liberties to be defined in the same manner universally; and it follows inexorably that a universally agreed-upon list of proper limitations to religious rights cannot be formulated by way of natural-law reasoning.

Closely allied to natural-law thinking are the impressive neo-Kantian efforts to justify rights (and their limitations). One of the most striking of the neo-Kantian legal philosophers is Alan Gewirth, who argues that one's "freedom" (embracing civil and political rights) and "well-being" (entailing social and economic rights) are grounded simply in the natural fact that one is a "prospective personal agent"—not in any special strengths or characteristics one may possess—and thus one ought to "act in accord with the generic rights of one's recipients as well as of oneself." Of course the intractable problem here is that human beings invariably maintain that their special advantages, not their common humanity, justify their desired conduct and warrant their special treatment. Genghis Khan, for example, will be delighted to point out that his right to rape and pillage derives from his personal strength and power, not from any quality of prospective personal agent that he shares with others (Montgomery 2009: 5.62). This is doubtless why on the international scale human rights are employed to protect one's own interests from the actions of others—and rarely to limit one's actions for the sake of others. Clearly, this would be the case with limitations on religious liberties: "*My* religion, being true, should have the right to proselytize, whereas *yours*, being false, if allowed to do so would invariably cause harm to others and to the society as a whole."

Positivism?

If natural-law theories cannot provide the guidance we need to arrive at sound limitations to religious freedoms, why not take the route offered by the legal philosophy which largely displaced jurisnaturalism in the nineteenth century: the positivism of Austin and Bentham—with their twentieth-century developments in the labors of H.L.A. Hart and Hans Kelsen? Even less needs to be said here than in respect to natural-law thinking.

If the "decrees of the sovereign" per se are the only genuine determinants of law (Austin, Bentham), or if the ultimate "rule of recognition" (Hart) and the *Grundnorm* (Kelsen) cannot be criticized from outside the given legal system, then there is no way whatever to identify universal standards of religious liberty, much less proper limitations to such standards. Rules (and this would perforce include Dworkin's "principles and standards") are then justifiable only within a given legal system (Montgomery 2002b, 2011a, 2011b, 2011c).

It should be obvious that this takes us right back to where we started—with cultures manifesting a given philosophy of human rights (for example, economic and social rights in preference to civil liberties) or a religion (for example, Islamic

---

"human nature" were presented as justification—a further reminder of the porousness of jusnaturalist arguments; see Montgomery (1994: 113–26, 1991: 98–110).

Shari'a) and defending *their* views over against the views of others—often in direct contradiction to the positions taken by other cultures and religious traditions. Legal positivism, whatever variety of it one prefers, necessarily drives religious liberty into the corral of a given jurisprudential tradition—with all the difficulties following therefrom.

A Transcendental Solution

The reason why neither natural-law theory nor legal positivism is capable of providing us with defensible limitations to religious liberties (or with the religious liberties themselves, for that matter) is a purely logical consideration. Religious freedoms and their potential limitations constitute an area of human rights, and human rights—if they are worthy of the name—will by definition be *inalienable* (in French, the classical tongue of rights analysis, *imprescriptible*). They will be absolute, unable in principle to be abrogated by others or even surrendered by the possessor. But rights of such a character (and any limitations upon them) would therefore have to have a *transcendent* character. Water does not rise above its own level and finite human beings will be capable of creating only societies, states, and laws of a finite, non-transcendental, non-absolute character. Thus Archimedes' principle that only a lever with a fulcrum outside the world would be capable of lifting the world; Rousseau's assertion that "it would take gods to give men laws" (Rousseau 1762: Bk. 2, chap. 7); and Wittgenstein's declarations that "the sense of the world must lie outside the world" and "ethics is transcendental" (Wittgenstein 1974: 6.41– 6.421; see also Wittgenstein 1965).

Genuine principles of religious liberty and their qualifications would need to come from a transcendent source: a revelation from the Source of those same values. Having set forth in detail elsewhere the argument for such a revelation (Montgomery 2002c, 2009), we shall not repeat ourselves here. We merely stress the logical fact that without such a transcendent revelation, the search for principles of religious liberty and the identification of legitimate exceptions to their application is a chimerical task without the slightest logical possibility of success.

Two objections to this line of approach are worth consideration. First: *Since a revelational solution to the problem is necessarily going to depend upon the truth of a particular faith position, would not that solution by definition be unworkable in a pluralistic world?* Would it not perforce be rejected out of hand by those not sharing the religious position of the revelation justifying the human rights position? The answer is simply that one must distinguish the *epistemological significance* of the revelational solution from its *pragmatic application*. It may well be that a secular or pluralistic society will resist even sound arguments justifying the revelation by which valid principles of religious liberty and their limitations are arrived at; but that does not mean that those same principles and limitations cannot be presented and advocated by common-ground arguments of a kind that will be acceptable in the pluralistic context in which the principles need to be implemented. Thus, to take but one example, it may well be prudent, once one has discovered revelationally the principle of freedom to change one's religion and the limitation upon it that conversion, even to a true faith, must never be forced, to persuade legislators in a society not committed to that revelational position that these principles are instrumentally and pragmatically good for the society—and that the disregard of them will surely produce a culture in which ideas in general suffer repression at the hands of ideological majorities.

Secondly, it may be argued that *to seek justification of religious freedom and appropriate limitations to it from a given religious revelation is to invite just the opposite: lack of religious liberty (to the advantage of the religion derived from the revelation) and limitations on religious liberty inevitably favoring that particular religious viewpoint*. To this we respond: that will depend entirely on the nature of the religion proclaimed by the verifiable transcendent revelation (Montgomery 1995: 105–88). Were the *Qur'an* to be justified as the necessary source of absolute principle (which cannot be done, owing to the aprioristic nature of Islamic truth-claims [Montgomery 1978: 81–99]), only conversions to Islam would be allowed and apostasy from Islam would be severely punished.[7]

But if the Bible can be shown to have the revelational quality essential for the provision of inalienable principles of religious liberty, the result is very different: freedom to convert is mandated by Jesus himself, since only a freely chosen relationship to God is worth anything spiritually (John 7:16–17, Matthew 23:37). To allow conversions in only one direction—or to prevent freedom of religious choice by restricting the available religious options only to the true faith—would be to abrogate the possibility of genuine faith decisions.

At the same time, biblical revelation provides meaningful limitations on unrestricted religious activity. Because of the Bible's respect for human life, religious rites imperiling life (human sacrifice, suicide cults) or health (refusal to permit blood transfusions or to rely on established medical remedies, psychedelic drugs as sacraments [Montgomery 2001b: 214–16]) are not to be permitted. The same will be the case for religious practices (for example, polygamy) that lower the value of familial life, these being contrary to the Bible's high view of the monogamous family (1 Timothy 3:2; Ephesians 5:31 – 6:4).

It is also vital to emphasize that, from the standpoint of biblical revelation, limitations to the general principles of religious freedom must always be applied *restrictively*. Whatever is not clearly contrary to biblical teaching and whatever cannot be shown to be socially deleterious should be permitted—and the burden of proof lies upon the one who would limit the freedom in question. Thus, in the

7 In France, where civil marriage must, by law, precede any religious ceremony, Muslims have been defying the law and some civil authorities have ignored the problem. However, the result is that a couple, having gone through only a religious ceremony, are not legally married at all, and thus the wife is at the mercy of Islamic practice, which, inter alia, permits her to be divorced (*talaq*) by the declaration of her husband, with (Shi'a) or without (Sunni) witnesses. See Sigrid Choffée-Harouel (2011).

matter of religious dress, no restrictions should exist save where total concealment of the person could encourage criminality or, in the case of public servants, where the dress could well give the impression that the state is supporting or favoring a given religious viewpoint—and certainly there should be no legal prohibitions relative to the wearing of non-obtrusive religious symbols.[8] Evangelism should be allowable without restriction; "proselytism" laws (as in Greece) can create an uneven playing field to the advantage of the established church and often treat the citizenry as immature children, incapable of making responsible religious decisions.[9] Blasphemy laws should be allowable only in instances where the potential speech is so offensive that it would produce riot and affray (Montgomery 2002c). Indeed, it seems impossible to find biblically justifiable reasons for legislation specifically limiting religious speech on ideological grounds—on the basis of its content. Existing civil and criminal penalties relating to fraud, deceit, undue influence, and the like would seem sufficient to deal with instances of overreaching by religious believers. The mere fact that a religious belief or practice is socially offensive or politically incorrect constitutes no legitimate ground whatever for its legal suppression. The Bible stands on the side of liberty, not on the side of its detractors (Riassetto 2010, Montgomery 2001a).

Appendix: Crucifixes in Italy

On November 3, 2009, the European Court of Human Rights in Strasbourg dropped a political/religious bombshell. In *Lautsi v. Italy*, Case No. 30814/06, the Court ruled that the Italian law requiring the display of crucifixes in public school classrooms throughout the country was incompatible with Article 9 (freedom of religion) and of Protocol 1, Article 2 (parental rights in the education of their children) of the European Convention of Human Rights.

---

8 The recent French parliamentary views on the wearing of the *burqa* or the *niqab* seem to accord with the philosophy expressed here. See the statement of the Commission Nationale Consultative des Droits de l'Homme, *Avis sur le port du voile intégral* (2010), adopted by the Assemblée plénière on January 21, 2010. See also the French *Code de l'Education,* Art. L. 141–5-1 (prohibiting in public schools student dress or symbolism manifesting "ostensiblement une appartenance religieuse"; law passed and implemented in 2004). It is also important to note that where there is an established church (e.g., "the Reformed branch of the Holy Catholic Church" in England), there can be no legitimate ground for repressing the symbols associated with that church—nativity scenes on public property, etc.

9 In the *Larissis* case which I successfully argued before the European Court of Human Rights (140/1996/759/958–60), we were nonetheless unfortunately unable to persuade the Court that a "superior" (in the instant case, a military officer) should be able to evangelize a "subordinate" (here, an enlisted man). Our position was—and is—that if one is mature enough to fight and die for one's country, one is mature enough to engage in the personal evaluation of religious claims evangelistically presented.

To say that the decision has created a flap would be a vast understatement. Politicians, churchmen–and the Pope–have been outraged. Since the Court's decision has been published only in French, and is therefore inaccessible to most of our readers, we shall comment briefly on it. Its relevance goes far beyond the boot of Italy.

The Italian crucifix law originated in 1860, and crucifixes have been a fixture in Italy's public school classrooms ever since. But a Finnish woman, one Soile Lautsi, a non-believer married to an Italian, objected to the fact that her two children were subjected to this religious symbol. She sued, and her case went through the Italian courts without success. Having "exhausted domestic [that is, national] remedies," she took the case to Strasbourg, and the Court agreed with her. In immediate reaction to the decision, the Italian foreign minister declared: "This is a death blow for a Europe of values and rights." The Vatican questioned the right of the European Court to interfere in a central matter of Italian belief and practice, calling the ruling "wrong and myopic."

The Italian government's lawyers had argued that the crucifix, as a national symbol, should not be removed from classrooms since it simply reflected the fact that Europe in general and Italy in particular have been deeply influenced by the tradition represented by the crucifix. So what was the Court's rationale for barring the crucifix?

First, the Court noted that in 1948, when Italy adopted its present republican constitution, it explicitly separated the state from the Catholic Church; and in 2000 the Italian Constitutional Court interpreted this as meaning that the state had to remain "equidistant and impartial" in relation to all religious and philosophical beliefs held by the citizenry. Secondly, the European Court of Human Rights, whilst agreeing that the crucifix is a multifaceted symbol, pointed out the obvious: that its predominant reference is religious, and specifically Christian. Therefore to display it in public school classrooms is to give a special, privileged position to one particular religion. Finally, the Court observed that school children are especially impressionable—vulnerable to influence, owing to their youth and inexperience.

Why should this case be of interest to those outside Italy—and particularly to Christian believers elsewhere? *Because the Lautsi case almost exactly parallels the cases brought to the U.S. Supreme Court and other federal courts which have resulted in the removal of prayers from public schools and biblical symbols, such as the Ten Commandments and nativity scenes, from public property.* After my late protagonist Madalyn Murray O'Hair succeeded in her fight to remove mandatory prayer and Bible reading from American public schools (*Engel v. Vitale*, 1962, *Abington School District v. Schempp*, 1963, and *Murray v. Curlett*, 1963), the evangelical community was appalled, arguing, as the Italian government was to do in *Lautsi*, that this was the end of "Christian America" and that, after all, the symbols involved need not be taken as primarily religious in nature but can be treated as simply part of the general cultural tradition.

This line of argumentation, however, is fundamentally flawed—and is as hurtful to Christian faith as it is to the political order. In both the U.S. and Italy, there is constitutional separation of church and state. It is simply *wrong* for citizens to be compelled to support a religion which does not reflect their personal beliefs. (Indeed, the crucifix itself can be an offense to some Christians, for example, very conservative Protestants who see in it a "graven image" contrary to the Second Commandment!) No one forced Italy to separate church and state in 1948; they could have continued as before and retained crucifixes—as does England, with the establishment of "the Reformed branch of the Holy Catholic Church" (the Anglican Church)—and where, consequently, Christian symbols cannot be removed from public schools or public property. But, politically, one cannot have one's cake and eat it too!

Even more importantly, the arguments of pro-crucifix and pro-nativity scene advocates demean Christian faith by trying to maintain these symbols by saying that they really are no longer specifically Christian—that they have become merely cultural or national in character! This is dreadful, for it is a denial of the saving message they convey. And prayers in the public schools will be *either*, if genuinely Christian—in the name of Jesus—offensive to non-believers, whose tax money also supports those schools, or, if merely general in nature (directed to an undefined Deity—the Great Puff of Smoke?), contrary to the biblical mandate that all prayer should be "in Jesus' name" and therefore unable to be prayed by Christians!

The great advantage of separating church and state is that a level playing field is created for all religious and philosophical positions, and on that field historic Christianity can triumph—and *will* triumph if the biblical gospel is effectively preached and the powerful apologetic evidence for its truth conveyed. Why? Because *only* the Christian faith (not the other world's religions, not the cults and sects, not the philosophers' speculations) can marshal the "many infallible proofs" supporting the truth of the written and the living Word (Acts 1:3).

But on March 18, 2011, the Grand Chamber of the European Court of Human Rights, by a vote of 15 to 2, overruled the earlier Italian crucifix judgment rendered unanimously by its Second Section, *so as to permit the display of crucifixes in Italian public schools*! It is clear that tremendous political pressure had been applied to reverse the original decision. The Court's reasoning—e.g., "a crucifix on a wall is an essentially passive symbol" (para. 72)—is based essentially on the view that the crucifix has lost any active evangelistic force and become (as the Italian State had to argue) merely a cultural symbol. Would serious believing Christians really want to support that kind of interpretation in order to justify secular governmental support of one's religious beliefs?

Bibliography

Abington School District v. Schempp [1963] 374 U.S. 203.
Avis sur le port du voile intégral [2010] Commission Nationale Consultative des Droits de l'Homme. (adopted by the Assemblée plénière on January 21, 2010).

Available at: http://www.cncdh.fr/IMG/pdf/10.01.21_Avis_sur_le_port_du_voile_integral.pdf [accessed: August 25, 2012].

Bauer, J. 1995. International Human Rights and Asian Commitment. *Human Rights Dialogue* [Online], 1(3). Carnegie Council for Ethics in International Affairs. Available at: http://www.carnegiecouncil.org/publications/archive/dialogue/1_03/articles/514.html [accessed: August 8, 2012].

Cannon, G.Q. 1879. *A Review of the Decision of the Supreme Court of the United States in the Case of Geo. Reynolds v. the United States*. Salt Lake City, UT: Deseret News Printing.

Choffée-Harouel, S. 2011. *La mairie avant la mosque*. Paris: Editions Jean-Cyrille Godefroy.

Declaration on the Elimination of All Forms of Intolerance and of Discrimination Based on Religion or Belief [1981] G.A. res. 36/55, 36 U.N. GAOR Supp. (No. 51) at 171, U.N. Doc. A/36/684.

Engel v. Vitale [1962] 370 U.S. 421.

Friedrich, C.J. 1963. *The Philosophy of Law in Historical Perspective*, 2nd edn. Chicago, IL: University of Chicago Press.

Hallaq, Wael B. 2009. *Shari'a: Theory, Practice, Transformations*. Cambridge: Cambridge University Press.

Howick, E.K. 2007. *Polygamy: The Mormon Enigma*. Silverton, ID: WindRiver.

Larson, Gustive O. 1971. *The "Americanization" of Utah for Statehood*. San Marino, CA: Huntington Library.

Llewellyn, K.N. 1930. *The Bramble Bush*. New York: Oceana Publications.

Lord Hailsham. 1975. *The Door Wherein I Went*. London: Collins.

Montgomery, J.W. 1975. *The Law above the Law*. Minneapolis, MN: Bethany.

Montgomery, J.W. 1978. How Muslims Do Apologetics, in his *Faith Founded on Fact*. Nashville, TN: Thomas Nelson.

Montgomery, J.W. 1991. *Wohin marschiert China?* Neuhausen-Stuttgart: Haenssler Verlag.

Montgomery, J.W. 1994. *Giant in Chains: China Today and Tomorrow*. Milton Keynes: Nelson Word.

Montgomery, J.W. 1995. *Human Rights and Human Dignity*, 2nd edn. Calgary: Canadian Institute for Law, Theology and Public Policy.

Montgomery, J.W. 2000. *The Transcendent* Holmes. Ashcroft: Calabash.

Montgomery, J.W. 2001a. *The Repression of Evangelism in Greece: European Litigation vis-à-vis a Closed Religious Establishment*. Lanham, MD: University Press of America.

Montgomery, J.W. 2001b. The Gospel according to LSD, in *Principalities and Powers: The World of the Occult*, revised edn. Calgary: Canadian Institute for Law, Theology and Public Policy.

Montgomery, J.W. 2002a. Whose Life Anyway?, in his *Christ Our Advocate*. Bonn: Verlag für Kultur und Wissenschaft.

Montgomery, J.W. 2002b. Modern Theology and Contemporary Legal Theory, in *Christ Our Advocate*. Bonn: Verlag für Kultur und Wissenschaft.

Montgomery, J.W. 2002c. Can Blasphemy Law Be Justified?, in *Christ Our Advocate*. Bonn: Verlag für Kultur und Wissenschaft.
Montgomery, J.W. 2002d. *History, Law and Christianity*. Calgary: Canadian Institute for Law, Theology and Public Policy.
Montgomery, J. W. 2009. *Tractatus Logico-Theologicus*, 4th edn. Bonn: Verlag für Kultur und Wissenschaft.
Montgomery, J.W. 2011a. Speculation vs. Factuality, in *Christ as Centre and Circumference*. Bonn: Verlag für Kultur und Wissenschaft.
Montgomery, J.W. 2011b. Law, in *Christ as Centre and Circumference*. Bonn: Verlag für Kultur und Wissenschaft.
Montgomery, J.W. 2011c. Human Rights, in *Christ as Centre and Circumference*. Bonn: Verlag für Kultur und Wissenschaft.
Murray v. Curlett [1963] 374 U.S. 203.
Philippot, D. 2011. Religion et travail: le choix du pragmatism. *Dernières Nouvelles d'Alsace*, March 9.
Reynolds v U.S. [1878] 98 U.S. 145, opinion by Morrison Waite, CJ.
Riassetto, I. 2010. Prosélytisme, in *Droit des Religions*, edited by Francis Messner. Paris: CNRS Editions.
Richardson, V. 2011. Same-Sex Marriages Give Polygamy a Legal Boost. *Washington Times*, March 20.
Rousseau, J. 1762. *On the Social Contract*, reprinted 1968. New York: Penguin Books.
Sircar, S.C. n.d. *Al-Shari'a (Sunni and Imamiyah Code)* (2 vols). Lahore: Law Publishing Co.
Wittgenstein, L. 1974. *Tractatus Logico-Philosophicus*. London: Routledge and Kegan Paul.
Wittgenstein, L. 1965. A Lecture on Ethics. *Philosophical Review*, 74(1), 3–12.

PART III
Enforcing and Motivating Human Rights

Chapter 8

No Human Rights without Retribution: Plights and Promises of Redress as if Nothing Happened

Hendrik Kaptein

Introduction

So much has been written on human rights that there must be really very good reasons to add anything more to an already enormously extensive literature. Might all these efforts not have been better spent on realization and protection of human rights in more direct fashions? So many scholarly and humane words and warnings, however suave or even persuasive, seem powerless against so much irrational cruelty in the world. It seems apparent that if human rights are really or even overridingly important, such rights ought to redirect human effort from the books to action on behalf of human rights.

Adding to this is the irony that almost all discussion of human rights is enabled by societies and jurisdictions offering real enjoyment of at least basic human rights like freedom of thought and expression and freedom of the press. All this still again presupposes enjoyment of human rights to freedom of association and to adequate means of material subsistence as presuppositions of whatever is required for a reasonable life, intellectual or otherwise.

Even ever more vociferous criticism of human rights in the so-called developed world presupposes enjoyment of the very same human rights as well, of course, as if such criticism is aimed at making an end to itself by abolishing preconditions of free speech. Thus MacIntyre (1984: 67) famously compared human rights with witches and unicorns, probably blissfully forgetting enjoyment of human rights enabling him to have published such a bold statement. Indeed there may be dangers of inflation and concomitant misuse of human rights, or semblances of it, to be discussed and countered (see on this Ignatieff 2001). This leaves basic human rights untouched of course. As said before enjoyment of such rights, by discussing them or otherwise, is like freely breathing air: happily unheeded as long as human rights are realized and enforced.

What a stark contrast indeed with human or in fact inhuman realities all around the world. Human rights violations abound, however difficult it may be to quantify amounts of violation or simply wanton violence against mankind. Little is done against this, which is all the more irresponsible or even criminal in the light of the officially proffered overriding importance of basic human rights. What is being done lacks clear guidelines. Some perpetrators of crimes against humanity are punished by the International Criminal Court or otherwise; most of them go free, like so many other offenders against human rights in a broader sense. Some victims may earn some or other marginal official compensation and/or restoration, under different and unrelated legal systems, criminal, civil, administrative and/or otherwise. Again, the overwhelming majority are left alone, without any clarity on what they are really entitled to.

So, and with all respect to discourse on the nature, extent, varieties and foundations of human rights, here some attention is to be paid to the question *what is to be done with human rights violations*—or for that matter with harmful violations of rights and rightful interests in general. Scholarly attention to this has probably been less plentiful than to human rights "as such" and to varieties of their implementations it well seems. Discussion of rational reactions to human rights violations is scattered among criminal law, civil law and other more or less legal and theoretical literature, without reaching any distinctive results. Varieties of retribution, redress, restitution and reparation passed muster, without any real implementation anyway. The lack of credible mechanisms to effect such redress means that the perceived cost of human rights violations is too low to deter offenders anyway.

Here it will be argued that redress of human rights violations, or in fact redress of any wrongful harm comes down to restoring victims to their rightful original positions, "as if nothing wrong happened"—even if they never enjoyed such rights ever before. Or, alternatively, it means that there may be a second chance for offenders to do the right thing, which implies that retributive redress is equivalent in principle to respecting rights. Such redress is not always fully realizable of course. This indeed is retribution in its original sense—"*retribuere*" originally meaning "to restore, give back, recompense." This is to be further explained in terms of "rolling back the past." This again implies that not trying to restore the enjoyment of human rights comes down to not respecting such rights at all. Of course this is not at all any license to commit any violations "because they may be undone after all." Doing the right thing to start with is the best option for everyone concerned. Potential victims are to remain free from any setbacks, however temporary. Full payback—if feasible at all—is rather more expensive for offenders than more or less simply sticking to the rules.

Further explanation and recommendation of this is done as follows. The next section offers development of resentment on wrongful harm in general to retribution as full redress, as presuppositions of respect and self-respect in any decent society or even as presupposition of any viable society at all. Then I provide a brief sketch of determination of harm and redress, in terms of counterfactual conditionals and the possibility in principle of later benefits compensating for earlier losses. Harm being determined in such fashion in principle, the question remains what distinguishes wrongful harm from harm in general. Next, I show that harmful consequences of human rights violations are incontestably wrongful in the first place and thus need to be redressed as fully as possible. Finally, I offer a succinct agenda concerning the plights and promises of redress, given so many practical limitations on the way to full realization of basic human rights (and rights in general), not just after harm is done. Prevention of any wrongful harm comes first, of course. Anyway not just the basic principles and practice of the International Criminal Court and many more national and international institutions need to be reformed along the lines of retribution as restoration.

From Resentment to Retribution and Respect

What is, or ought to be, the prime human experience, thought or even emotion concerning this so severely limited real existence of human rights, in stark contrast to so overwhelmingly many violations? Resentment about such violations of course, this complex combination of negative judgments and feelings. There may be compassion for victims as well, though such victims generally are too remote both geographically and emotionally to really upset minds and hearts of fellow human beings in more safe and comfortable circumstances.

Also such positive resentment, compassion and hopefully some positive consequences by acting upon them are marginal in so many individuals, societies and cultures determined in part by judgments of inferiority concerning "others." Negative resentment found in nationalisms, ethnocentrisms, religious fanaticisms and worse look for innocent culprits and scapegoats, in the illusion of transferring guilt and annihilating it by harming or even killing such supposedly inferior or even criminal "subhumans." At least in part this is the ancient mechanism of transference of guilt, however much Christianity and other religions tried to religiously redirect this.

Actually this kind of "we versus them" sentiment is more or less well hidden in contemporary revivals of nationalism even in the Western world, more or less explicitly implying lesser value and worth in strangers, with attendant consequences for their supposedly lower status in terms of human rights and otherwise. Even more generally resentment often is a consequence of not feeling sufficiently respected, or even simply of lack of self-respect with all attendant violent consequences, however deeply mistaken such subjective disrespect may be.

Still better hidden behind semblances of legal rationality is resentment against offenders in criminal justice, in the Western world and otherwise. Part of such justice is driven by primitively instinctive sentiments of payback in terms of tit for tat, a natural consequence of resentment indeed. In more civilized forms this is institutionalized as retribution, letting offenders suffer because they wrongly made others suffer (if they did so at all). Criminal justice may be indispensable in the real world, but not for such reasons. What is retribution by hurting criminal offenders more than just causing more suffering in the world?

Here it is taken for granted that retribution to be effected by letting offenders suffer is deeply mistaken. Offenders' suffering may be a byproduct of restorative activities by these same offenders, not always willing as they are to voluntarily realize full redress. But the very idea of offenders' suffering making up for victims' suffering is a category mistake at best, whatever quasi-philosophical or even theological attempts to justification of such suffering have been proffered (see on this more extensively Kaptein 2004).

Then of course even in decent societies there is so much more resentment more or less hidden behind (not always) polite appearances. In fact negative resentment is overwhelming in so many lives even in the so-called developed world, as complexes of judgment and feeling however irrational and ultimately harmful to selves and others that respect is insufficiently paid, that rightful desserts are not earned, that others receive what ought to be enjoyed by so resentful subjects themselves, that opportunities are wrongfully withheld, that others undeservedly ended up higher in ranks and hierarchies, and so on and so on. Such sentiments may be apposite at times, as reactions to real injustice, but then most of the time they are to no good at all of course, again including scapegoating others.

How to do away with so much destructive resentment, then? How can we redirect such negative energies? Still there is no viable society without resentment in a rather different and more positive sense, related not to false semblances of subjective wrongs but to unquestionable norms of human society. This may be briefly explained as follows.

Imagine somebody not taking any notice at all at being wrongfully harmed. Thus an offender may negligently hurt a victim, for example by stumbling over her without apparent necessity. A normal and mentally healthy reaction would be expression of personal resentment, or heartfelt disapproval of being wronged. Bystanders may supplement this with expression of moral resentment as expression of compassion and solidarity. Without such experiences and expressions of resentment, potential victims set no limits to what others may do to them, just as they will feel left alone by the rest of the world in the absence of anyone else's expression of moral resentment. There may be wide-ranging varieties of wrongful harm and resentful reactions to it of course. Still basic patterns will be identical.

Resentment may be misplaced, among other things because offenders could not have done otherwise. If "hard" determinism excluding any freedom of actions and attendant liability holds good, no offender could ever have done otherwise. This again excludes resentment, a well-nigh unimaginable option. Anything would go, no negative reaction to it would ever be apposite.

Such absence of any limits to offenders in order to respect victims is incompatible with any viable society lived by respecting and self-respecting fellow human beings indeed. This is Strawson's justly famous anti-determinist (or better, compatibilist) argument as first set out in 1962 and further explained in 1983, here in a nutshell of course. Indeed if any determinism really excluding free will would be true, any human rights talk or for that matter any thought and action would be meaningless anyway. Then thoughts and things happen as they happen, without any option of changing them for better or worse. So resentment on really wrongful harm cannot be done away with, not even in principle. And certainly not so if resentment is to lead to positive consequences, supplementing and surpassing its function as expression of limits to be observed.

Indeed Strawson's argument may be further developed as follows. What would be optimal reactions to resentment as a necessary consequence of wrongful harm? To start with, offenders noticing such resentment ought to offers apologies and, if need arises, forced to do so some other way by communities thus giving further form to their moral resentment. Words, however sincerely meant, may not be enough, so next offenders ought to remedy wrongful harm done some other way. Again, they may not do this voluntarily. So personal and moral resentment may be driving forces behind making offenders pay. If they do so in the end, to the satisfaction of both victims and others concerned, reconciliation may be the naturally positive consequence.

This is retribution in its original sense, as payback. Offenders are not so much to suffer for what they did wrong, but they are to pay for it, by restorative measures and/or by payment of money from their own pockets. Thus the original balance may be restored. This is far superior of course to making offenders suffer by punishment or otherwise, without any really positive result for victims or others. Still imposition of restorative measures may lead to hardships for offenders, a probably not unwelcome byproduct of redress by such offenders themselves. Such deserved hardships may also serve to make an end to any remaining resentment, personal and/or moral.

Though both Kant and Hegel espoused comparable lines of thought in holding offenders liable for retributive reasons, as famously culminating in Hegel's philosophy of law (1821: section 100), one important difference with the view expounded here is this change from destructive retribution effected by making offenders suffer to constructive retribution by making offenders pay back.

If full retribution as redress has been effected, forgiveness may be superfluous. Forgiving someone for something presupposes some or other debt not made good. So no debts imply nothing to be forgiven, probably apart from forgiving in the sense of communicating former victims' reconciliation with their harmful histories, including offenders. This is rather idealistic of course as well. Still there ought to be no mercy as long as there are any realistic options for redress left. Remember that nobody is entitled to being forgiven anyway.

This ideal of handling wrongful harm is not often realized of course. Also even with the best of intentions there may be so many variables intervening with desirable sequences from wrongdoing to reconciliation. Thus there may not always be full liability for harm done, even if there is free will in principle. Wrongfulness of harm done may be debatable, according to legal, moral or whatever normative standards. And/or there may be no real harm at all. If there is really wrongful harm and full liability for it no full redress or even no redress at all may be available, as a consequence of the nature of the harm and/or as a consequence of offenders' inability to offer adequate redress. Think (just think!) here of causing paralysis, blindness and other irreversible physical and/or mental injury.

Still there is no respect and self-respect without sincere attempts to live up to sequences of resentment and redress. Offenders are respected in ascribing agency and liability to them, just as victims are respected by not leaving them alone with harm they did not deserve. Thus respect and self-respect do not just presuppose some or other freedom of action as explained above, but also consequences of such freedom of action in terms of adequate reactions to wrongful harm. Not to be discussed here is resentment's important and equally oftentimes unheeded counterpart: gratitude as one more cement of decent society.

Please note that these preconditions and realizations of respect and self-respect do not presuppose any religious, let alone quasi-religious concepts and conceptions of sin, repentance and atonement. Quite to the contrary. However important such parts of religion may be and apart from dangerous fanaticisms as noted above, it would seem a debasement of any religion to take it that adequate answers to wrongful harm done may only be found in the word of God.

Both believers and non-believers had better first heed their human duties and obligations before turning to God in order to find right answers in fact already given with human existence—created by God, by nature or in whichever way. So beware of any religious excuses in terms of false forgiveness and otherwise in attempts to evade human responsibilities and act upon human resentment as victim and as offender if any positive need rises. God may forgive everything in the end, human beings had better not.

Resentment and its positive consequences is one important and in fact indispensable expression of compassion or even love. Offenders not held liable may end up being treated as things instead of as fellow human beings. Moral resentment as active solidarity with victims is love (*agape*) in a still more direct sense. Feeling and acting upon it all is trying to realize the (God's?) kingdom on earth, however, remote it may ever remain.

So resentment is not just a bad thing. Quite to the contrary. That is, as long as it is properly understood and acted upon, as a consequence of wrongful harm. As Kant famously noted, if only in his posthumously published writings (after 1804: 36):

> Niemals empört etwas mehr, als Ungerechtigkeit; alle anderen Übel, die wir ausstehen, sind nichts dagegen.
>
> [Nothing fills more with indignation than injustice does; all other evils borne by us are nothing compared to it.]

A driving force, such rightful resentment one might hope.

What is Harm—And Who is to Redress it?

Indeed the complex concept of harm deserves some further explanation. Harm is a much wider concept than wrongful harm of course. Fair competition and so much other more or less rightful human conduct may lead to major and even irreparable harm, just as unspeakable harm may be irreversibly done by moral wrongs committed by parents to children. Though legally irrelevant in many cases, still such harms may be major and well-nigh irreversible factors in human lives, even compared to harm for which legal redress may be obtained. Also, such harm, however strongly felt, may be difficult to define at all, just as measures and extents of subjective harm may be hard to determine.

Discussion here is to be limited to wrongful harm, to be redressed some or other way. Leaving further determination of wrongfulness to a later section, harm is here to be understood as "the difference between the world including a cause leading to a less valuable world, and a world without such a cause and its consequences, other things equal."

This of course is a counterfactual conception of harm, as discussed by Feinberg, Coleman and others (see Gardner 2012). This conception competes with a number of others, among which differential conceptions are predominant: harm as the negative difference between the harmful situation and the situation before harm set in. Here this discussion is not really relevant, however much the counterfactual conception seems superior in more than a few respects – which is not to imply that it is completely unproblematic (see again Gardner 2012 for a good overview).

The difference implied in this counterfactual conception must be negative some or other way, in terms of material, monetary and/or emotional losses. In simple cases like harm caused by theft of a pushbike, things may be none too complex. Redress comes down to return of the bike "as it was" plus adequate compensation for the victim's temporary inability to ride the bike. Many cases of legally wrongful harm may be handled like this. Harm may also be future harm, not just as a consequence of breach of contract. Rightful opportunities may be wrongfully harmed. Thus temporary bodily and/or emotional harm may result in inability to work.

Bodily and/or emotional harm may not be undone at all, given the state of the art of medicine and psychotherapy. Thus a youthful road accident victim may receive compensation not so much on the basis of any really incalculable prediction of two different futures, but on the basis of what is needed to secure a humanly acceptable future, given the handicaps caused by the accident.

Oftentimes payment of money is the only "remedy," in order to compensate for at least part of the harm done, however indirectly. But money cannot pay for everything of course, certainly not so in cases of serious damage done to physical and/or mental health or even to life. Though many jurisdictions do not allow for compensation of wrongful death, harm done by it is beyond any imaginable compensation of course.

Still the ideal of redress is recreation of victims' original positions, as if nothing bad happened at all. To return to less dramatic harm: the pushbike owner may well forget about the theft after he receives the bike back, plus compensation for temporary loss, or even receives a new bike at the thief's expense. The victim's knowledge of the thief having to dearly pay for the wrongful harm done may also make an end to any resentment on the violation of the victim's rights, as already briefly explained.

This leads to a still stronger reason to make offenders and nobody else pay for wrongful losses inflicted. One reason for this is restoration of relationships of respect and self-respect after harmful wrongdoing, as previously explained. Victims are to be taken seriously as wrongfully harmed, to be paid for in a wide sense by offenders who accept liability and thus may be regarded as categorically more than just passive parts of nature, by others and by themselves.

But a probably less noticed consequence of the counterfactual conception of harm is that duties to redress by offenders are more or less equivalent to such offenders' duties to refrain from doing harm in the first place. Or: there is a very strong agent relationship concerning redress if harm is taken to be the difference between a rightful and a wrongful world. Redress indeed comes down to creating the original rightful situation, as if the norm prohibiting inflicting harm was not violated at all. Or: full redress by offenders is materially equivalent to compliance with relevant norms.

This leads to a still stronger agent relationship than quasi-Kantian conceptions like Weinrib's (2012) imply. Again the pushbike theft may serve as an example:

> Original norm: Stealing is wrong
>
> Specific implication: x (the offender) ought not to steal this bike, or:
>
> x ought to leave the rightful situation as it is
>
> After the offense: x still ought not to have stolen the bike, or:
>
> x ought to recreate the rightful situation, as if he had abided by the norm.

Thus offenders get a second chance to do what they ought to do. This makes duties to offer redress equivalent to original duties not to harm in principle. (As a consequence such duties are not just on a par with freely incurred obligations as pertaining to breach of contract and the like.)

So offenders are in a special position in undoing harm, not just as a consequence of needs to restore victims' and offenders' respect and self-respect as outlined above. These are much stronger reasons for making offenders pay in the first place than that third parties are not to pay for costs they did not create and/or deserve to bear. Thus the principled identity of doing the right thing and restoring rightful realities pleads against any spread of losses as a consequence of wrongful harm, for economic and/or other reasons (but see also the last section for state and international liability for human rights and thus for human rights violations).

Also note that this conception of the agent relationship concerning wrongful harm does not depend on any unjust enrichment and attendant duties to restitution as a consequence of wrongful harm done. Though the bike case suggests this, it may easily be changed in terms of wrongful harm without any offenders' gains, with the very same result: full payback is identical to doing the right thing from the start. Think here of grievous bodily harm (apart from offenders' doubtful satisfaction in having wrongfully harmed).

What makes redress of harm like this possible at all? How may history be reversed, the past rolled back in a positive sense? This at least presupposes something positive offered now and/or in the future "to make up" for something negative in the past, however much negative consequences may last, sometimes for a whole lifetime.

To again start with stolen pushbikes: restoring things as they ought to be may indeed make victims simply forget that they were wronged at all. Though harm and redress are not coincident in time—or there would be no harm at all—human experience of time and human oblivion does the job of combining them in principle. It is also enabled by human capacities to perceive the past in terms of the present and the future. Negative pasts may be compensated by better present and future circumstances. Or even: real redress changes perceptions of the past for the better, against the fatalism of history as forever unchangeable. "Yes it did happen, but no more so, in a way …"

Man is more than past, present and future. As Kant (1787: 408f.) and others rightly expressed it, being a person implies consciousness of identity in time. Kant's even better-known concept of persons as ends in themselves, as *Menschheit*, again relates to harmed persons being entitled to rightful conduct by others, including forbearance of wrongful harm.

Thus redress is equivalent to prevention of harm as well, in changing the courses of history and of the future for the better. In fact and at least in subjective senses all experience of harm is present and future, a remembrance of harmful things past and/or as direct experience of continuing harm as a consequence of physical handicaps or otherwise. Redress thus ought to be aimed at redirecting such experience for the better, ideally as if no harm happened at all.

Or less harm maybe, as stolen pushbikes are no paradigms for real harm done to human beings. Wrongful death, by murder or otherwise, cannot be undone in principle by whatever measures of redress. "The creditor is no longer there …" just as surviving fellow human beings have to live with a loss for ever. The list of such irreversible losses is long. Still something may be done even in such dramatic cases, in order to undo at least parts of harm done, however marginally so.

This ideal identity of forbearance and redress surely does not imply that living by the rules does not matter as long as any harm done is fully compensated for. At least so far as offenders are concerned, doing the right thing to start with is rather less expensive in the great majority of cases than compensating harm done afterwards. Victims may well prefer undisturbed lives, whatever learning there may be in experiencing harm and however far-reaching redress may be.

Harm may be aggravated by the passage of time. Even in simple cases like theft victims' prolonged impossibility to make good use of belongings concerned makes things worse and worse. A few minutes without a rightfully owned pushbike or whatever is nothing compared to having to rent another bike for months, and so on. Thus doing the right thing from the start or redressing things as soon as possible remains the best thing to do. (Whether legal practice and for that matter human practice in general really reflects this is quite another matter of course.)

On the other hand wrongful harm may have been done so long ago that passage of time made such harm less felt or even disappear altogether. Still negative resentment may survive any possibly related harm and lead to new wrongful harm done against "culprits" or their descendants, however remote. This is major harm in itself then, like so much more destructive resentment (see the second section).

Then there are practical limitations to full-scale redress in so many cases of wrongful harm. Even if offenders may be able to offer full redress, the question remains whether burdens of payback may be borne by them to a full extent. Thus an offender having wrongly pulled an emergency train brake may be ruined by having to pay full compensation, probably too high a price to be paid for such an offense, however serious. Who is or are to pay for the rest, then? (See again the last section on the need for public compensation funds.)

"Ought implies can" and/or at least "ought implies some or other reasonable balance" might indeed be countered against this supposed equivalence of doing the right thing from the start and offering full redress after wrongdoing. Take the emergency brake case: the original rule ("to be pulled in emergency cases only") is easy to live by and a rational rule for a couple of more reasons. *Ex post facto* however, the price to be paid for still sticking to the rule may become rather high. Thus regarded the original rule may be translated as "Do not pull the emergency brake for nothing and pay (say) 250,000 euros at that." (In fact this amount of damages to be paid was estimated in a civil case concerning a train wrongly brought to a halt in the Netherlands.)

Or are these extra costs to constitute the probably desired punitive effect of redress by offenders? As noted before, such plights of redress and their less than pleasurable consequences for offenders may be welcome to victims and others. Still there is no principled justification for it yet. "But offenders deserve it" may be brought in against this. Right, but then material equivalence of doing the right thing from the start and offering full redress as if nothing happened was specifically designed to explain this kind of retributive dessert. Full circle? Not yet, but still there may be some work to be done here, scholarly and otherwise.

Note that this strongly agent-related conception of liability does not by itself imply any ready-made solution to related problems of free will and intention as preconditions of duties to redress either. Think of a bus driver's lack of attention unintentionally killing several passengers, or any small fault however avoidable in principle but still leading to serious harm. Such offenders may not be burdened with full costs of harm done, apart from their inability to pay for such costs in most cases. Also there may be serious harm as a consequence of marginal wrongdoing only. Again, insurance and/or public fund money may pay for at least part of the costs. Possibly complex issues of causation need to be solved as well (see also Kaptein 1999).

Do such offenders' duties to redress as a well-nigh logical consequence of norms protecting against wrongful harm do away with the rather more complex sequence from wrongful harm and resentment to reconciliation as outlined earlier? Probably not so, for several reasons. Most offenders and victims may not be aware of any direct connection between norms protecting against wrongful harm and offenders' duties to recreate rightful situations as if nothing happened. This direct connection may not be really strong anyway, as discussed in terms of the emergency brake case, and thus may need to be supplemented by a more explicitly retributive "logic" of wrongful harm and offenders' duties to make up for it—as indeed outlined earlier.

Also, important expressive and signaling functions of personal and moral resentment cannot be done away with. Remember respect and self-respect presupposing expression of resentment as setting limits to what may be done to oneself and to others, just as offenders need to be notified of their wrongdoing and of their duties to realize adequate redress. Other factors in the sequence of resentment on wrongful harm to redress and reconciliation are important for respect and self-respect as well.

Indeed offenders having to restore original rightful realities is an issue of retributive justice as explained earlier. Thus there are no direct implications concerning distributive justice of such rightful realities. Of course such realities may be deeply unjust in themselves, but this is another issue, relating of course to human rights issues in several respects. Thus a pushbike thief may think he is entitled to owning and riding a bike. Being too poor to buy one himself he resorts to stealing, thus realizing some sort of distributive justice by violating retributive justice. May this be justified, not just concerning pushbikes but also concerning basic material presuppositions of a decent life? Maybe so, in extreme circumstances, not to be further discussed here (but see the last section on the need for more distributive justice in the world as well).

A main point is and remains that retributive justice is nothing special, at least not concerning redress of wrongful harm. Retribution is nothing else than doing the right thing after all, however much more troublesome this may be afterwards, compared to doing the right thing in time, or better—from the start. Again: why then is the need for retribution universally understood as the necessity of making offenders suffer? What kind of wrongheaded resentment may be behind this? Again: how can we redirect human energies in more constructive and creative directions? (Contractual retributive justice may be another matter, not to be further discussed here.)

Still this all may not really impress the practical minded. A natural reaction may be: all of this philosophizing is too complex, however logically sound and even mandatory it may seem on paper. But then practical philosophy may be and in fact ought to be more than so-called futilitarianism. Without elementary good reasons regarding retribution and redress by offenders any practical remedies lack clear guidelines in principle.

Respect for Human Rights is Respect for Retribution

Having ever so slightly clarified concepts and conceptions of harm and offenders' duties to offer full redress, one major remaining question is what makes harm wrongful at all. Indeed so much harm as experienced by man all over the world is not wrongfully inflicted, by legal, moral or whatever relevant standards. Think here of physical and emotional suffering due to illnesses caused by not always traceable internal or external factors. So what are standards of wrongfulness here? Different legal and moral systems imply different criteria, yet still there may be incontestably common ground, constituted by human rights (rights of man, fundamental rights) and their supposed universal validity.

Sure enough ever-expanding catalogues of human rights, on paper and in (international) jurisdictions may lead to doubts concerning their real standing. Still a common core may be assumed. Human rights are presuppositions of a human life worth living, in whatever minimal sense. Benn expressed this as follows (in 1967): "Human rights, in short, are statements of basic needs or interests." No life can be worthwhile without enforceable guarantees, against governments and others, to physical integrity, freedom of thought and action and minimal means of subsistence. Thus the Declaration of Independence of the United States posits inalienable rights to life, liberty and the pursuit of happiness. "The three p's" are often mentioned, as the fundamental rights to "person, property and promise." Or: there is no means of subsistence without some or other kind of personal property and enforceability of contract. The further development of human rights led to well-known distinctions between liberty rights, political rights, and social, economic and cultural rights (see on this more extensively Kaptein 1993).

Human rights may not be curtailed in favor of other rights and interests without overriding necessities, to be expressed in terms of human rights themselves, otherwise such rights would not be fundamental rights. Also, fundamental necessities of life and thus fundamental rights are relatively invariant in different cultures, though social, economic and cultural rights may have a less absolute status.

But still, why respect basic human needs and interests and thus human rights? Among so many more important reasons, because man is a Kantian end in himself, as already noted, or even because man is god himself, as so movingly suggested not just by Epictetus (around 100 AD) and other Stoics. Also enjoyment of such rights is a basic presupposition for respect and self-respect, the highest human good according to Rawls (1999). Remember respect and self-respect also presupposing resentment on wrongful harm and adequate reactions to it, as outlined earlier. Who could not resent being thwarted in human rights? Nobody could, without giving up dignity as a person.

Human rights are not just an issue of personal dignity, but of any viable and decent society as well. Thus criticisms against human rights as too individualistic miss the point. Any human society ought to consist of fellow human beings respecting each other. At least such mutual respect and self-respect presupposes full individual enjoyment of human rights. Otherwise there would be nobody to be really respected, just as there would be nobody really able to respect anybody else from anything like a really self-respecting standpoint. Again, human rights are not enough, certainly not so for any viable and decent society. But anti-human rights criticism as voiced by communitarians and other "anti-individualists" is self-contradictory in the end. There can be no decent society at all without mutual respect at least in terms of human rights (see on this as well Kaptein 1993).

Human rights imply duties of everybody concerned not to thwart or even violate them. This is another side of human rights presupposing human society. Indeed such rights certainly are not an issue between citizens and official bodies only. Everybody and every body is expected to respect human rights and to offer full redress after violation of them. Still official bodies are on different footings here, as they of course are to actively further human rights like rights to freedom of expression, political rights and rights to material subsistence for which individuals cannot be held responsible directly.

Still such individuals can contribute to official bodies' respect for human rights, by making good use of political liberties in favoring governments taking human rights seriously—not just for its own citizens but all over the world.

Criminal justice on the other hand is in part designed to protect individuals against other individuals and bodies in terms of human rights as well, however implicit this may be in many jurisdictions. Other kinds of law and legal practice ought to serve comparable purposes, though legal realities still leave something to be desired even in the so-called developed world.

Indeed human rights are violated on grand scales, particularly so in the developing world. If anything is wrongful harm, this is it. Human rights need not even be expressly at stake: so many crimes are direct or indirect human rights violations as well. Again, as in any case of wrongful harm, full retribution as if nothing happened is the only really adequate answer. Here too duties to retribution are on a par with duties implied by human rights as such. Thus retribution is a presupposition of human rights in the real world or even a human right in itself. Human rights make no real sense without retribution.

Human rights or for that matter rights in general are not respected at all if there is no enforcement of them by whatever adequate measures, retributive or otherwise. Furthering human rights thus means redressing human rights violations as well, not just trying to guarantee them for the future. Here too offenders ought to do what they should have done in the first place. A second chance is no less a chance for enjoyment of human rights, or whatever rights in principle. If human rights are to be taken seriously, protection and redress are fundamental human duties, overriding other human pursuits in principle. Again respecting human rights in advance, like avoidance of any wrongful harm, is superior to any realization by retribution as if nothing happened, however perfectly executed.

Agenda

How to implement this, in a world so obviously unjust at least in terms of human rights? Indeed remarks here are limited to human rights issues, leaving alone realization by retribution or otherwise of so many other rights and rightful interests. Even within these confines, the task of realization by retribution seems superhuman, still apart from the need to pay full attention to realization of human rights even if there has been no violation of them at all yet. But doing nothing is no option of course, just as it is clear enough that actual efforts fall far short of what ought to be done. That is, what ought to be done if human rights are to be taken seriously in having priority over other rights and interests.

Indeed all too common objections against securing human rights all over the world will be only briefly mentioned here. Thus it is oftentimes assumed that nobody is really responsible for strangers, at least not in the sense of any duty of care for human beings not belonging to the same national, ethnic and/or religious group. This is nationalism and worse of course, as briefly expounded earlier. Such a stance is nothing else than blunt denial of the very idea of human rights to be enjoyed by any human being qua human being.

Again, a probably unwelcome implication would be that such nationalists and worse are not entitled to human rights themselves either, at least not in their own universalist terms and as long as they are to be qualified as human beings. Human rights are for everybody, so denial of human rights to anyone implies human rights for nobody at all.

The very idea of human rights implies the need to broaden moral points of view, from kin, people, religion and nation to humankind as such. Still it may be difficult to even imagine that one's own descendants are not entitled to more human rights than others in principle. Such equality entails consequences for distribution of human goods and services in order to protect basic human rights all over the world. Few if any citizens of the world appear to be really ready to bear such consequences (see on this Singer 1995).

This is the deep discord of modern man in well-to-do circumstances "being everywhere," by modern means of travel and telecommunication, but still being primarily "home alone," by withholding solidarity from so many others missing elementary preconditions for living, not just in terms of human rights grossly and continuously violated. *Philia* is not so readily developed into *agape* here as well.

Also there are vociferous objections like: we earned our own money and riches by good hard work ourselves, why give them away to strangers for nothing? Leaving aside the silliness of the "for nothing" here it is to be noted earning any serious money is made possible by institutional structures offering protection and opportunities in terms of human rights and otherwise without which nothing could be earned and accumulated at all. This kind of deeply mistaken distributive or even retributive justice cannot stand in the way of sharing of at least some profits with others, in order to at least safeguard basic preconditions for decent lives—which is what human rights are about.

A mirror image of this is to claim that it happened by "their own fault," as if so many fellow human beings being killed, maimed, starved and deprived of other basic human rights are to blame for this themselves. Even vague notions of collective responsibility are invoked, like "they simply do not want to improve things, so leave them alone."

Or, if real need to do something about human rights violations is conceded, "why me" and other kinds of special pleading may pop up in last attempts to ward off unwelcome costs. This varies from "Personal exertions and sacrifices won't make any real difference" to "Let the state and/or international organizations see to this, which is not any individual's business." At least any more or less well-to-do fellow citizen in the so-called developed world may make good use of political rights to further governments and other official bodies taking human rights seriously, just as personal funding of human rights development aid may do much good.

These well-nigh endless varieties of special pleading may be confounded with rather more meaningful issues of priorities and factual possibilities. Does it really make sense to try at any expense to realize human rights, by redressing violations and otherwise, in far away and hostile environments? Might means to be spent on that be better used on more viable projects less far away? And so on.

Even apart from so many self-servingly senseless objections against furthering human rights in the world, part of which is securing just and effective redress, such retribution faces serious problems of course. For the greater part these difficulties are still graver varieties of problems with retribution in general, as briefly discussed earlier—which does not make such problems less serious of course.

Ideally, perpetrators of crimes against humanity and other human rights violators are to be taken to task in being forced to fully redress what they did wrong. This is what retribution as realization of duties *ex post facto* by offenders themselves amounts to after all. But then most offenders simply go free of course and even if they are brought before some or other court they may get away with it by lack of legally sufficient evidence.

Second, so many human rights violations cannot be redressed at all as if nothing happened. The dead will not be resurrected, physical, mental and emotional handicaps incurred as a consequence of human rights violations cannot be done away with by whatever measures of redress, however consoling and comforting for victims. This is nothing new of course, though it may again serve to show the superiority of not violating such rights in the first place and forcing everybody concerned to really respect them.

Third, there may be complex issues of causation concerning human rights violations as well. On the one hand there are completely clear cases of state officials calmly and deliberately orchestrating large-scale torture and murder of "enemies of the people," including women and children. On the other hand there are historical vagaries concerning well-nigh intractable causal links between factors like slavery in the past and extreme poverty constituting material human rights violations today—however deeply wrong such slavery was of course (but see also Nozick's radical conception of backward-looking transgenerational justice, as expounded by him in 1974).

Fourth, this again is related to wrongful harm, however serious, "disappearing" in ever receding pasts, in lifetimes and through successive generations. Harm may be aggravated by doing nothing about it, just as it may sooner or later disappear into oblivion. Slavery may still be strongly resented by victims' descendants, but then such resentment may do more harm than any real influence of wrongful pasts may still do. This is not to belittle slavery of course, which is still a reality all over the world today. Still the principle is and remains that not realizing full redress for human wrongs is equivalent to continuing violation of human rights.

Fifth, so many human rights violations however obvious and however obviously to be ascribed to specific and fully intentional offenders taken to task may not be redressed by such offenders themselves in any way. Nobody is able to pay up for immeasurable losses caused by killing, maiming and other monstrous crimes. Even life sentences executed until the very end cannot make up for any such harm—just as any punishment as infliction of suffering may satisfy victims and others in some sense but still cannot redress any harm by itself. Penal servitude would be a better answer in principle, however little it may make good as well (see again Kaptein 2004).

So who is to pay for the rest? To the extent that offenders may not be forced to offer adequate retribution, for whatever reasons? May not states and/or international bodies be liable, at least because they did not live up to their primary duty to protect citizens and other human beings against violation of human rights? Then such liability may imply states' and/or international bodies' duty to supplement redress in as far as feasible.

The agent relationship is important here as well, as states and international bodies not protecting human rights against offenders violate such rights as well. Again this puts the redress of human wrongs on an equal footing with protection and promotion of human rights. Such redress is essentially more than just aid, developmental or otherwise. Advanced national jurisdictions try to implement this principle (for more on this, see Kaptein 2012).

To be sure, there may be disagreement on ultimate responsibilities and liabilities here. But then the enormous scale of direct and indirect human rights violations in the world, including the well-nigh universal absence of redress, retributive or otherwise, urges anybody to at least try to do something about it. Otherwise the supposed universality of human rights is not taken seriously at all.

Anybody taking the slightest notice of chilling statistics on unnecessary suffering and death in the world as summarized by Ziegler (2011) may realize that something needs to be done, not just in terms of human rights and retribution for human wrongs, but also and primarily in terms of distributive justice, withheld from so many fellow human beings.

This requires institutional and other reforms. Even basic declarations on victims' rights concerning human rights violations as issued by the United Nations in 1985 fall rather short of requirements of redress as retribution. Even on such lofty paper victims of human rights violations are left alone with major parts of wrongful harm done to them, just as offenders and others to be held liable go free in principle. The International Criminal Court and other International Courts of Justice, criminal or otherwise, ought to be further developed in terms of retribution as real protection of human rights. Crimes against humanity in the first place are to be sanctioned by adequate redress at the cost of perpetrators, including states and other official bodies.

However doubtful effects of development aid may be, the best solution may not be to further curtail or even stop it but to better inquire into ends and means and do something about it, passing over so many vested interests in this field. Even if so many human rights violations cannot be redressed, securing a materially more acceptable future for fellow human beings may also serve as a kind of compensation for having been deprived of human rights.

This all leaves national and international reforms in more fortunate parts of the world probably less important, including well-nigh endless discussion of it. Still serious crimes and torts may be human rights violations as well, implicitly or even explicitly so. Apart from this, any wrongful harm ought to be redressed by offenders in the first place, though state liability may supplement this on national levels as well. What stands in the way? Criminal justice wrongly focused on making offenders suffer, instead of forcing them to do what they ought to do after all, too strict separations between criminal justice and tort law, and so on. But again, in terms of scale this may be more or less left as it is, however far from ideal it may be (see again Kaptein 2004, for detailed reform proposals).

To briefly return to issues of respect and self-respect, probably the fundamental values in life, presupposing not just unhindered enjoyment of human rights but so many and partly intractable factors; real self-respect is also furthered by real respect for others, however remote emotionally and geographically. What else is having and acting upon a real conscience? *Conscientia*, "knowledge together," the active consciousness that we are not alone in this world and thus may do something good even for complete strangers without any self-serving intentions at all. This is what Kant—and not just Kant of course—meant by *Menschheit*.

So we should strive to turn all personal resentment, so much negative energy, into moral resentment, against real wrongs, wherever committed. This requires more than scholarly writing and its rationality. It requires less vanity and more imagination.

And remember the main message here. Not redressing human wrongs is nothing more or less than letting them continue. If retribution really is restoration of original rightful situations by offenders themselves in the first place, then anything done about that is on equal footing with protection and furtherance of human rights in general—the one thing to do from a moral, or more simply, a human point of view.

So in the end one may feel ashamed about writing one more hopefully intellectually stimulating chapter, while effort spent on it might have been better directed to help create a better world – not just in furthering human rights but also in making up for any wrongs done by oneself in the first place. Even preachers may forget about their own direct liabilities of course, however petty in comparison to real injustice.

To further belittle this contribution, working on a really better world for all does not just require basic insight into justice—hopefully furthered here—but also the will to give up part of our unnecessary intellectual and other luxuries. Otherwise even Camus' words as written down by him in 1940 (at 135) would be completely futile in the end:

> We must mend what has been torn apart, make justice imaginable again in a world so obviously unjust, give happiness a meaning once more to peoples poisoned by the misery of the century. Naturally, it is a superhuman task. But superhuman is the term for tasks men take a long time to accomplish, that's all.

Bibliography

Benn, S.I. 1967. Rights, in *The Encyclopedia of Philosophy*, edited by J. Edwards. New York: MacMillan and The Free Press.

Camus, A. 1940. Les amandiers, in A. Camus. 1954. *L'Eté*. Paris: Gallimard, and in *Lyrical and Critical Essays*, edited by P. Thody. 1967. New York: Alfred A. Knopf.

Epictetus. 1926. *Diatribai*, in *The Discourses as Reported by Arrian*, edited by W.A. Oldfather. London: Loeb Classical Library, Heinemann.

Gardner, J. 2012. Corrective Justice, Corrected. *University of Oxford Legal Research Paper Series*, 31, 1–26

Hegel, G.W.F. 1821. *Grundlinien der Philosophie des Rechts*. Berlin: Nicolaische Buchhandlung (and later editions).

Ignatieff, M. 2001. *Human Rights as Politics and Idolatry*. Princeton, NJ: Princeton University Press.

Kant, I. [1781] 1787. *Kritik der reinen Vernunft*. Riga: Johann Friedrich Hartknoch (and later editions).

Kant, I. After 1804. Bemerkungen zu den Beobachtungen über das Gefühl des Schönen und Erhabenen, in *Akademie-Ausgabe*, vol. XX. 1942. Berlin: De Gruyter.

Kaptein, H.J.R. 1993. The Morals of Post-Modern Human Rights. *Archiv für Rechts- and Sozialphilosophie*, 51, 154–65.

Kaptein, H.J.R. 1999. Causation, Criminal, in *The Philosophy of Law: An Encyclopedia*, edited by C.B. Gray. New York and London: Garland Publishing, 93–4.

Kaptein, H.J.R. 2004. Against the pain of punishment: On penal servitude and procedural justice for all, in *Crime, Victims and Justice: Essays on Principles and Practice*, edited by H.J.R. Kaptein and M. Malsch. Aldershot: Ashgate, 80–111.

Kaptein, H.J.R. 2012. Victims of inconclusive criminal evidence against offenders: State liability and some more restorative remedies, in *Restorative Justice and Criminal Justice: Exploring the Relationship*, edited by L. Gröning and J. Jacobsen. Stockholm: Santérus Academic Press Sweden, 61–92.

MacIntyre, A.C. [1981] 1984. *After Virtue: A Study in Moral Theory*. London: Gerald Duckworth & Co.

Nozick, R. 1974. *Anarchy, State and Utopia*. New York and Oxford: Basic Books and Basil Blackwell.

Rawls, J. [1971] 1999. *A Theory of Justice*. Cambridge, MA: Belknap Press of Harvard University Press.

Singer, P. 1995. *How Are We to Live? Ethics in an Age of Self-Interest*. New York: Prometheus Books.

Strawson, P.F. 1962. Freedom and resentment. *Proceedings of the British Academy*, also in *Freedom and Resentment, and Other Essays*, edited by P.F. Strawson. 1973. London: Methuen.

Strawson, P.F. 1983. *Skepticism and Naturalism: Some Varieties* (The Woodbridge Lectures). New York: Columbia University Press.

United Nations. 1985. *United Nations' Declaration on the Basic Principles of Justice for Victims of Crime and Abuse of Power*.

Weinrib, E.J. [1995] 2012. *The Idea of Private Law*. Oxford: Oxford University Press.

Ziegler, J. 2011. *Der Aufstand des Gewissens: Die nicht-gehaltene Festspielrede 2011*. Salzburg: Ecowin Verlag.

Chapter 9

The Motivation to Protect and Advance Human Rights: A Faith-Based Approach

Dallas Miller

Introduction: The Foundation of Human Rights—Secular or Religious?

Secularist thinkers continue to pursue the Enlightenment project of eliminating religion from public discourse. To some, religion is a contributing factor to many of today's societal problems. An example is Mark Juergensmeyer's (2000) book *Terror in the Mind of God: The Global Rise of Religious Violence*. Others, such as Anthony J. Lisska (1996), seek to establish a natural law theory devoid of religious content based on the assumption that Enlightenment philosophy alone is the fundamental theory on which human rights are based. However, at the same time it appears that religion is alive and well in the twenty-first century. Works such as Johnston et al. (1994), *Religion, The Missing Dimension of Statecraft*, have become mandatory reading in many diplomatic and political circles. While secularizing modernity believes it has made "progress" since the Enlightenment, it is surprising to many that religion is still a factor and increasingly so in many areas of thought.

While the debate between Enlightenment thinkers and religious adherents continues in today's intellectual and academic circles, it is also seen in the modern human rights movement. In her recent *New York Times* article "The Sacred and the Humane," Anat Biletzki (2011), a philosophy professor at Tel Aviv University, clearly describes the wide gulf between secularists and religionists when it comes to important issues of human rights. Biletzki states that in the area of both justification for human rights and motivation to protect human rights the "religious way" is inadequate and must give way to the secular. After summarizing the religious justification for human rights and comparing that with the secular justification she acknowledges the challenge that secularists face. However, she simply asserts without argument that when it comes to a conflict between religious and secular justifications for human rights, it is the secular that must prevail. After describing the various secular alternatives of Immanuel Kant, H.L.A. Hart, Alan Gewirth and others, Biletzki asserts that the differences between them may be intricate and problematic, but they are all equal to or better than religion in justifying human rights. From this, the author makes the rather bold claim that "there is no philosophically robust reason to accept the claim that human dignity originates with God" and therefore religious claims to justify human rights are to be ignored in favor of the secular.

In this chapter, we will first show that secularism has serious difficulties in motivating realistic human rights protection. This weakness in secular human rights theory can be strengthened by looking at a faith-based approach to human rights. We will then offer three arguments to show that a faith-based approach may very well be a superior alternative.

The Failure of Secularism to Motivate Human Rights Protections

Justification or the philosophical foundation for human rights is not the focus of this chapter. Nevertheless, it is difficult to deal with human rights theory without some comment on the foundational aspect of human rights.

It is not my intention to critique Biletzki's secular approach to *justifying* human rights or the secular grounding of human rights generally. Others have undertaken such a critique and have performed it well. Authors such as Michael J. Perry in *Toward a Theory of Human Rights* (2007) and John Montgomery in *Human Rights and Human Dignity* (1986) provide some of the best analysis and critiques of attempts to justify human rights from a secular basis alone.

That aspect of Biletzki's article which is of interest here has to do with the *motivation* to protect human rights. She asserts that religiously motivated people fail to really work well in the field of human rights:

> The end-product, the human rights *activity*, is similar, even identical; but the reason, the intention, the motivation for it are distinctly different. Does that matter?
>
> I think it does. I dare say that religion, even when indirectly in the service of human rights, is not really working for human rights. Although there is recognition of the human as sacred, it is not the concept of *rights* that propels the religious person. For him, the human status of sacredness draws from divine creation and directive, from man (and woman) having been created in God's image, and therefore has nothing to do with a human right …
>
> The parallel turn to God puts our actions under his command; if he commands a violation of human rights, then so be it. There is no meaning to human *rights* under divine commandment. A deep acceptance of divine authority – and that is what true religion demands – entails a renunciation of human rights if God so wills.

It is interesting that Biletzki's (2011) critical analysis of religiously motivated human rights advocates in the abstract fails to acknowledge motivation from the secularist side. A review of all major systems that seek to justify human rights principles reveals that they all suffer from a common problem, that is, the inability to properly motivate individuals to advance and protect human rights ideals. One author, Montgomery (1986: 214) has summarized this problem as follows:

> … not a single major philosophy of human rights is able to supply the motivation needed to carry out even its own best ideals. Utilitarianism, were it to identify and prove what is truly useful for human beings (which it does not), would still not be able to motivate them to choose the useful. Neo-Kantian rights theories tell us, inter alia, that we ought to act in accord with the generic rights of the recipient as well as of ourselves (Gewirth); but we are given no inner stimulus to ethical universalization. Policy orientation is incapable of motivating the individual or the society to carry out what it claims (and, incidentally, has not proven) to be desirable policies. Marxism is caught in the vicious conceptual circle of believing that external economic factors are the ultimate source of all violations of human dignity; its refusal to face the dark side of human nature leaves it powerless to find any means of changing human beings from within so that they will no longer exploit each other.

Biletzki touches on the two aspects of human rights that have plagued human rights scholars: human rights theory (justification for human rights) and human rights activism (motivation to advance and to protect human rights). Various attempts to bridge the gap have been made. Those who would describe themselves as human rights activists spend their time defending the vulnerable and oppressed and, when necessary, appeal to international declarations or covenants. The appeal to principles contained in international law by activists is often as far as it goes. They rarely, if ever, seek to justify those principles. On the other hand, human rights theorists do little in the work of activism but seek to establish and support principles that undergird human rights law. Philosophers and political theorists rarely get past the justification of human rights issues. These two groups involved in human rights work display the practical and urgent as opposed to the theoretical and abstract. They display the two sides of the same human rights coin.

However, keeping the two aspects of human rights from deep division is a challenge. In principle these two aspects of human rights work should be well integrated. A practical problem arises when, the human rights activist, in her struggle to protect and advance certain human rights of individuals who are being oppressed, faces difficult issues of justification. Not all the answers are found in the law or the legal principles of international human rights law. If one does not have a proper philosophical grounding in the justification for human rights it can affect the motivation of the activist. For example, if the human rights theorist does not have a valid answer to the cultural relativist who says that human rights activism is not warranted because the principle is not universal the activist ultimately fails.

Political theorist Jack Donnelly seeks to bridge the gap between theory and activism in human rights by way of consensus. His point is that human rights are universal in the sense that they are "almost universally accepted – at least in word, or as ideal standards." Donnelly (2003) claims that the fact that there is near universal acceptance of enumerated rights in international law by the community of nations makes it easy to defend or justify rights on a practical basis. Though near universal acceptance of human rights is a practical step in a good direction, more is needed when one faces the criticisms a rights relativist could easily muster. For example, there is an argument that Donnelly's view is flawed because of the naturalistic fallacy: Donnelly seems to move from the descriptive to the normative or from the "is" to the "ought." Geisler et al. (1990) explains that one can only derive an "ought" from an "is," if the "is" already consists of a moral property. Moving from a moral opinion (is) does not necessarily form a moral property (ought). Universal acceptance does not automatically turn into a universal moral principle. This view is also fallacious because of *consensus gentium*, that is, if all people agree on something it is necessarily true. One cannot establish absolute moral principles in this fashion, and this intellectual shortcoming can work against motivation.

Michael Freeman (1994), who analyzes Donnelly's consensus model and finds it lacking, also reviewed several Kantian and neo-Kantian attempts to justify human rights along with the postmodern human rights theories of Richard Rorty. The reviewer seems to despair that neither Donnelly's consensus model nor neo-Kantian ethics has an answer for the cultural relativist. How can the human rights activist or theorist avoid the charge of moral imperialism without vindicating the philosophical underpinnings of his own principles? On the practical side the answer arrived at by Freeman (1994: 499) is as follows: "Faced with oppressive governments and their cultural relativist apologists, the doctrine that human rights is [*sic*] a precarious historical contingency is a gift to tyrants."

In reviewing Richard Rorty's postmodern approach to ethics on human rights activity Freeman appears even more despairing. Rorty argues that human rights advocates should simply rest on their sentiments or passion and the courage of their convictions! To this rather vacuous support for human rights activism Freeman (1994: 514) responds:

> Undoubtedly, non-rational human qualities, such as sympathy and imagination, are important components of the moral psychology of human rights activism. Human rights practice, however, raises theoretical problems both because human rights violators seek to justify their actions with reasons, and because reflective human rights supporters may find themselves perplexed by moral dilemmas.

To the enlightened secularist, justification of human rights principles is a challenge. Without a proper grounding, motivation becomes even more difficult, yet both are necessary in terms of holistic human rights activity. In answer to the secularist, we wish to put forward three arguments to show why a faith-based justification assists in the motivation to protect and advance human rights. One argument is jurisprudential, one is historical, and one is pragmatic. At the same time we describe the urgency of the human rights situation, especially for the poor in the world. The conclusion drawn from this analysis is that there must be room for a faith-based approach to justify and protect human rights ideals.

A Faith-Based Answer

The Jurisprudential Argument

The modern human rights movement is said to have commenced with the adoption of the Universal Declaration of Human Rights (UDHR) by the United Nations General Assembly on December 10, 1948. This document was adopted without a single dissenting vote by the General Assembly, which is significant, in light of the division between the West and the Soviet Empire that was emerging at the time. While the UDHR is not a binding treaty as later human rights conventions were to become, it has considerable moral authority. It was an announcement to the world, similar to the American Declaration of Independence, that the nations who voted for the Declaration would commit themselves to the goals of freedom, the rule of law and self-government, while at the same time safe-guarding and protecting human rights.

The drafting of the UDHR was originally entrusted to a subcommittee of three members of the 18-member United Nations Commission on Human Rights. The subcommittee consisted of the Chairman of the Commission, Eleanor Roosevelt, Vice-Chairman P.C. Chang, head of the Chinese delegation to the United Nations, and Dr. Charles Malik, the Secretary of the committee, a Lebanese philosopher and diplomat. René Cassin later joined this group and contributed greatly to the final version of the UDHR. The diplomatic skills of Eleanor Roosevelt helped steer the document through difficult political and national objections. It is safe to say that without her leadership the UDHR would not have achieved its final form and would not have met with universal approval. A common thread appears to have been woven through the worldview of each of the main contributors to the UDHR. A recent biographer, Glendon (2010: 24), describes Eleanor Roosevelt's motivation:

> In view of the importance that Eleanor Roosevelt attributed to religion throughout her life, how can one explain that few contributors to the Roosevelt literature have connected her religious beliefs to her well-known empathy? Roosevelt was famously committed to helping the hungry, the homeless, the jobless, the dispossessed, and the victims of war, disease, and injustice. How did that relate to her faith? Jean Elshtain put her finger on the right answer in 1986: "Eleanor Roosevelt's deeply devout and intensely felt religious convictions, her determination to bear witness and to serve as Christ did, and her unabashed openness about all of this, is more of a scandal to us than to her contemporaries."

P.C. Chang was a Chinese Renaissance man who had been a playwright, a musician, educator and diplomat. He was well versed in Chinese culture and was very conversant with Islamic and Western culture. While an adherent to Confucianism, Chang saw the aim of the process in drafting a universal document on human rights to "subdue people with goodness." Charles Malik, the third member of the drafting committee, knew the Christian scriptures well and saw the aim of Chang as a different way of saying what Paul said to the Roman Christians: "Seek not to overcome evil with evil, but overcome evil with good [Romans 12:21]" (Glendon 2002).

This group of three represented both East and West and none of the members of the committee were provincial in their outlook. Roosevelt and Malik were both committed Christians and Chang was a widely read individual whose Confucian philosophy of subduing people with goodness was harmonious with some aspects of New Testament teaching.

The original drafting committee was expanded to include the French lawyer René Cassin, who ultimately received the Nobel Peace Prize for his significant role in the drafting process. The final version of the UDHR was largely due to his legal skills and world view. In replying to the Soviet criticism of rights of individuals over the state, Cassin used a classic natural law argument (Glendon 2002):

> I was very much struck by the statement of our colleague from The Union of Soviet Socialist Republics who several times used the word "interference." … I must state my thoughts very frankly. The right of interference is here; it is here in the (UN) Charter … Why? Because we do not want a repetition of what happened in 1933, where Germany began to massacre its own nationals, and everybody … bowed, saying "Thou art sovereign and master in thine own house."

Cassin's background was truly eclectic. He knew a life of religious bigotry, having grown up during the infamous Dreyfus Affair. He received a devoutly Orthodox Jewish education at the insistence of his devoutly religious mother. From his father, he received the secularist spirit of the French Revolution. Superintending over this was the influence of Catholic friends of his youth who helped him acquire a great respect for Christian thought. Later in life when reflecting upon the philosophical origins of the UDHR, Cassin (1971: 15) asserted that there clearly is a connection between the Jewish Decalogue and the modern human rights movement:

> The first article of the Declaration–for the sake of achieving unanimity–does not contain the affirmation of the "divine origin of man," which several delegations would have wished to insert. It does proclaim, however, that "all human beings are born free and equal in dignity and in rights. They are endowed with reason and with conscience, and should act towards each other in a spirit of brotherhood." Thus, though man is mortal and civilizations come and go, from Biblical times

> to our days, there has been a fixed pivot for the thoughts of all generations and for men of all continents: the equal dignity inherent in the human personality.

Cassin (1971: 25) pays homage to the plurality of other religious influences but concludes with an emphasis on Judeo-Christian Scriptures and its positive impact on history and society:

> Centuries have passed. Judaism has, throughout unparalleled trials, preserved its passion for justice and its desire to contribute to the defense of the rights of men of all races and origins, along the lines of the very principle with which it was entrusted two thousand years ago. The Ten Commandments, the first Code of essential duties of man, have suffered many an outrage in history and continue to suffer. Their moral authority remains intact.

It appears clear, therefore, that the original drafting committee of the UDHR included individuals who were either well-trained in Christian philosophy or who were at least exposed to the Judeo-Christian worldview such that they rebutted and refused to allow a secular or Marxist ideology of human rights to prevail. They also were sure to include terminology that precluded enforcement of Islamic law against apostasy (Glendon 2002: 70).

The universal nature of human rights comes through the UDHR strongly. The drafters seemed to conclude that in order to have a document with strong moral weight, it needed to speak authoritatively on the subject of human rights. The principles of human rights were portrayed as *universal* thereby applying to all nations and all cultures. While present-day relativists and postmodernists pose a problem for universal human rights values it was similar at the time of the drafting of the UDHR. On the eve of the United Nations General Assembly's vote to adopt the Universal Declaration of Human Rights a strongly worded criticism of the document was included in a submission to the draft committee. The American Anthropological Association submitted a statement to the committee stating that respect for the individual must include a respect for cultural differences between individuals. Li (1998) reminds us that by adopting a universal statement or declaration on human rights that applies to all nations and all cultures the American Anthropological Association was of the view that the UN General Assembly would unjustly and unfairly critique cultures. Fortunately, this criticism was ignored, thereby strengthening the foundation for human rights and encouraging their advancement.

The UDHR marked a commencement of stage one of the modern human rights movement. On the heels of the UDHR, the *International Covenant on Civil and Political Rights* and the *International Covenant on Economic, Social and Cultural Rights* were adopted by the UN General Assembly in 1966. By 1976 after sufficient states had ratified the two covenants the three documents then took on the force of international law and became known as the International Bill of Rights. It was at this point that human rights standards and human rights commitments could seriously be discussed. Later in the twentieth century, according to Buergenthal (2006) international treaties and conventions addressing torture, genocide, women's rights, racial discrimination and children's rights rounded out the entire panoply of international human rights standards and norms. This period has been described as the first stage of the modern human rights movement. It was at this stage that standards of protection of human rights and human rights norms were articulated and adopted.

A second stage seems to have occurred both simultaneously and after the completion of the first stage. This second stage saw some Western nations and many developing nations criminalize basic human rights violations and saw the constitutional protection of basic political and civil rights which included due process rights and women's rights. Since the 1960s more and more nations of the developing world brought their national laws into conformity with international human rights norms. One scholarly article describes the conclusion of these first two stages of the modern human rights movement: "As a result, hundreds of millions of the most vulnerable and abused became entitled to global standards of justice and equity under local law" (Haugen et al. 2010: 21). At least that was the assumption.

Reality Check: The Actual State of Human Rights Protections

With the human rights movement having made great strides since the adoption of the UDHR, it is important to ask what is the current state of protection for the weak and vulnerable throughout the world? Notwithstanding the strides made in stages one and two of the human rights movement, it is apparent that much work needs to be done in the area of advancing the rule of law and protection of the poor and ensuring that basic human rights protection exists in the majority of the world. A recent study on the state of the law and its ability to protect the poor in the developing world has disclosed some sobering conclusions.

The United Nations Commission (2008) on Legal Empowerment of the Poor was established by the United Nations for the express purpose of focusing on the link between poverty and the rule of law and human rights. Its findings are quite revealing in terms of the lack of basic human rights protection for much of the world's population. The Commission found that at least four billion people are excluded from the rule of law and basic human rights protection. In other words, the majority of humanity appears to be on the outside looking in. They are unable to count on the protection of basic human rights and the rule of law and thereby cannot count on legal protection to lift themselves out of poverty. Lest the successes of stage one and stage two of the human rights movement blind us to the real problems, one of the conclusions of the Commission (2008: 3) will bring us back to reality:

> Most poor people do not live under the shelter of the law, but far from the law's protection and the opportunities it affords. Informal local norms and the

> institutions govern their lives and livelihoods, and where they are not excluded from the legal system, they are often oppressed by it. Because the poor lack recognized rights they are vulnerable to abuse by authorities that discriminate, seek bribes or take the side of powerful interests who may wish to prevent the poor from competing economically or seek to evict them from their land.

As a result of its work, the Commission has concluded that strengthening the rule of law in nations is paramount to protecting the human rights of the poor. This is the number one priority to eradicate poverty (2008: 20):

> Legal empowerment is anchored in the basic principles of human rights articulated in the Universal Declaration of Human Rights – and the subsequent global and regional international human rights conventions – beginning with Article 1: 'All human beings are born free and equal in dignity and rights.' The implications of this simple statement could not be more profound. Indeed, out of familiar and established principles, comes a radical agenda of legal empowerment, not a technical fix, but an agenda for fundamental reform. All citizens should enjoy effective protection of their basic rights, assets and livelihoods, upheld by law. They should be protected from injustice, whether caused by their fellow citizens or government officials, all of whom – high and low – must be bound by the law.

The Commission realizes that the task of providing legal protection to the vast majority of the world's population through strengthening of the rule of law and protecting and advancing their human rights is not easy. It calls for a multifaceted approach that is consistent with international human rights obligations but gives identity and voice to the poor as part of the reform process. The solution cannot be imposed from outside the country's legal regime, but must be built from the bottom up. The poor themselves must own the reforms and must participate in them in order for those reforms to be effective. Reforming the public justice systems in countries where a large percentage of the population is poor and vulnerable must be the cornerstone of any program to extend basic human rights protection.

The report from the Commission truly expresses a dark side or a failure of the human rights movement. The serious need to empower the poor and establish the rule of law in these parts of the world to give basic human rights protection to those who are not protected now is a monumental task that few human rights advocates are prepared or able to address alone. The task is so large that the Commission itself calls on a broad spectrum of groups to help. From civil society groups and community-based organizations to religious communities, all are requested to focus on this core fundamental challenge to extend the ideals and protection of the UDHR to the majority of the world who do not presently enjoy such protection. While calling on governments as "duty bearers" in human rights terms, the Commission also asks religious communities to play a unique and vital part in translating the moral imperatives of legal empowerment into concrete action (2008: 10).

The report of the Commission on Legal Empowerment of the Poor unwittingly has simply assumed the justification for human rights, but nevertheless touched on one of the key aspects of motivation to protect human rights.

In today's world we have a virtual human rights industry. Never before in human history have we had more international organizations, more boards, laws, tribunals, councils, scholars and activists involved in human rights. At the same time it would appear that we do not have fewer victims or fewer oppressed and vulnerable subjects of human rights abuses. Indeed, there appears to be widespread injustice in all quarters of the globe. The current state of affairs illustrates once again the interplay between human rights justification and human rights motivation. To illustrate this dilemma a review of a historic human rights issue is worth noting.

The Historical Argument

The illegality of slavery is clear. Although slavery was commonplace in much of human history, individuals like William Wilberforce in England following many years of battle saw the passage of an Act of Parliament that ended the British slave trade in 1807. Wilberforce's tireless work and that of his many supporters was the catalyst that saw the beginning of the end of an institution that had plagued civilization from its beginnings.

Many, such as Belmonte (2002) have described William Wilberforce as the greatest social reformer in the history of the world. Today we would call him a human rights activist who had a firm theory or justification for his human rights activity. He grasped the idea that all men are brothers and that we are our "brother's keepers." He took seriously the Christian injunction that we must love our neighbor as ourselves and that the golden rule applied to all of our relationships. In other words, he had both the human rights justification and motivation to end a practice that was so evil and so pervasive that our modern sensitivities have difficulty comprehending its display. As a Member of Parliament he saw the passage of an Act ending the international slave trade in 1807 and days before his death in 1833 an Act of Parliament was passed freeing domestic slaves. Stetson (2007: 12) has said that it is without question that Wilberforce's lifelong tireless work was grounded in his Christian conviction:

> "Let everyone," he wrote, "regulate his conduct … by the golden rule of doing to others as in similar circumstances we would have them do to us." This meant that he would serve others, even those with whom he had little or nothing in common, even those who could not repay. It grounded abolitionism and every other philanthropic and human rights concern he addressed.

The work of Wilberforce in the early nineteenth century was translated into international law outlawing slavery in all respects: the *Slavery Convention of the League of Nations* (1926), *the Universal Declaration of Human Rights* (1948), the *Supplementary Conventions on the Abolition of Slavery, the Slave Trade and*

Institutions and Practices Similar to Slavery (1956). These nearly universally adopted Conventions appear to make the world of the twenty-first century far different from that of the world into which Wilberforce was born.

However, the brute facts of our world tend to show otherwise. Today it is estimated that there are more than 27 million slaves in the world. These are individuals who are bought, sold, trafficked in the sex trade, held captive, brutalized and exploited for a profit. The twenty-first century version of slavery is much different from what history tells us slavery was like before it was abolished in the nineteenth century. In today's world there is no such thing as legal ownership of human beings as there was in the past. In the past, ownership of a slave entailed some responsibility; but today people simply control other human beings. They control their slaves by violence and deception. Today for slaveholders, not having legal ownership means that they have no responsibility, just control: Bales (2004) asserts they have all the benefits of ownership without any of the legal responsibilities.

Contemporary human slavery appears to be a more insidious problem and a more pervasive problem notwithstanding that it is illegal. Kevin Bales (2004), the world's leading expert on slavery and Director of Free the Slaves, charts the differences between the old slavery and the new slavery. The key differences between the old and new slavery break down as follows:

Old Slavery	**New Slavery**
Legal ownership asserted	Legal ownership avoided
High purchase cost	Very low purchase cost
($40,000—$80,000)	(less than $100)
Low profits	Very high profits
Shortage of potential slaves	Glut of potential slaves
Long-term relationship	Short-term relationship
Slaves maintained	Slaves disposable
Ethnic differences: important	Ethnic differences: not important

A real-life example of how slavery operates in the world today is worth noting in detail to gain a picture of the challenge of motivating human rights activists. In India, which has some of the strongest anti-slavery laws in the world, the vast majority of the 27 million enslaved human beings live under bonded labor. Bonded labor or debt bondage occurs when people give themselves into slavery as security against a loan or when they are unfortunate enough to inherit an indebtedness from a relative.

The Pragmatic Argument—A Real-Life Human Rights Problem

Notwithstanding the illegality of the brutal practice of slavery, illegal both from a national law perspective in every nation in the world and prohibited internationally, this abhorrent practice and human rights abuse continues to flourish in some areas of the world. An example of the pervasiveness of this abuse can be found in the country of India where today's slavery rests on generations of human rights abuse. In a recent documented case, Haugen (2005: 94–5), a not uncommon practice of multigenerational slavery has emerged. A 70-year-old man named Narakalappa recounts how he was born to slave parents who had sold themselves into bondage to pay off a debt for medical expenses. By selling themselves into slavery they did not realize that they would be forced to work in a plantation virtually all their waking hours and receive no compensation, while the original minor debt accrued interest at an alarming rate. When Narakalappa was born into slavery he became a second-generation slave, the property of the plantation owner just like his parents. Receiving no education, Narakalappa was doing the work of a grown man and this forced labor was all he would ever know:

> Narakalappa later married a woman in the village, where hundreds of other plantation slaves lived, and they had children together. His first wife passed away from an illness, and he married again, this time to Ashok's mother.
>
> Over the decades people simply forget about paying off a debt and accept slavery as their purpose in life. They are born into slavery and will always be slaves. There is no sense that things can change. And the caste system in India feeds upon this mind-set. Those of higher caste need those of lower caste; otherwise, there is no one beneath them to stand upon. Many, not just slave owners, benefit from the existence of a class of slaves.
>
> The owners continued to perpetuate the abuse of the younger generation. When children tried going to school instead of working in the fields, the owners beat up the parents until the kids felt guilty enough to quit school. That's what happened with Muni Raj.

It is difficult to comprehend who would advocate on behalf of the enslaved in India or other parts of the world. A violation of human rights so pervasive and so ingrained in a culture requires a human rights activist who not only is properly grounded but who also is firmly motivated to combat such a pervasive injustice. Notwithstanding the protests from human rights activists like Biletzki (2011) and the claim of Juergensmeyer (2000: 225) that "Modernity not only signalled the demise of the church's institutional authority and clerical control, but also the loosening of religion's ideological and intellectual grip on society," it does appear religious faith may have something to contribute to human rights discourse and protection. In discussing the foundational aspect of human rights, Jerome J.

Shestack (1998: 206, 224), chair of the International League for Human Rights for 20 years, does more than allow for this possibility:

> Thus, religious doctrine offers a promising possibility of constructing a broad intercultural rationale that supports the various fundamental principles of equality and justice that underlie international human rights. Indeed, once the leap to belief has been made, religion may be the most attractive of the theoretical approaches. When human beings are not visualized in God's image then their basic rights may well lose their metaphysical *raison d'être*. On the other hand, the concept of human beings created in the image of God certainly endows men and women with a worth and dignity from which the components of a comprehensive human rights system can flow logically.
>
> Some religious philosophers, holding dignity to be the inherent quality of the sacredness of human beings, believe that an entire rights system can flow from that concept.

Conclusion: A Faith-Based Approach for Human Rights Motivation

Perhaps, rather than writing religion out of the human rights equation as does Biletzki, there should be an effort to look more closely at what a robust, fully engaged philosophy of human rights infused with religious ideas would look like. This is to take up the challenge of Shestack. It is also the challenge of Pope John Paul II when he stated according to Glendon (2011: 44):

> It has been rightly pointed out that the 1948 Declaration does not present the anthropological and ethical foundations of the human rights which it proclaims. It is clear today that at that time such an undertaking would have been premature. It is thus the task of the various schools of thought–in particular the communities of believers–to provide the moral bases for the juridic edifice of human rights.

To move in this direction at this point in history is truly a daunting task. It comes at a time in world history when the sense of accountability to God is in radical decline. The secularist, imbued with Enlightenment thinking, wants to eliminate a faith perspective and certainly any reference to God from the human rights equation. As someone who lived in Africa and witnessed many human rights abuses, Charles R. Taber (2002: 101) makes this comment on developing a theory of human rights with a faith perspective:

> The sad irony of the West is that it erected its high tower of human rights, adding to the list through the centuries, all the while enthusiastically sapping the only foundation on which it can rest securely. Without such a transcendent foundation the structure of human rights is a house built on sand. It is irrevocably precarious

> and irreparably fragile. What other foundation could sustain the concept? Humanity as its own ultimate point of reference does not do it, as can be seen in the current erosion of the rights of all kinds of persons who are not "fully human": the unborn, the severely impaired, the dying, the incarcerated, even the unemployed. It is all too easy to call into question the rights of anyone who is not fully able, who is not fully productive, who is not fully in tune with society and its expectations.

The need, therefore, for a faith perspective or for theological reflection in the area of human rights may be very opportune. While a comprehensive review of religion and human rights is not possible in this chapter, reference to the Judeo-Christian faith as a motivation to advance human rights will be made. Historically, it is this faith perspective that seems to be the motivation of those who sought to abolish slavery and therefore is the focal point of our response to Ms. Biletzki.

If one were to look at the mission in the Old Testament, it is clear that God's blessing through the Abrahamic Covenant was to be a blessing to all nations (universal in scope) and it was to be accomplished by God's people "keeping" the way of the Lord by doing what is right and just (Genesis 18:19). And if we only looked at the heritage of God's people in the Old Testament and its impact in today's human rights field, there is a tremendous foundation. In his book, *The Gifts of the Jews*, Thomas Cahill (1998: 248) chronicles this foundation:

> Nor can we imagine the great liberation movements of modern history without reference to the Bible. Without the Bible we would never have known the abolitionist movement, the prison-reform movement, the anti-war movement, the labour movement, the civil rights movement, the movements of indigenous and dispossessed peoples for their human rights, the antiapartheid movement in South Africa, the solidarity movement in Poland, the free-speech and pre-democracy movements in such Far Eastern countries as South Korea, the Philippines, and even China. These movements of modern times have all employed the language of the Bible; and it is even impossible to understand their great heroes and heroines–people like Harriet Tubman, Sojourner Truth, Mother Jones, Mahatma Gandhi, Martin Luther King, Cesar Chavez, Helder Camara, Oscar Romero, Rigoberta Menchu, Corazon Aquino, Nelson Mandela, Desmond Tutu, Charity Kaluki Ngilu, Harry Wu–without recourse to the Bible

When we come to the New Testament and the gospel of Jesus Christ, building on the Hebrew law and prophets—Jesus rejected all forms of discrimination. He insisted that all human beings should be treated the same way—as bearers of great worth. He dealt with women, children, lepers, the ritually unclean, and foreigners in a manner that was truly egalitarian. He lifted the marginalized, far past the goals of any affirmative action plan in today's world.

Christ extended the category of "neighbor" to all humankind and insisted that the two Great Commandments applied equally to all. He taught his disciples to love their enemies. He upheld the marginalized and ostracized Samaritan as the hero in the story that gave definition to the question "Who is my neighbor?" (Luke 10:25–37).

The apostle Paul, following Christ, in his letter to the Galatians emphatically and specifically rejected three grounds for discrimination. He said in Galatians 3:28 there is neither Jew nor Greek; slave nor free; male nor female; we are all Abraham's seed, one in Jesus Christ. Paul touched on the three most contentious grounds for human rights abuses historically and indeed in today's world: ethnicity, social status, and gender. Peter in Acts 10 goes through a radical learning process. He came to accept that God chose his people through race not grace. In other words, he thought the only way to God was through the Jewish life, practice and religion. Through a dramatic object lesson in Acts 10, Peter witnessed the birth of the idea of universal human rights and respect for the individual. After witnessing a threefold vision where he learned a lesson in the universality of human kind, Peter described his experience, "I now realize how true it is that God does not show favoritism but accepts men from every nation who fear him and do what is right. You know the message God sent to the people of Israel, telling the good news of peace through Jesus Christ, who is Lord of all" (Acts 10:34–6). It was this vision which led Peter to accept the idea that all humankind, not only Jews, were fit receptacles for God's grace. From this point on, Peter understood that the gospel was all about grace, not race!

Throughout human history there appear to be three areas in which discrimination and abuse of human rights occur so easily. These areas are sexual equality, slavery, and racial equality. While certainly not perfect and with much to account for, Christians have also historically been at the forefront to break down the barriers of discrimination (Schmidt 2004; Mangalwadi 2009, 2011).

Assuming a case has been made for a Christian view of human rights, one that provides both a solid justification for human rights as universal, equal, and unalienable, and provides motivation for the advancement and protection of human rights—how does a Christian philosophy of human rights work itself out in the case study of slavery referred to earlier?

First, the solution to the problem of much of the world's population outside the protection of the law is to ensure that a functioning public justice system exists. Without a public justice system that works, victims of human rights abuses like Narakalappa will never get justice. Yet the example cited above occurred in a nation with one of the strongest laws against slavery, in a world where there are multiple international treaties making slavery illegal! As well, there are many millions of other Narakalappas in India and other nations.

With the wisdom of hindsight and looking back over 60 years some have argued that this result is possibly due to a lack of motivation in the right areas and misplaced priorities by the human rights community. Haugen et al. (2010: 21) argues for public justice systems as the starting point:

> The human rights community exists in part to intervene on behalf of the victimized, particularly where power actors otherwise have little incentive to

> act on their behalf. Yet during the modern human rights movement, the human rights community has largely neglected the critically important task of building public justice systems in the developing world that work for the poor.

He goes on to metaphorically state that a nation with up-to-date laws in compliance with international human rights standards but no functioning justice system is like a warehouse of vaccines for a desperately sick population but no way to retrieve the vaccines from the warehouse and administer it to the populace. The picture we are seeing is one of catastrophe and it explains why, after generations of human rights work and rhetoric, more than half the world's population is unprotected by the law and is vulnerable to human rights abuses:

> Two generations of global human rights work have been predicated, consciously or unconsciously, upon assumptions about functioning public justice systems in the developing world which, if incorrect, effectively undercut the usefulness of those efforts for their intended beneficiaries. What matters to the hundreds of millions of intended beneficiaries of these laws is their enforcement. Absent an effective enforcement mechanism, the great work of the first two generations of the modern human rights movement can deliver to the poor only empty parchment promises (Haugen et. al. 2010: 30).

Just as victims of slavery in the eighteenth and nineteenth century only saw relief when social reformers and human rights advocates like William Wilberforce saw results, such is the case today in the twenty-first century. Victims of slavery, such as Narakalappa and millions of others, await the work of a modern-day Wilberforce.

One such example is Gary Haugen and the human rights organization he founded, and leads, International Justice Mission (IJM). In response to the needs of victims like Narakalappa, IJM seeks to make public justice systems work for the poor and vulnerable who are routinely victims of human rights abuses. It has been the experience of many human rights workers in the developing world that they cannot readily go to the police on behalf of victims of injustice either because the police are poorly trained, lack the resources or will, or are hopelessly corrupt. The problem with police on the front lines of a public justice system is characteristic of a larger problem in seeking to protect human rights and provide a public justice system that works for the poor. The unresponsiveness of many public justice systems in the developing world prompted IJM to develop a collaborative casework model that seeks to remedy the most basic problems. The collaborative casework model aims to investigate basic human rights abuses, work with local authorities, and help them in securing relief for victims and bringing the perpetrators to justice. In addition, the collaborative casework model facilitates care for the victim and as cases work through the system problems can be corrected and thereby public justice systems are enhanced and basic human rights protection for the poor becomes a reality.

This approach seems to have succeeded as it has provided tangible relief for identifiable victims and shown perpetrators that they must face accountability, and it assists in showing government leaders where the strengths and weaknesses in the public justice system are and thereby helps to improve the system. The collaborative casework model provides a system whereby progress can be evaluated and success can be measured (Haugen and Boutros 2010).

The good news about the collaborative casework model is that by using this casework approach Narakalappa and two succeeding generations of slaves were freed from the horror of slavery. A man enslaved for over 70 years, his son, and grandsons have been freed. This illustrates that the real work of human rights needs to be part of a new mandate by the human rights community. This new mandate is not centered in the United Nations headquarters of New York City or Geneva, but rather one where a team of motivated and properly grounded human rights lawyers and activists in collaboration with law enforcement officials and social workers live and work among the 4 billion persons not currently receiving the protection of the rule of law and human rights (Haugen and Boutros 2010).

This new approach to providing basic human rights protection for the poor is working. It is born out of a foundation for human rights that is steeped in the most solid view of humanity and it is propelled by a motivation similar to that which drove William Wilberforce. The collaborative casework model is consistent with and proceeds from the mandate of "loving your neighbor" and "doing unto others as you would have them do unto you." The results achieved are similar to what was observed by the atheist writer Matthew Parris (2008) when he confirmed the value of the work of Christians in Africa:

> Now a confirmed atheist, I've become convinced of the enormous contribution that Christian evangelism makes in Africa: sharply distinct from the work of secular NGOs, government projects and international aid efforts. These alone will not do. Education and training alone will not do. In Africa Christianity changes people's hearts. It brings a spiritual transformation. The rebirth is real.

The Change is Good

If one were to compare the early stages of the human rights movement since the UDHR it would look much like Raphael's *School of Athens*. In each case one sees the best that secularism has to offer. In the case of the UDHR and succeeding international covenants, high sounding platitudes, important statements on human dignity and aspirational ideals are included without any reference to religious foundations. In the painting by Raphael, Plato and Aristotle and the self-sufficiency of mankind to know the truth through intellectual efforts are portrayed. However, in each case much more is needed from outside man's best efforts. Observers of the *School of Athens* often do not realize there is a companion painting which appears only in Rome with the original. It is called *The Adoration of the Sacrament*. The detailed description by Wilkin (2011) is worth repeating:

> In this painting, as in the *School of Athens*, most of the figures are identifiable: the four Latin doctors of the Church–Ambrose, Jerome, Augustine, and Gregory the Great; medieval teachers Thomas Aquinas and Bonaventure; spiritual leaders Dominic and Francis; artists Fra Angelico and Bramante; and the poet Dante. Flanking Christ are the Virgin Mary and John the Baptist; around them one sees Abraham, Moses, David, Jeremiah, Peter and Paul, John the Evangelist, and other biblical saints. The *School of Athens* is laid out on a horizontal axis, with its several groups extending like an animated frieze across the width of the picture. The *Disputa*, however, is arranged on a vertical as well as a horizontal axis, and then two axes converge on the host. The world below and the world above communicate with each other, and the entire scene is crowned by a golden light that streams from above.

As Raphael's *The Adoration of the Sacrament* enhances and fulfills the *School of Athens* so does a faith-based human rights philosophy fulfill the ideals of the UDHR and provide motivation for the modern-day human rights movement. It is only through this type of foundation that the ideals of the UDHR and the modern human rights movement can be fully grounded and ultimately achieved. To look at the *School of Athens* is to see only a segment of Raphael's work; indeed, it is similar to seeing the modern human rights movement through an Enlightenment lens. A careful analysis of the two paintings illustrates the *School of Athens* as laid out on a horizontal axis and closed off from the light above. As strong as the intellect and humanism portrayed in this painting is, it is limited. On the other hand, the *Adoration of the Sacrament* focuses on the eternal without taking away from the true humanism illustrated in the *School of Athens*. It is arranged on both a horizontal and vertical axis and the two axes come together on the Host, which symbolizes the Incarnation of Christ. Because of the vertical and horizontal, the *Adoration of the Sacrament* allows for the light from above to permeate the entire painting. What human reason alone through the *School of Athens* is unable to project, the *Adoration of the Sacrament* can allow the observer to see.

Similarly, in the human rights movement today, what is needed is not a singular focused "enlightenment" view of human rights. Both in the area of justification for human rights and in the area of motivation and protection of human rights, a broader view than that represented by Anat Biletzki is needed. Those who suffer human rights abuses and those who lack basic human rights protection are badly in need of a complementary approach to human rights. This is an approach where the positive aspects of Enlightenment humanism is bolstered and supported by a faith-based approach which allows for a view of humankind that is both horizontal and vertical and provides an eternal stream of light to shine on the condition of the real world.

Bibliography

Bales, K. 2004. *Disposable People*, revised edn. Berkeley, CA: University of California Press.

Belmonte, K. 2002. *William Wilberforce: A Hero for Humanity*. Grand Rapids, MI: Zondervan.

Biletzki, A. 2011. The Sacred and the Humane. *New York Times*, July 17. Available at: http://opinionator.blogs.nytimes.com/2011/07/17/the-sacred-and-the-humane/ [accessed: October 31, 2012].

Buergenthal, T. 2006. The Evolving International Human Rights System. *The American Journal of International Law*, 100, 783–807.

Cahill, T. 1998. *The Gift of the Jews*. New York: Doubleday.

Cassin, R. 1971. From the Ten Commandments to the Rights of Man, in *Of Law and Man*, edited by S. Shaman. New York: Sabra Books.

Donnelly, J. 2003. *Universal Human Rights in Theory and Practice*, 2nd edn. Ithaca, NY: Cornell University Press.

Freeman, M. 1994. The Philosophical Foundations of Human Rights. *Human Rights Quarterly*, 16.

Geisler, N. and Moreland, J.P. 1990. *The Life and Death Debate: Moral Issues of Our Time*. Westport, CT: Praeger.

Glendon, M. 2010. God and Mrs. Roosevelt. *First Things*, May.

Glendon, M. 2011. The Bearable Lightness of Dignity. *First Things*, May.

Haugen, G. 2005. *Terrify No More*. Nashville, TN: Thomas Nelson.

Haugen, G. and Boutros, V. 2010. And Justice for All. *Foreign Affairs*, May/June. NY: Council on Foreign Policy.

Johnston, D. and Sampson, C. 1994. *Religion: The Missing Dimension of Statecraft*. New York: Oxford University Press.

Juergensmeyer, M. 2000. *Terror in the Mind of God: The Global Line of Religious Violence*. Berkeley, CA: University of California Press.

Li, X. 1998. Post Modernism and Universal Human Rights. Available at: http://www.secularhumanism.org/library/fi/li_18_4.html [accessed: October 31, 2012].

Lisska, A. 1996. *Aquinas' Theory of Natural Law: An Analytical Reconstruction*. Oxford: Clarendon.

Mangalwadi, V. 2009. *Truth and Transformation: A Manifesto for Ailing Nations*. Seattle: YWAM Publishing.

Mangalwadi, V. 2011. *The Book That Made Your World: How the Bible Created the Soul of Western Civilization*. Nashville, TN Thomas Nelson.

Montgomery, J.W. 1986. *Human Rights and Human Dignity*. Grand Rapids, MI Zondervan.

Parris, M. 2008. As an Atheist, I Truly Believe Africa Needs God. *The Sunday Times*, December 27.

Perry, M.J. 2007. *Toward a Theory of Human Rights*. New York: Cambridge University Press.

Schmidt, A. 2004. *How Christianity Changed the World.* Grand Rapids, MI: Zondervan.
Shestack, J. 1998. The Philosophic Foundations of Human Rights. *Human Rights Quarterly*, 20, 201–34.
Stetson, C. 2007. *William Wilberforce: A Practical View of Christianity*. McLean, IL: Trinity Forum.
Taber, C. 2002. In the Image of God: The Gospel and Human Rights. *International Bulletin of Missionary Research*, 26(3), 98–102.
United Nations Commission on Legal Empowerment of the Poor: Making the Law Work for Everyone. 2008. Volume 1.
Universal Declaration of Human Rights [1948] G.A. Res. 217 A(III), U.N. Doc. A/810.
Wilkin, R.L. Culture and the Light of Faith. *First Things*, February. NY: Institute on Religion and Public Life. 31–6.

Chapter 10
Why is Man the Primary and Functional Way for the Church?: The Involvement of Christian Teaching in Contemporary Human Rights Discourse

Dobrochna Bach-Golecka

Introduction

The aim of the present chapter is to analyze the impact of Christian teaching, and more specifically Catholic doctrine, upon contemporary human rights discourse. Thus, there are certain assumptions and limits in the scope of our undertaking. Historically, it was Christian doctrine, irrespective of denomination, that had the greatest influence on the emergence and evolution of human rights. The Jewish, Greek, and Roman heritage of Christianity helped to cultivate the cardinal ideas of dignity, equality, liberty and democracy that ground the modern human rights paradigm. Christianity also helped to shape public and private, penal and procedural rights (Witte and Alexander 2010, Wolterstorff 2012).

Within an ontological perspective (concerning what really exists), it is the Catholic Church that invokes the argument of truth (*veritas*) as she claims the right to be a teacher for mankind not only of faith but of morals as well. Nevertheless, this insistence on the role of the Church as a witness to truth does not have an exclusivist character as it is understood as a proposal, within the context of the autonomy of the state and combined with a positive evaluation of present pluralistic societies where secularity is treated as a place of communication between different communities of believers (Pontifical Council for Justice and Peace 2004).

Last but not least one may invoke technical arguments for the restriction of the scope of the present analysis: namely, that it is for the Catholic Church to provide the most elaborated, coherent and systematic approach to social affairs. While other Christian denominations may not present a comparable doctrinal outcome, still they often engage in cooperative effort in order to issue a common standpoint (document) on a particular issue. A special emphasis on the doctrine of the Catholic Church may be explained also through the organizational arguments as she has the most institutionalized hierarchical structure and the Holy See is represented on the international forum, unlike any other religious community (Arangio-Ruiz 1996). Those features give the Catholic Church unique opportunities for action on an international plane. Moreover, one may state that the Catholic Church is original within the enforcement sphere as it provides a set of differentiated and highly elaborated means for ensuring compliance with the prescribed rules.

As far as the essence of this chapter is concerned, it deals with the role of religious communities within a society. Theoretical analysis is followed by the examination of the recent involvement of the church in the practice and protection of human rights.

There are three fundamental assumptions concerning the impact of religious community upon the social surroundings. Firstly, following the analysis of Immanuel Kant, the church is regarded as a means of ensuring the validity and observance of moral norms. Hence, a religious (ethical) community is a fundamental basis of morality. This role may be termed as a *general function.*

Secondly, the impact of the church upon the society is largely determined by her teaching on social problems. In this context, many religious communities provide their members guidance as well as specific criteria concerning required personal conduct within the public sphere. This role may be termed as a *specific function.*

Thirdly, the church acts as an entity entrusted not only with the task of helping her members to obey religious standards but also with the burden of controlling the level of norms-observance. This role may be termed as an *implementation function.*

General function: Church as the Fundamental Basis for Morality

The general function of the church (religious community) is understood as providing the fundamental basis for morality. This role of an ethical community may be presented using the example of the reflections developed by Immanuel Kant, and complemented with the recent theory of Jürgen Habermas on permanent interpretative communities. Therefore, it is possible to state that there is not a direct opposition between religious reflection upon the human inclination towards evil and the Kantian evolution of philosophical thought (Benedict XVI 2007).

There are still some misperceptions concerning the philosophy of religion in Kant's theory, connected to the simplified vision of the religious crisis of the Enlightenment. According to this vision there are only two possible standpoints: either to follow the way of reason (*ratio*) and exclude faith and religion as those spheres cannot be proved in a rational way or to accept faith which is outside the speculative discourse. Nevertheless it seems that Kant would not approve this alternative and would treat it as a false one. According to him the thesis of the existence of God had not originated from the speculative reason and therefore cannot be proved or falsified by this reason.

Hence the analysis of the idea of God in the theory of Kant should be performed with a strict division of the sphere of theoretical (speculative) reason and practical reason. There is not a theoretical knowledge of God; there is no possibility of proving the existence of God or falsifying such a thesis. Therefore, Kant disapproves of the argumentation of Descartes, based on the writings of St. Anselm that would treat existence (being) as the characteristic feature of God

(Cahn 2009): just as the essence of a triangle is having three angles, the essence of God is being, existence.

Kant's theory on God would not be connected to the transcendent idea of God as the primordial or original being (*ens originarium*), as the most complete being (*ens summum*) or as the most real being (*omnitudo realitatis*). Rather, according to Kant, there is a need for the acceptance of the thesis of the existence of God within the sphere of practical reason and morality. One should accept the moral origin of the world and the creator of the world, in order to follow the moral law and to specify the final aim (purpose) of human beings (Guyer 2000). This final purpose includes an objective part (attaining the highest good within human freedom) as well as a subjective part (attaining happiness).

The acceptance of the existence of God in the moral sphere is crucial for securing a connection between the moral law and a drive towards happiness and in order to establish a real (possible) character (*ausführbar*) of the moral law. Hence the notion of God is individual and subjective (Byrne 2007). It is connected to the sphere of moral law: God is understood as the creator of world, the highest judge and moral law-maker. One may state that the image of God in the philosophy of Kant is rooted in the Christian religion; still it does not represent a coherent orthodox content. God is not treated as a father but rather as a creator of moral law or a judge. Similarly, the Incarnation is understood primarily as *logos*, as the complete personification of moral law and Jesus is the one who fulfilled the law in a perfect way. Seung stresses Kant's conviction of a truly moral character of Christianity in comparison with other religions, which emphasize subordination to external rules (Seung 2007). In Kant's theory it was due to Jesus that the old, external law of subordination has been transformed into new, internal law of inner disposition.

Kant's philosophy of religion differs from the natural Stoic religiosity, understood as solitary human efforts to cultivate the earth, as it includes hope in God's grace. Similarly, it corrects various notions of Christian piety to include only prayers originated in moral needs, by excluding those stemming from purely emotional or pathological desires.

According to Kant, the possibility of knowing God within theoretical reason would transform moral law into a coercive system of pathological fear and forced submission. By contrast, the existence of God within practical reason would mean an additional motivation (*Triebfeder*) for moral actions. Man is acting morally not only because of the fear of law (*Achtung vor dem Gesetz*), but also due to hope that God would subscribe a proportionate happiness to particular moral actions. Therefore, the notion of moral law presupposes the doctrine of free will, and the existence of an immortal soul and God (Wood 2009). Human self-consciousness and acceptance of the validity of moral law may thus be regarded as a linkage between human and divine spheres. According to Kant moral law is a sign of God's existence as God left in human beings His image within the categorical moral law while Himself remaining hidden in transcendence.

Hence Kant's image of religion was linked to the sphere of moral disposition rather than theoretical cognition. The philosophy of religion developed by Kant in the late stage of his life was formulated within his reflections upon the mysterious nature of radical evil, deeply entrenched in the heart of man (Despland 1973). Those insights had led Kant to transform his previous statements on moral law. The hope for moral progress was no longer founded on the existence of the inner law within a human being, as there is an interior evil as well.

Moral law is not fully respected by people as human beings are free and not fully rational. They tend to follow not only the requirements of reason but are also directed by the senses; they seek happiness and try to realize their self-interest. Those irrational traits of human behaviour were treated by Kant as signs of imperfection or examples of the action of evil which are particularly destructive in social relationships (Bobko 2007). Evil emerged as a result of the improper use of freedom and consisted of the malfunctioning (*perversitas*) of the human heart. Inclination to do evil coexists alongside a similar inclination to perform good actions. Hence, rational ethics is not sufficient to guarantee a proper implementation of moral law.

Every human being is subject to evil as social relationships are particularly vulnerable. Therefore, in order to combat the destructive force of evil there is a need for unity. A proper response for the mystery of evil is religious faith. Faith requires respect for and the implementation of moral law; still it is intrinsically connected with hope for God's assistance for human beings in their struggle for attaining good. God may diminish the obstacles or increase strength necessary to combat evil. Nevertheless hope should not be treated as certainty. Moral religion, in comparison to religion of cult, is based on the assumption of human activity and responsibility, on cooperation of people with God, aiming at attaining good.

The notion of religion in the philosophy of Kant is linked primarily to the sphere of morality and fulfilling moral obligations; even piety is aimed at strengthening the virtuous attitude of the believers. Hence, there is a connection between religion, morality and the rational sphere. Ethical community should be formed not due to the historical faith, based on revelation, but rather as a fulfilment of a rational idea of such a community (Firestone and Jacobs 2009).

According to Kant the notion of church, religious community or God's people (*Gottesvolk*) should include certain characteristics: it should have a universal (general) character, it should originate from pure reasons, connected with morality and not superstition or mysticism (Kant 1998). Moreover, ethical community should be based on the principle of freedom within the inner perspective (among its members) as well as within the outer perspective, in relation to political power. The fourth feature of religious community is its mutable character, allowing for an evolutionary adjustment to external conditions, alongside with the preservation of permanent essential features.

In the theory of Kant the ethical community may be compared to the community of family which is subject to a common, invisible moral father. It is the holy son who knows the will of the father and proclaims it to human beings. The son is connected with people by the brotherhood of blood, therefore they worship the father in him and enter voluntarily into universal and permanent association of hearts.

Kant distinguished three aspects of human beings: vocation, representation and choice. The aspect of vocation is linked to unconditional submission of humans to the moral law given by God, yet still without encroaching on the category of freedom (Hare 1996). Hence people are not determined by nature, but they depend on moral obligations while respecting laws of freedom. The aspect of representation is connected to the human necessity of external help in order to fulfil moral rules. People should supplement their abilities with God's assistance. Therefore, the aspect of choice is linked to the process of human acceptance of representation and salvation done in human substitution. In effect, human will is inclined towards good according to God's grace.

Mankind should respect a higher moral authority than its own current insights; this foundational authority is a transcendent, sovereign, majestic and holy God. The notion of God's holiness means that there exists an unconditional border between the human and the divine. This border shows the finitude of human nature, limits of human reason and human actions. Hence, the life of men should concentrate on search, and not possession. Similarly, the task of a philosopher lies in defining the limits of human actions, rather than in attempting to transcend them.

The implications of God's holiness and His overwhelming omnipotence stretch into a redeeming activity, gracious Providence. Transcendence communicates with humans through the means of moral law; a call to freedom, conscientiousness, honesty and practice of justice. Within this context lies the notion of an ethical community (*Gottesvolk*, church) as the possibility of respecting the norms of moral law is dependent on the process of uniting the good-willed people. Moral progress is not an individualistic process as there is a further need for men to create a community under a common moral law with the aim of strengthening the inner disposition of its members to fulfil all duties as divine commands (Wood 1970). Thus, the need to form a religious community is derived from the social character of the highest good. Within this meaning the moral project of Kant is of a universal character and may be applied within the contemporary multilateral society (Donagan 1993).

The role of religion within the contemporary liberal democratic state has recently been recognized in the works of Jürgen Habermas (Junker-Kenny 2011). He stressed that since communication networks within liberal civil society are of a flexible and unstable character, there is a need for more permanent communities of interpretation, able to formulate possible answers to socially crucial problems. Thus the process of public discourse may be enriched by inclusion of proposals submitted by various civil groups, among them religious communities (churches). According to Habermas those ethical entities are particularly well-prepared for addressing such pathologies of modernity like deformations of small organized groups or failures of individual life-plans and presenting solutions based on the principle of equal participation as well as mentalities of solidarity and compassion.

The responsibility of the church within the public sphere is linked primarily to the process of forming the conscience of an individual and to raising his or her moral sensibility (Demmer 2000). Hence, it is entrusted with the task to articulate within the social arena the moral insights growing out of faith's effective story (*Wirkungsgeschichte*) and to build consensus around them.

Specific Function: Church as the Criteria-Giving Entity

It would grossly exceed the frames of this chapter to try to present the doctrinal content of the teaching of the Catholic Church. Nevertheless, it does not even seem to be necessary to embark upon such an arduous attempt since the essence of the relevant teaching of the church concerning the analysis of the social life is contained within the specifically delineated body of so-called Catholic social thought (Brady 2008). This has been developed since 1891, the year of the first papal encyclical letter on social issues *Rerum Novarum*, yet the teaching has been inspired by the ordinary sources of the church: the Bible and tradition. The fundamental root of Catholic social thought is the commandment of love: to love God as the source and inspiration of all good action and secondly one's neighbour as the expression of a similar attitude. Charity should be the distinguishing mark of Christ's disciples (Jn 13:35).

Catholic social teaching has been developed as a reflection upon the crucial social issues (Charles 1998). It began with the encyclical letter *Rerum Novarum* (1891) on the conditions of the workers in early capitalism; the other documents responded to various phenomena like the economic malaise of the Great Depression in *Quadragesimo Anno* (1931), vibrant optimistic economic environment in *Mater et Magistra* (1961), *Pacem in Terris* (1963) and *Gaudium et Spes* (1965) or examined the issue of the development of nations in *Populorum Progressio* (1967), *Octogesima Adveniens* (1971) and *Sollicitudo Rei Socialis* (1987). Some encyclical letters concern specific issues like *Laborem Exercens* (1981) on labour, *Centesiums Annus* (1991) on capitalistic models of economic life (Barrera 2001).

As far as the social institutions and type of arrangement of public authorities are concerned it may be stated that such institutional details are not specified in the teaching of the church. The Bible contains rather general statements on the notion of public authority. Some texts from the New Testament, like the tax (*tributum*) pericopes (Mt 22:15–22; Mk 12:13–17; Lk 20:20–6), aim to separate the public sphere (*ius publicum*) and the sphere of religion (*ius sacrum*). The general message stemming from the Scriptures is that the faithful should strongly remember their heavenly citizenship (*politeuma*) and then wholeheartedly engage in the activities of everyday life (Phil 3:20).

This urge for social involvement may be regarded as a characteristic of the Catholic religion. The contemporary understanding of the commandment to love one's neighbour is connected with such terms as human dignity, equality of men and women, human rights and solidarity. Differences among people do occur and this differentiation may lead to some beneficial results, such as the encouragement of charity (solidarity). Solidaristic actions, considered as the practice of sharing with others, are linked not only to material goods but to spiritual ones as well.

Charity may be understood in different ways, as the exercise of pastoral counselling or psychological healing, as well as the development of political and social justice projects (Graham 1990). Nevertheless it seems that charity should be linked to an individual attitude of contrite heart and repentance (*metanoia*). This notion of charity has a twofold nature: on the one hand it means a practical (materialistic) concern to help others in their needs, poverty and weakness; on the other hand, it is dependent on a spiritual sphere, on the ability of empathy, of giving emotional support and understanding. Therefore, it is possible to discern an intellectual aspect of charity linked to the individual perception of God's loving process of creation and constant sustenance of the world. Charity (*caritas*) is a human imitation of God's providence. In other words, God in His transcendence invites people to share in His mutuality by empowering them with freedom. It is with the use of human imagination that freedom may result in the attitude of faith and moral endeavour which give concrete shape to human mutuality (Rossi 1983: 170).

Charity may be understood as an individualistic engagement still Christians are called to take up the attitude of co-responsibility. The faith has an intrinsic profound community element within itself (Benedict XVI 2007) and solidarity forms an expression of interdependence among people, the supreme model of unity of the human race which is the reflection of the intimate life of one God in three Persons (John Paul II 1987, Njoku Uzochukwu 2006). Moreover, actions of solidarity have a profound impact on social relations; as Peter Geach states:

> [N]othing blinds the heart more than malice; and contrariwise a disposition to construe one's neighbour's words as meaning something true or reasonable pays off in increased mutual understanding. (Geach 1977: 86)

Solidarity should be practiced within the ordinary circumstances of social life. Nevertheless the contemporary culture contains a large number of negative factors working against the awareness of the common good and the eagerness to further it. Such an environment is being described as a structure of sin. It can be characterized as follows:

> whenever the church … condemns as *social sins* certain situations or the collective behaviour of certain social groups, big or small, or even of whole nations and blocks of nations, she knows and she proclaims that such cases of *social sin* are the result of the accumulation and concentration of many *personal sins*. It is a case of the very personal sins of those who cause or support evil or who exploit it; of those who are in a position to avoid, eliminate or at least limit certain social evils but who fail to do so out of laziness, fear or the conspiracy of silence, through secret complicity or indifference; of those who take refuge in the supposed impossibility of changing the world, and also of those who

> sidestep the effort and sacrifice required, producing specious reasons of a higher order. The real responsibility, then, lies with individuals. (John Paul II 1984)

The introduction of the category of social sins may be regarded as a helpful means for understanding the contemporary reality and for naming the roots of evil. There are two general attitudes of sinful behaviour: an urge for power (*libido dominandi*) and an all-consuming desire for profit.

As far as an economic perspective is concerned, recent phenomena include: the pace of technological change; rapid movement of capital; the rise of corporate power, standardization processes; and the acceleration of economic inequalities, insecurity and poverty. These phenomena undermine the proper functioning of democracy and diminish the level of civic participation. Moreover, the contemporary vision shows a profound internalization of market values in everyday life (market idolatry), with the prevailing trends of materialism, consumerism and expectations of immediate gratification; the extreme individualism and suspicion of community and solidarity. Market values place at the central position an individual, regarded as a worker, owner or consumer, and highlight the importance of mobility, newness and youth. Within the religious perspective individual security may be achieved through the process of involvement in community affairs and through sharing while market values place the only guarantee of security in accumulation.

Therefore, it is possible to distinguish the values present in Christian teaching (Gospel values) and values promoted through economic mechanisms (market values). The former relate to the notions of stewardship, the dignity of human beings, spheres of sanctity; and they stress the linkage between an individual and community and the validity of obligations towards the community (Collin and Wright 2007).

Implementation Function: Church as the Discipline-Providing Body

The essence of Christian social teaching may be encapsulated in the words of St. Paul: "Serve one another, rather, in works of love, since the whole of the Law is summarised in a single command: *Love your neighbour as yourself*" (Gal 5:13–14). Every Christian is regarded as a unique creation, as a human being and not a doing, called to live by the Spirit in normal secular surroundings. Within the sphere of spirituality it is possible to discern special criteria for judging the consistency of one's behaviour with the presence of Spirit (Byron 2007). The criteria have been recorded by St. Paul (Gal 5:22–3) as the following: love, joy, peace, patience, kindness, generosity, faithfulness, gentleness, self-control. There are also the opposite-side criteria, pinpointing self-indulgence and works of the flesh—activity not informed by God's indwelling Spirit, such as fornication, gross indecency and sexual irresponsibility, idolatry and sorcery, envy, disagreements, drunkenness, orgies and similar things.

Therefore the recommended path of action consists of a proper spiritual attitude, capable of recognizing the gifts received and of taking individual responsibility for one's life. A Christian response to sin is a change of behaviour, a conversion. This should include the recognition of interdependence among people as a moral category and practicing the virtue of solidarity. It should be remembered that it is difficult to accomplish much by a solitary action hence there is a need to organize small groups of committed people. Still one should remember that individual choices tend to make a difference.

There are various institutional arrangements for assuring norm-observance within the church as provided in the canon law. Still those mechanisms should be regarded as a means of helping and not of forcing as membership in the church is based on the voluntary decision of a given individual. The institutional structure of the church is based primarily upon the individual ministry of the priests, working within the parishes, being the fundamental territorial structure of the religious community. While attending religious ceremonies, every member of the church is being instructed about the specific content of the teaching of the church. Moreover, there are also means provided for in a strictly individual manner. One of them is the sacrament of reconciliation which may fulfil various tasks. Firstly, it is an individual examination of one's conscience; secondly, it comprises an external viewpoint made by the priest about the situation of the penitent; thirdly, it provides psychological relief after receiving the forgiveness of sins; fourthly, is restores the broken relationship between the penitent and the community of believers.

One of the best metaphors describing the nature of the Catholic Church defines her as the Mother of all people. Hence, the conduct of the church should resemble family relations, full of dialogue, listening and communicating with others. Therefore, this dialogue should be participatory, public, patient and forgiving (O'Brien 2007). The church should indulge in the science of bridge building, avoiding the attitude of confrontation and practicing conversation, openness and humility (Mannion 2007).

Catholic Teaching on Human Rights

The Catholic involvement in the promotion of human rights may be analyzed on various levels. The most fundamental perspective is the focus on individual behaviour as it is always a unitary, specific human being that is called to perform good deeds. Therefore, the canon law contains specific provisions concerning the promotion of human rights in personal conduct (canons 208–23, Helmholz 2010).

It is possible to discern a positive and a negative aspect of an individual's involvement in the protection of human rights. The latter involves situations of non-observance of human rights which are treated as evil actions, with the requirement of penitential behaviour, confession and reconciliation. The former includes direct and conscious involvement in the protection of human rights. It may be observed that people more engaged in religious practices are more engaged in social affairs and, specifically, in the promotion of human rights.

Catholic teaching contains a profound social element which should be discernible among the attitudes and actions of those most seriously involved in the religious practices (McCarthy 2009). Hence people who often attend the religious celebrations (a few times a week) are those who are most familiar with the teaching of the church, and also Catholic social doctrine. They have also an opportunity to get familiar with various groups (like religious or charity groups, pastoral councils or parochial family clinics) active at the level of the parish, either passively or actively. It seems that the level of the parish is the place of crucial importance for developing the necessary social skills, motivations and abilities for the future involvement in various external social activities (Bach-Golecka 2010). The people regularly practicing and attending religious celebrations are also very motivated toward moral behaviour, in accordance with Christian standards. Those conditions result in their performing various social functions, like membership and work within non-governmental organizations, electoral activity on the local and central level, and an inclination towards donating to charities or a high level of trust in local authorities.

The other perspective visible within the Catholic involvement in human rights is a local (regional) standpoint. One may indicate as the best relevant example specific teaching of the local Conference of Bishops. Pastoral letters usually concern a specific issue of crucial importance for a given community at a particular time, like peace and violence, work and unemployment, protection of life and a ban on abortion. Those letters may be regarded as a means to promote human rights within a local church (society within a state) and are supplemented by the teaching (mostly encyclical letters) of the Pope. Those documents are also used in a pastoral role, namely to promote a culture of human rights on two levels: firstly, by encouraging an attitude conducive to moral behaviour (civilization of love); and secondly by warning of the dangers of contemporary culture promoting evil (civilization of evil).

The normative role of the church concerns the specification of rights. Catholic teaching underlines that human rights should be understood as universal, inviolable and inalienable rights. The church proclaims Christian foundations for human rights (Hehir 2010, Pontifical Council for Justice and Peace 2004). Moreover, it is possible to discern a specific and original understanding of the content of human rights, like the right to life from conception to its natural end, the right of the child to develop in the mother's womb from the moment of conception (hence opposition to in-vitro-fertilization); the right freely to establish a family and to have and rear children through the responsible exercise of one's sexuality (against the practices of forced fertilization and the right to become a parent being dependent on public authorities). One should promote not only human rights but corresponding responsibilities (duties) as well: in human society, to one man's right there corresponds a duty of other persons to acknowledge and respect the right in question. According to the Catholic teaching on human rights a collective form of rights should be promoted alongside individual human rights. Rights of peoples and nations should be respected as they are human rights within a community life (*koinonia*—living together). Those should include a fundamental right of existence, right of language and culture, right to self-determination which should be performed in accordance with the principle of equality of states and free cooperation and solidarity among peoples aiming at the attainment of the highest goal of the common good of mankind.

The monitoring role of the church aims at controlling the everyday practice of human rights promotion. Catholic teaching contains provisions to handle a discrepancy between the proclamation and violation of human rights (letter and spirit) as well as on the dangers of an excessive affirmation of equality, as it can give rise to an individualism in which each one claims his or her own rights without wishing to be held responsible for the common good. The church also calls us to respect certain privileges of the poor within the principle of the preferential option for the poor, namely to create conditions for marginalized voices to be heard, to assist the most vulnerable and to assess lifestyles, policies and social institutions in terms of their impact on the poor. People more fortunate should renounce some of their rights so as to place their goods more generously at the service of others.

The active role of the church is linked to direct engagement in the promotion of human rights and denunciations of violations of human rights. Those actions may be performed with the use of the ordinary forms of papal diplomacy through the permanent representatives of the Holy See to states and international organizations (D'Onorio 2000). A vivid example of the direct involvement of Vatican representatives in the process of human rights protection may be the peace negotiations to resolve the conflict between Chile and Argentina over the Beagle Channel (Lindsley 1987, Moncayo 1993).

The communication role of the church involves the use by the Pope and his representatives of various instruments designed to communicate with the outside world (Kent and Pollard 1994). One may point out permanent events like messages delivered annually for the World Day of Peace or addresses to diplomatic corps at the Vatican as well as less regular events like communications during formal visits in other states during the Pope's pilgrimages, sermons during special events (World Youth Days) or delivering speeches at the forum of international organizations. There are various goals of such actions: to distribute the essence of the social teaching of the church through mass-media, to warn against the dangers of contemporary culture (like neopaganism, totalitarianism, religious indifference, consumerism, religious or ethnic violence), to convince and find allies with similar attitudes and to promote similar values.

Conclusion

In contemporary society, the church may be seen as an institution deeply involved in the promotion of solidaristic behaviour, based on the recognition of the interdependence among people (Corecco 1999). The roots of such an attitude are based on a specific vision of human nature. Within Catholic social teaching the notion of development is understood as a complex term, including not only economic aspects but also cultural, social and moral ones (Njoku 2006). Therefore, any action towards the improvement of the economic situation of the people should necessarily address those other perspectives.

The church may be regarded as a "holistic entity," performing various fundamental functions within a given society. Firstly, it gives unique reasons for moral behaviour and thus supports the rule of law within a state. Secondly, it is constantly examining the contemporary social relations with the aim of warning its members of possible dangers and evils. Thus, it performs the monitoring function and a crucial preventive task. Thirdly, the church administers its moral role through its specific instruments, which are means of helping the attainment of moral goals. Those mechanisms include the sacraments, defined as a method of obtaining God's assistance in the pursuit of good and human rights.

Bibliography

Arangio-Ruiz, G. 1996. On the nature of the international personality of the Holy See. *Revue Belge de Droit International*, 29(2), 360–71.

Bach-Golecka, D. 2010. Catholic religion and social capital: The case study of Poland. *Universitas Gedanensis*, 40(2), 115–28.

Barrera, A. 2001. *Modern Catholic Social Documents and Political Economy*. Washington: Georgetown University Press.

Benedict XVI. 2007. *Encyclical Letter Spe Salvi*. Vatican: Libreria Editrice Vaticana.

Bobko, A. 2007. *Myślenie wobec zła. Polityczny i religijny wymiar myślenia w filozofii Kanta i Tischnera*. (Thinking On Evil. The Political and Religious Perspective in the Philosophy of Kant and Tischner). Kraków-Rzeszów: Instytut Myśli Józefa Tischnera.

Byrne, P. 2007. *Kant on God*. Aldershot: Ashgate.

Brady, B. 2008. *Essential Catholic Social Thought*. New York: Orbis Books.

Byron, W.J. 2007. *Individuarian Observations: Essays in Catholic Social Reflection*. Scranton, PA and London: University of Scranton Press.

Cahn, S.M. 2009. *Exploring Philosophy of Religion: An Introductory Anthology*. New York and Oxford: Oxford University Press.

Charles, R. 1998. *Christian Social Witness and Teaching: The Catholic Tradition from Genesis to Centesimus Annus*. Leominster: Gracewing.

Collin, C. and Wright, M. 2007. *The Moral Measure of the Economy*. New York: Orbis Books.

Corecco, E. 1999. *Canon Law and Communio: Writings on the Constitutional Law of the Church*. Vatican: Libreria Editrice Vaticana.

Demmer, K. 2000. *Shaping the Moral Life: An Approach to Moral Theology*. Washington: Georgetown University Press.

Despland, M. 1973. *Kant on History and Religion*. Montreal and London: McGill-Queen's University Press.

Donagan, A. 1993. Common morality and Kant's Enlightenment project, in *Prospects for a Common Morality* edited by G. Outka and J.P. Reeder. Princeton, NJ: Princeton University Press, 53–72.

D'Onorio, J.B. 2000. *Le Saint-Siège dans les relations internationales*. Paris: Cujas.

Firestone, C.L. and Jacobs, N. 2009. *In Defence of Kant's Religion*. Bloomington, IN: Indiana University Press.

Geach, P.T. 1977. *The Virtues*. Cambridge: Cambridge University Press.

Graham, G. 1990. *The Idea of Christian Charity: A Critique of Some Contemporary Conceptions*. London: Collins.

Guyer, P. 2000. *Kant on Freedom, Law and Happiness*. Cambridge: Cambridge University Press.

Hare, J.E. 1996. *The Moral Gap: Kantian Ethics, Human Limits, and God's Assistance*. Oxford: Clarendon Press.

Hehir, J.B. 2010. The modern Catholic Church and human rights: The impact of the Second Vatican Council, in *Christianity and Human Rights: An Introduction*, edited by J. Witte and F.S. Alexander. Cambridge: Cambridge University Press, 113–34.

Helmholz, R.H. 2010. Human rights in the canon law, in *Christianity and Human Rights: An Introduction*, edited by J. Witte and F.S. Alexander. Cambridge: Cambridge University Press, 99–112.

John Paul II. 1984. *Apostolic Exhortation Reconciliatio et Paenitentia*. Vatican: Libreria Editrice Vaticana.

John Paul II. 1987. *Encyclical Letter Sollicitudo Rei Socialis*. Vatican: Libreria Editrice Vaticana.

Junker-Kenny, M. 2011. *Habermas and Theology*. London and New York: T&T Clark International.

Kant, I. 1998. *Religion within the Boundaries of Mere Reason*. Cambridge: Cambridge University Press.

Kent, P. and Pollard, J. 1994. A diplomacy unlike any other: Papal diplomacy in the nineteenth and twentieth century, in *Papal Diplomacy in the Modern Age*, edited by P. Kent and J. Pollard. Westport, CT: Praeger, 14–20.

Lindsley, L. 1987. The Beagle Channel Settlement: Vatican mediation resolves a century-old dispute. *Journal of Church and State*, 29(3), 434–55.

Mannion, G. 2007. *Ecclesiology and Postmodernity: Questions for the Church in Our Time*. Collegeville, MN: Liturgical Press.

McCarthy, D.M. 2009. *The Heart of Catholic Social Teaching: Its Origins and Contemporary Significance*. Grand Rapids, MI: Brazos Press.

Moncayo, G. 1993. La médiation pontificale dans l'affaire du canal Beagle. *Recueil des Cours*, 242, 197–434.

Njoku Uzochukwu, J. 2006. *Examining the Foundations of Solidarity in the Social Encyclicals of John Paul II*. Frankfurt am Main: Peter Lang.

O'Brien, G.D. 2007. *Finding the Voice of the Church*. Notre Dame, IN: University of Notre Dame Press.
Pontifical Council for Justice and Peace. 2004. *Compendium of the Social Doctrine of the Church*. Vatican: Libreria Editrice Vaticana.
Rossi, P.J. 1983. *Together Toward Hope: A Journey to Moral Theology*. Notre Dame, IN and London: University of Notre Dame Press.
Seung, T. 2007. *Kant: A Guide for the Perplexed*. London and New York: Continuum.
Witte, J. and Alexander, F.S. 2010. *Christianity and Human Rights: An Introduction*. Cambridge: Cambridge University Press.
Wolterstorff, N.P. 2012. Christianity and human rights, in *Religion and Human Rights: An Introduction*, edited by J. Witte and M.C. Green. Oxford: Oxford University Press, 42–55.
Wood, A.W. 1970. *Kant's Moral Religion*. Ithaca, NY: Cornell University Press.

Index

For Product Safety Concerns and Information please contact our EU representative GPSR@taylorandfrancis.com Taylor & Francis Verlag GmbH, Kaufingerstraße 24, 80331 München, Germany

Batch number: 10725973

Printed by Printforce, the Netherlands